Biblical Shalom for Sustainable Holistic Transformational Development in Nigeria

A Study of Two Rural Communities in North Central Nigeria

Stephen Z. Yashim

Langham

MONOGRAPHS

© 2020 Stephen Z. Yashim

Published 2020 by Langham Global Library
An imprint of Langham Publishing
www.langhampublishing.org

Langham Publishing and its imprints are a ministry of Langham Partnership

Langham Partnership
PO Box 296, Carlisle, Cumbria, CA3 9WZ, UK
www.langham.org

ISBNs:
978-1-83973-054-2 Print
978-1-83973-203-4 ePub
978-1-83973-204-1 Mobi
978-1-83973-205-8 PDF

British Library Cataloguing-in-Publication Data
A catalogue record for this book is available from the British Library.

ISBN: 978-1-83973-054-2

Cover & Book Design: projectluz.com

The quest for a holistic transformation of rural communities through a sustainable framework in Africa has indeed been a challenge over the years. A participatory appreciative dialogue approach has been developed by Stephen Z. Yashim as a working and sustainable method for holistic rural community development to facilitate the application of biblical shalom. His qualitative engagements with the sampled participants during the data collection and the results obtained afterward have proven beyond reasonable doubt that the proposed framework is worth adopting as a supplement to the existing frameworks that are still not yielding adequate results. I am convinced Yashim's model in this book is relevant for the African context. Hence, the rural communities will get involved in meaningful services with biblical guidance for their own development, and they will appreciate and feel recognized for their contributions with the help of God almighty.

Ruth Enoch Adamu, PhD
Department of Arts Education (Religion Education),
University of Jos, Plateau State, Nigeria

I highly recommend this practical book with its detailed case studies for any Christian who wants to improve their work in community development. As a result of this innovative approach in two Nigerian villages, using appreciative inquiry and dialogue with the biblical narrative, each community mobilized and accomplished a project using their local resources. I will also use this book as a handy reference when I need a summary of the theories of global and community development, theologies of development and *missio Dei*, analysis of worldviews, and the concepts of biblical shalom.

Mary S. Crickmore
West Africa Ministry Team Leader,
World Renew

Rev. Dr. Stephen Yashim's research *Biblical Shalom for Sustainable Holistic Transformational Development in Nigeria* is not only relevant to the Nigerian context but addresses a global phenomenon. The study which advocates for an application of biblical shalom by means of participatory dialogue with the biblical worldview for sustainable transformation of rural communities was born out of shortcomings of the traditional approaches to human needs which were based on mere relief and not transformation.

The study is well presented, logical, and coherent. The necessary and relevant concepts are well researched and discussed regarding developments within the field of community development. I have read this work with great excitement. It is commendable for academic and practical use by promoters of human dignity.

Ephraim Yoms, PhD
Director, People Oriented Development,
Evangelical Church Winning All (ECWA),
Jos, Plateau State, Nigeria

This study is dedicated to:

Rev. Barje Maigadi, PhD, of ECWA Theological Seminary, Jos,
who introduced me to
the theology of development with passion.

Mary Crickmore, of World Renew,
who inspired my interest to
facilitate transformational development in rural communities.

Rev. Idowu Akintola, PhD, of New Estate Baptist Church, Abuja,
who influenced my final decision to
pursue the PhD program.

Sa'adatu S. Yashim, my wife,
who has and is still sacrificially supporting me holistically.

Contents

Foreword

A new field of study has gradually emerged seeking to unify the sacred and secular; human environment and religious contexts; as well as development principles and faith convictions. This kind of development is not new in historic Africa; but the coming of Christianity left a gap that was filled by historic religious views of adherents. A return of this field of study is therefore a welcome idea that effectively fills such void.

This field of study has come in various forms such as inter-disciplinary research like religious study (theology) with social sciences. One of the efforts in this direction in Nigeria was made popular by Professor Emeritus Adetoye Faniran who brought theology and geography together, establishing an academic body called "Sacred Earth Ministry." One of his monographs, *Tenants on Earth*, captured the context of this inter-disciplinary perpective. It sought to affirm that the world is created by God and its management needs to take God's plan and purpose for creating into cognizance for sustenance of the earth.

This study by Rev. Dr. Stephen Zahiop Yashim takes another dimension. It seeks to harmonize the biblical worldview and socio-religio-cultural perspectives as they relate to community development, resulting in the transformation of the society holistically. The study affirms the responsibility of the people to their sustatined development, and the role the Bible plays in transforming attitudes toward nature and the human environment.

This study achieves its objective in affirming the need and benefit of conscious engagement of biblical worldview in dialogue with the community's worldview. An aspect, however, that may need subsequent focus would be the dynamics in ensuring such biblical worldview is implicated for development. This resource is a significant contribution to the role worldviews play in our management of resources, ethics, and principles guiding development. Engaging the biblical worldview will, in no small way, enhance the achievement of transformational and sustainable development of society.

Moses Audi
Professor of Theology and World Christianity Scholar
President, Baptist Theological Seminary, Kaduna

Acknowledgments

Everyone that contributed to the success of this study deserves to be publicly acknowledged. Much as I'd wish to, I cannot publicly acknowledge each person. Permit me however to mention a few.

Dr. Rev. Barje Maigadi, planted the seed of interest in the Theology of Development. Dr. Maigadi also gave me practical guidance as I conducted the research and wrote the dissertation. I also acknowledge the roles of the second reader, Dr. Lami B. Ibrahim, and the external examiner, Dr. Rev. Ephraim Yoms.

Professor George E. Janvier provided me with relevant books that assisted me in this study. Professor Janvier sourced for the funds and shipped the books from the United States of America.

Dr. Rev. Idowu Akintola used his sphere of influence to facilitate the payment of my tuition fee for six semesters. Rev. Nathan Chiroma, PhD, used his sphere of influence to facilitate my acceptance to access the library of the University of Stellenbosch, South Africa. Professor Jurgens Hendriks facilitated and assisted me to be accepted to access the library of the University of Stellenbosch, South Africa after I completed participation in the African Doctoral Academy in January 2017 at the same University.

The New Estate Baptist Church, Abuja, under the leadership of Rev. Idowu Akintola, paid my tuition fee for the PhD program. The New Estate Baptist Church, Bwari, granted me a three-year study leave to undertake the PhD program.

The directors and staff of Christian Rural and Urban Development Association of Nigeria (CRUDAN), People Oriented Development (POD) of the Evangelical Church Winning All, and Rural Development Counsellors for Christian Churches in Africa (RURCON) for graciously granting me access to their respective libraries.

Mary Crickmore, the West African team leader of World Renew, used her sphere of influence to give me support. Through Mary's assistance World Renew paid for my visa, air travel to, and housing in Stellenbosch, South Africa. World Renew also funded the field research.

Hon. David Chatjock linked me with the Kurmin Gwaza community. Rev. Joseph J. Hayab linked me with the Kurmin Jatau community. The district heads of Kurmin Gwaza and Kurmin Jatau granted me leave to undertake the study in their domains. Ten people in Kurmin Gwaza and ten people in Kurmin Jatau communities participated in focus group discussions for the study. Rev. Nathan Nwachukwu, and the members of Shalom Baptist Church, GRA, Jos provided me with spiritual and moral support during my stay in Jos in the course of this study.

I received financial and moral support from: Mrs. Sarah I. B. Miner; Mr. Olusegun and Deaconess Folashade Adigun; Mr. Yusuf and Deaconess Tabitha Y. Gandu; Deacon Musa and Mrs. Briskila M. Birat; Mr. William and Deaconess Martha W. Kolo; Mr. Raphael Olatayo; Rev. Samson and Mrs Opeyemi Ojo and the United Baptist Church, Bwari, Abuja; and Rev. Thomas B. Nache and the Victory Baptist Church, Dutse Alhaji, Abuja.

My wife, Sa'adatu, and my children, Caesar Gankon (who died before the study was completed) and Sandra Didiya, made sacrifices and gave me immense support from the home front.

Abstract

The issue of the transformation of rural communities through sustainable transformational development in Africa, especially in Nigeria, has been a challenge over the years. Many Christian relief and development organizations have been making giant strides through the application of participatory problem-solving approaches but it seems their efforts are not yielding adequate results. Therefore, it has become necessary to look at a supplementary approach.

This study therefore considers the possibility of applying a participatory appreciative dialogue approach as a supplementary approach for facilitating biblical shalom for sustainable transformational development in Kurmin Gwaza and Kurmin Jatau, two rural communities in North Central Nigeria. This is based on two assumptions: first, that the application of a participatory appreciative approach to facilitate dialogue between the communities' worldview and the biblical worldview on holistic transformational development can be a means of creating sustainable development in rural communities in Nigeria with general application to the African continent; and second, that when a biblically transformed worldview is adopted by a rural community it will advance a new way of life resulting to a continuous application of biblical shalom in the life of the people.

The study of transformational development is multidisciplinary. Therefore, insights from anthropology, sociology, hermeneutics, theology, philosophy of education, and organizational development gained from review of literatures were applied.

The participatory appreciative dialogue approach demonstrates potential for facilitating biblical shalom in a process of holistic transformational development in both Kurmin Gwaza and Kurmin Jatau communities. Therefore, this study argues for the application of participatory appreciative dialogue, as a supplementary approach to the participatory problem-solving approach, to facilitate biblical shalom for holistic transformational development in rural communities.

Key concepts such as transformational development, worldview, rural communities, appreciative dialogue, and biblical shalom are predominantly used to achieve the objective of this study.

Abbreviations

AI	Appreciative Inquiry
CCMP	Church and Community Mobilization Process
CD	community development
CDO	Community Development Officer
CRDOs	Christian relief and development organizations
CRUDAN	Christian Rural and Urban Development Association of Nigeria
DCC	District Church Council
ECLA	Economic Commission for Latin America
ECWA	Evangelical Church Winning All
EMS	Evangelical Missionary Society
FBO	faith-based organization
LePSA	Learners-centered, Problem-solving, Self-discovery, and Action
NPE	National Policy on Education
PAT	People Oriented Development Animation Technique
PEP	participatory evaluation process
PLA	Participatory Learning Action
PME	Participatory Monitoring and Evaluation
POD	People Oriented Development
PRA	Participatory Rural Appraisal
RRA	Rapid Rural Appraisal
RURCON	Rural Development Counsellors for Christian Churches in Africa

CHAPTER 1

Introduction

The issue of facilitating the well-being of rural communities through sustainable transformational development in Africa, especially in Nigeria, has been a challenge over the years. Many Christian relief and development organizations (CRDOs) have been making giant strides through the application of participatory, problem-solving approaches but it seems their efforts are not yielding adequate results. The CRDOs aim at mobilizing, empowering, and building capacity through the process of learning and skills acquisition for the people to identify, plan for, and take action to address community needs and problems. In addition to these aims the primary goals of these CRDOs include reaching non-Christian communities to demonstrate God's love, to model a kingdom of God community, and to present the gospel in word and in deed. However, the approaches do not seem to adequately engage the people's worldview on development in a direct and appreciative dialogue with the biblical worldview on holistic transformational development.

This study assumes that the application of a participatory appreciative approach to facilitate dialogue between the communities' worldview on development and the biblical metanarrative can be a means of creating sustainable development in rural communities in Nigeria, with general application to the African continent. It also assumes that a biblically transformed worldview on holistic transformational development will advance a progressive application of biblical shalom in the life of the people. Therefore, this study considers the possibility of applying a participatory appreciative dialogue approach as a supplementary approach, which may be more effective in engaging the worldview of Kurmin Gwaza and Kurmin Jatau, two rural communities in North Central Nigeria on development.

Development is a multifaceted process that involves growth, refinement, and maturation that establishes and sustains the physical, psychological, emotional, social, and spiritual well-being of human beings. Growth implies increase. Refinement refers to improvement. Maturation describes the process of achieving optimal ability. Therefore, development is considered to be a multifaceted process that leads to the increase, refinement, and maturity of human abilities to cultivate and sustain human well-being. In this study holistic transformational development is understood to be a process that aims to apply biblical shalom progressively to the time Jesus Christ returns to establish the new heavens and the new earth. A holistic transformational development process can increase the experience, the refinement, and the sustenance of the ability to apply biblical shalom in all spheres of human life consistently over time. The ultimate goal of holistic transformational development is the actualization of the state of biblical shalom. Biblical shalom is God's shalom as revealed in the biblical metanarrative. It is a state of just, peaceful, harmonious, and enjoyable relationships with each other socially, with ourselves psychologically, with our physical environment, and with God spiritually.[1] Therefore, based on the aforementioned assumption, this study attempts to demonstrate a participatory approach, referred to here as participatory appreciative dialogue, to apply the vision of biblical shalom through the process of sustainable holistic transformational development in two rural communities, Kurmin Gwaza and Kurmin Jatau in Kaduna State, North Central Nigeria.

The study presupposes four things. First, human beings lost the state of biblical shalom due to the fall of man into sin, hence the need for it to be reinstated. Second, there is a process through which biblical shalom can be reinstated for humankind to re-experience it. Third, participatory appreciative dialogue is a process through which biblical shalom can be applied for humankind to re-experience full life. Finally, the application of biblical shalom is a progressive process not something that can be experienced fully in an instant.

It has been mentioned earlier that the CRDOs in Nigeria engage in facilitating holistic development in rural communities by applying participatory, problem-solving approaches in community development. These participatory

---

1. Myers, *Walking with the Poor*, 175.

problem-solving approaches include: Participatory Learning Action (PLA), Rapid Rural Appraisal (RRA), Participatory Rural Appraisal (PRA), Participatory Monitoring and Evaluation (PME).[2] The basic principle of these different approaches is to build the capacity of stakeholders at the grassroots community level to mitigate their problems and overcome challenges.

Definition of Key Terms

Biblical shalom, sustainable holistic transformational development, and rural communities are the three key concepts in this study. These concepts are briefly defined below.

Biblical shalom: The term biblical is an adjective that describes that which is in accord with the teaching of the Bible. It is applied to the term shalom in this study. Shalom is a state of harmonious relationship between the inter-related and interdependent creation within itself and with God its Creator. Therefore, biblical shalom, as applied in this study, refers to the state of equilibrium in creation and human society that exists based on the operation of the interconnected, interdependent, and harmonious relationships God designed for all creation within itself and with God who is the Creator as revealed in the Bible.

Sustainable holistic transformational development: The term sustainable is an adjective that describes the ability to continue a process over time. The term holistic is also an adjective that describes the belief that parts of something are intimately interconnected and are explicable only by reference to the whole. The term transformational is an adjective that describes the act of producing improvement or change in a situation. Development connotes the idea of making the present state of affairs in a community more functionally beneficial for life and wholeness for the community, transformation toward the best human future. Therefore, sustainable holistic transformational development denotes a process through which the interconnected, interdependent relationships of every aspect of creation, and its relationship with the Creator, can continue to be sustained in accord with the Creator's design over time.

---

2. The PLA, RRA, PRA, and PME are various methods of research that apply a people-centered approach that allows the people in a target community for development and to actively participate in the process of enhancing development. Chapter 2 discusses these approaches in more detail.

Rural communities: A rural community, as applied in this study, consists of a group of people with homogeneous characteristics and living in dynamic relationships in a geographical area described as rural. A geographical area that lacks social and infrastructural facilities that are in cities such as good roads, safe sources of potable water, hospitals etc.

Research Problem

The research interrogates the participatory problem-solving approaches applied by CRDOs in rural communities in Nigeria postulating that previous CRDOs methods seemed not to have been adequate in enabling the application of biblical shalom for sustainable transformational development. The key problem the study identifies from the reading of previous literature and by critical observation of CRDOs is that initial approaches are rather deficient in facilitating direct dialogue between the target audiences' worldview on the development and the biblical worldview on holistic transformational development. The above observation is reinforced in by Ephraim Yoms's PhD dissertation measuring the holistic effort of ECWA's People Oriented Development Programme.[3] In Yoms's research, focused on some selected rural communities in North Central Nigeria, the outcome is that the persistence of poverty in People Oriented Development communities (PODs) was due to lack of a more fruitful approach to development.[4] Given the above identified concern, this study investigates what other approaches are there for CRDOs and proposes the application of a biblical shalom by means of participatory dialogue with a biblical worldview on transformational development as a supplementary method for sustainable transformational development of rural communities in Nigeria.

---

3. Yoms, "Transformational Development."

4. Yoms. He posits that "it is difficult to conclude that POD interventions have sufficiently led to TD" (iii) Yoms argues that it is "lack of an appropriate approach to development probably contributes to the persistence of poverty in these communities" (218). Thus, Yoms recommends that, "More research on the concept of Transformational Development is needed considering the fact that there are several studies (books and articles) within the field community development" (224).

Research Question

How effective can an application of biblical shalom be by means of a participatory appreciative dialogue approach for sustainable transformational development in rural communities in Nigeria? This study examines how the worldview of Kurmin Gwaza and Kurmin Jatau rural communities on development can be engaged in a direct appreciative dialogue with the biblical worldview on holistic transformational development in order to initiate and sustain a holistic transformational development for the progressive application of biblical shalom.

The study of transformational development is multidisciplinary. Therefore, this study applied principles and insights from practical theology, to provide a Christian theological framework; philosophy of education, to provide the epistemological framework; organizational development, to provide the model for the appreciative approach; anthropology, to provide the framework for analyzing the communities' worldview on development; biblical theology to provide the normative for the transformation of the communities' worldview on development; and hermeneutics to facilitate the development of a contextual theology of development that impacts the application of biblical shalom.

Background of the Study

Holistic transformational development can be historically traced from the biblical account of creation and all through the biblical metanarrative to the present day. God gave humankind a mandate at creation to be God's vice-regent or co-creator with God.[5] God gave humankind the responsibility to rule over all creation on earth and to cultivate the garden in which God placed humankind.[6] The responsibility includes the classification of all other creation (Gen 2:19). This responsibility to classify all of creation was a holistic act of development. It involved the social, cognitive, and physical well-being of all creation including humankind. This act was a means of making humankind's habitat functionally meaningful for life and wholeness for the human community.

---

5. Miller, *Discipling Nations*, 76, 163–171.
6. Gen 1:26–30; 2:15–20.

The fall of humankind into sin distorts the state of shalom that humankind enjoyed at creation (Gen 3:8–19). The effort of human beings to make their economic, physical, social, political, and spiritual well-being on earth to be functionally meaningful since the fall of humankind into sin has continually been pursued with different sheds of strains and struggles. Three global theories are reviewed in chapter 2 to provide a perceptual understanding of the efforts being made to improve and promote human well-being on earth. Sometimes the efforts yield some degree of success, while at other times they result in gross failure. God decrees that humankind, as a result of the fall, will continue to struggle with great stress as it executes its development responsibility.[7] In other words, humankind will have to now struggle with great stress in its bid to experience life and wholeness as was divinely intended at creation.

At creation God had engaged human beings as his vice-regents to participate with him in cultivating and maintaining creation. After the fall of human beings into sin God initiated a divine action, described as the mission of God, to re-establish his shalom in creation. The mission of God includes processes aimed at making the state of creation more sensibly beneficial for human life and wholeness in spite of the effects of the fall. The biblical metanarrative shows that God chose to engage his chosen people to participate with him in this mission to re-establish his shalom in creation.

Purpose and Objectives of the Study

The purpose of this study is to advocate for the application of biblical shalom by means of participatory appreciative dialogue with the biblical worldview on transformational development for sustainable transformational development of rural communities in Nigeria. Hence the study facilitates the engagement of the worldview of two rural communities in North Central Nigeria, Kurmin Gwaza and Kurmin Jatau, on development in a participatory appreciative dialogue with the biblical worldview on holistic transformational development.

---

7. Gen 3:17–19.

This approach is proposed as a supplement to the approaches CRDOs apply as indicated earlier.[8] The study has four objectives:

1. To facilitate the engagement of the communities' worldview on development in a participatory appreciative dialogue with the biblical worldview on holistic transformational development.
2. To lead each community in the study site to recognize and appreciate their place in God's design for the application of biblical shalom in their communities.
3. To equip each rural community in this study with the requisite skills to sustain the process of participatory appreciative dialogue with the biblical metanarrative to facilitate worldview transformation to sustain holistic transformational development for the progressive application of biblical shalom in their community.
4. To inspire each rural community in this study to design plans and take concrete action for holistic transformational development and for the progressive application of biblical shalom in their respective communities.

Importance of the Study

Knowledge and insights gained from this study can be applied to sustainable, holistic, transformational, development efforts and the progressive application of biblical shalom in rural communities, particularly in the Nigerian context and generally in the African context. The following stand to benefit from the outcome of the study:

1. Members of the rural communities in which the empirical study took place.
2. Mission scholars and researchers. The study proposes a supplementary approach of facilitating the process of holistic transformational development from a biblical perspective. The

---

8. See page 4 above.

      results are intended to stimulate further investigation on the applicability of the participatory appreciative dialogue approach in other sociocultural contexts.

3.   Christian development practitioners, denominational church leaders, mission administrators and local church leaders in Nigeria, Africa, and beyond the shores of Africa may benefit from the result of this study.

4.   Christian non-governmental organizations (NGOs), referred to in this study as Christian relief and development organizations (CRDOs), involved in rural development, and donors that support such organizations may benefit from this study. It may help the organizations in the design of policies aimed at applying the participatory appreciative dialogue approach to facilitate a sustainable holistic transformational development process in rural communities for the progressive application of biblical shalom. It may help donors to understand what is involved in the participatory appreciative dialogue approach to facilitate holistic transformational development for the progressive application of biblical shalom. Such understanding may help donors to make informed commitments as they provide support for such programs.

Limitations and Delimitations

This study applies a qualitative research design that engages selected research participants in focus group discussions or dialogue to describe, analyze, and interpret their experiences.[9] The study applies a focus group discussion technique, which is usually limited to between ten and twelve participants. Thus, this study is limited to ten research participants, a number considered adequate for this study. Bonnie Goebert, states that "Focus groups have more to do with concentrated and creative listening than numbers" and that focus groups are the ideal place to begin understanding what it is going on in

---

9. Michael Quinn Patton states that "qualitative inquiry typically focuses in depth on relatively small samples selected purposefully." Patton, *Qualitative Research*, 230.

the psyches of the study group.[10] "The contemporary focus group interview generally involves 8 to 12 individuals who discuss a particular topic under the direction of a moderator who promotes interaction and ensures that the discussion remains on the topic of interest."[11] This study seeks to understand the worldview of the communities on development therefore ten participants are considered adequate for a more concentrated and creative listening, in order to have more depth of understanding of the worldview of the communities in their historical context. Focus groups are constituted to be inclusive, having representations of the different segments of the society in which the study is undertaken.

Two specific geographical areas, namely Kurmin Gwaza and Kurmin Jatau, rural communities in Jaba, Kaduna State, North Central of Nigeria, were chosen to participate in the study. The limiting of the study to these two rural communities allows the researcher to do a more detailed study of the research problem and also provide an opportunity to compare the outcome of the study from the different communities.

Conclusion

This study engages two Jaba rural communities in a qualitative research design that applies focus group discussions or dialogue technique. The study facilitates a participatory appreciative discussion in a process aimed at facilitating the application of biblical shalom for sustainable holistic transformational development in the selected communities. The study uses both secondary and primary data, secondary data obtained through literature review and primary data obtained through qualitative empirical focus group discussions.

---

10. Goebert, *Beyond Listening*, ix, 4.
11. Stewart, Shamdasani, and Rook, *Focus Groups*, 37.

CHAPTER 2

Literature Review

Introduction

Development theories or development ideologies guide the strategies organizations engage in facilitating development.[1] Richard Peet and Elaine Hartwick, write that, "development theories reflect the political positions of their proponents, the places where they developed, their philosophical perspective, and whether they are predominantly economic, sociological, anthropological, historical, geographic, and so on."[2]

This chapter reviews three major global theories and approaches to development and reviews the approaches applied by three Christian relief and development organizations (CRDOs) in the process of facilitating holistic development in rural communities. The review demonstrates the strengths and weaknesses of the theories and approaches. The review also demonstrates how the theories and approaches relate to the issue of holistic development in rural communities. In the light of this review the inadequacies identified in the theories reviewed are highlighted. These inadequacies informed the necessity for this study. Thus, the review of literature in this chapter provides the backdrop upon which the study is situated. Three major global theories, modernization, dependency, and world-system theories are reviewed. The principles, the methodologies, the target, and the goal of each of these theories is the focus of the review. The approaches to community development (CD)

---

1. Hettne, *Development Theory*, 3.
2. Peet and Hartwick, *Theories of Development*, 21.

applied by Christian Rural and Urban Development Association of Nigeria
(CRUDAN), People Oriented Development (POD) of the Evangelical Church
Winning All, and Rural Development Counsellors for Christian Churches
in Africa (RURCON) are reviewed. The approaches are critiqued in the light
of three broad models of approaching CD to highlight both strengths and
weaknesses of the approaches of these CRDOs and highlight the inadequacy
this study addresses. The review of the approaches and methods of CRDOs
in rural communities in Nigeria is done through a document analysis of the
three selected CRDOs. In this chapter there is also a review of literature on
subjects essential for this study. The subjects include: biblical theology of development, the doctrine of shalom, the anthropological concept of worldview,
rural sociology, and appreciative dialogue.

Emergence of Global Development Theories

Roland J. Hustedde, writes that theories can provide explanations for people's
behavior and a framework from which to explain and comprehend events.[3]
Global theories of development are ideas of development that identify and
draw logical explanations for factors that can generate economic, social, and
political progress in nation states. These theories were conceived within particular historical and cultural contexts. Examining the history of development Gilbert Rist, argues that the "concept which is supposed to command
universal acceptance" was constructed within a particular historical and
cultural context.[4] Theories of development, according to Oswald de Rivero,
originates from the West's ideology of progress that was born during the Age
of Enlightenment but that the theories of development began to be discussed
in the early 1950s.[5] Bryant L. Myers, in a review of the trajectory of development, also posits that development as a concept that describes human efforts
to improve the well-being of the poor was used for the first time in the early
1950s. Myers writes that, "the idea of development in terms of helping a nation escape from poverty dates to the immediate aftermath of World War

---

3. Hustedde, "Seven Theories," 20.

4. Rist, *History of Development*, 2.

5. Myers, *Walking with the Poor*, 26.

II."[6] Bjorn Hettne, writes that development theories emerged from tentative attempts to understand the problem of "underdevelopment" in non-Western countries, initially, from the point of view of the West.[7] Jeffery Haynes,[8] Rist,[9] and Jennifer A. Elliott,[10] posit that discourses on international development as a planned activity and as a field of study can be linked to a speech made by President Truman of the United States who, in 1949, considered poverty in underdeveloped areas to constitute a threat to prosperity and peace within those areas and for the world as a whole.

However, the field of development study has become interdisciplinary and as a result it "has seen many changes in thinking regarding the meaning and purpose of development (ideologies) and in development practice in the field (strategies of development)."[11] Joseph Iloabanafor Orji also states that the concept of development has evolved from the orthodox idea of development being synonymous with economic growth to broader concepts in more recent times, which accommodate non-economic issues.[12] Ideas about development have developed over time, according to Rist, from different particular vantage points or perceptual vision or horizons.[13] A horizon is a perceptual vision "that includes everything that can be seen from a particular vantage point."[14] Therefore, theories of development have evolved over time and each theory presents a perception of development from a different point of departure. For example, the point of departure can be from the perspective of the "developer" who is committed to the task of facilitating development in another context different from their own or from the perspective of the "recipient" of the development effort by the "developer." The recipient "is forced to modify his social relations and his relationship to nature in order to enter the promised new world."[15]

---

6. Myers, 23.

7. Hettne, *Development Theory*, 2.

8. Haynes, *Religion and Development*, 2.

9. Rist, *History of Development*, 70–79.

10. Elliot, *Introduction to Sustainable Development*, 26.

11. Elliot, 26. Parenthesis is in the original.

12. Orji, *New Approaches*, 1.

13. Rist, *History of Development*, 2.

14. Gadamer, *Truth and Method*, 301.

15. Rist, *History of Development*, 2.

Jorgen Larrain, notes that each development theory puts different emphasis on development from the perspective of different disciplines such as economics, political science, sociology, psychology, and geography.[16] Larrain, categorizes the different approaches into three categories: (1) Approaches that emphasize sociological theories to explain development from a sociological perspective.[17] (2) Approaches that emphasize psychological motivation as the motor forces of economic growth.[18] (3) Approaches that emphasize economic factors in the process of development.[19] The models of development that arise from these different disciplinary perspectives view development perspectives that reflect a firm belief in human reason, technology, and money as the means of facilitating development. The earlier development theories did not consider development from religious or spiritual perspectives. Development theory or theories that lay emphasis on development from religious or theological perspective are a recent development.

Though the history of the concept of development can be traced back to antiquity, the concept of development and social change have existed in most human societies throughout history.[20] Larrain states that academic interest in studying development can be traced back to shortly after the Second World War.[21] However, Jeffrey Haynes, states that at that time "most Western governments and development agencies saw religion as part of the problem, not as a potential aspect of its resolution" but recently development thinking has come to "include various religious expressions that are now widely seen as potentially important components of achieving development gains."[22] Myers argues that the biggest gap in the ideas on development by different scholars "lies in the absence of religion and things spiritual in their explanation for why people are poor and what can be done to help them."[23] John Rapely accedes that spirituality or religion has been a development taboo but is surfacing in

---

16. Larrain, *Theories of Development*, viii.

17. Larrain, 88.

18. Larrain, 94.

19. Larrain, 95.

20. Harrison, *Sociology of Modernization*, 1–3; Larrain, *Theories of Development*, 1.

21. Larrain, *Theories of Development*, 11.

22. Haynes, *Religion and Development*, 1.

23. Myers, *Walking with the Poor*, 45.

development thought.[24] Therefore the role of religion and the spiritual nature of human beings as an essential factor in facilitating development have mostly been ignored in the formulation of the theories of development.

Myers proposes a theory of development from a Christian perspective. Myers's Christian theory of development has one overarching goal, two objectives, and two principles. The overarching goal is the kingdom of God. The kingdom of God is characterized by the experience of God's shalom, which includes just, peaceful, harmonious, and enjoyable relationships with each other socially, with ourselves psychologically, with our physical environment, and with God spiritually. The twin objectives are changed people and changed relationships. Changed people who have discovered their true identity and vocation in the light of biblical revelation, and changed relationships characterized by just and peaceful coexistence in the light of the transforming effect of the gospel of salvation in Christ. The two principles are that the development process belongs to stakeholders, and that relationships matter in the process of development. The stakeholders are God, the church, the holistic development practitioner, working together, and the Evil One, who is actually working against development by causing distraction, division, and destruction.[25] The stakeholders in the process of holistic development are those who are actively involved in one way or another in the processes of facilitating that development in a given context. Myers's framework for understanding development from a Christian theological perspective is assumed in this study and therefore useful for the analysis of the primary data collected and collated in this study.[26]

There is a large number of development theories, however the review in this section is limited to three major ones that are global in scope and helpful to the practice of development. The review of these global development theories provides a broad backdrop against which the approaches of CRDOs in Nigeria can be understood. The review of the concept of development is limited to the period when it began to be considered with academic interest and to three selected theories.

---

24. Rapley, *Understanding Development*, 178.

25. Myers, *Walking with the Poor*, 202.

26. This provided the conceptual framework for analyzing the biblical transformation of the worldview of the study communities on development in chapter 5.

The three global theories reviewed in this section include the modernization theory, the dependency theory, and the world-system theory. First, modernization theory is described as a classical theory rooted in the concrete experience of Western economic history, a Eurocentric view on development.[27] Second, dependency theory, is described as a theory influenced by Marxian philosophy and as a reaction to the modernization from the perspective of the nations described as underdeveloped or developing nations and offering an alternative approach to development. Finally, world-system theory, is described as a neo-classical theory of development that subsumes the development of any nation in a world economic system.

Note that this study was undertaken in two rural communities as indicated in chapter 1. Global development theories do not provide a framework that can be applied in the process of holistic transformational development in rural communities. Therefore, how the application of these theories of development engage or do not engage rural communities in the process of facilitating holistic development is the concern.

The review is further limited to broad descriptions of the basic principles and methodologies of the selected theories and the historical context of their development. The review includes the historical beginning of the selected theories and evaluation of the relationship that exists between their theoretical approaches and rural communities if any. In view of the fact that the reviews are not exhaustive but limited, it is imperative to state its objectives to justify the reasons for the limitations.

The first is to highlight the assumptions each theory has about development, and the goal and philosophy directing the actions taken toward development. Bjorn Hettne writes that development theories "originally grew out of concern with so-called underdeveloped countries on the implicit assumption that the conditions in these societies were unsatisfactory and ought to be changed."[28] Adamu Kevin Kesuwo[29] and Abdulhameed A Ujo,[30] in their respective reviews of the concept of development from different perspectives, conclude that development is concerned with three things. (1) life sustenance

---

27. Hettne, *Development Theory*, 5.

28. Hettne, 3.

29. Kesuwo, *Insight into Development*, 4–5.

30. Ujo, *Theory and Practice*, 5–7.

concerned with basic human needs; (2) self-esteem or self-respect pursued through different means that will satisfy this need; and (3) freedom from alienating material, social, natural, psychological, emotional, institutional, and "dogmatic beliefs." The second objective is to consider the hermeneutical basis for the assumptions made for each theory. By hermeneutical basis we mean the basis upon which development is interpreted in the theory. Hermeneutics based on the natural sciences seek scientific explanation whereas hermeneutics based on social sciences seek understanding of human phenomena.[31] The third is to review the processes applied for development and identifying the actors and their roles in the process. Finally, it is to evaluate the outcome in terms of the holistic scope, transformational effect, and sustainability in rural communities, if any.

The review of these selected theories of development suggests that the basic principle of the theories is that development occurs through the process of economic growth. Each theory applies a pragmatic approach to enhance economic growth through the use of its chosen tool. All of these theories target national, political, or commercial institutions to formulate policies for the application of its methodology. The goal of each of these approaches is a temporal utopian experience of economic, physical, social, and political life.

Modernization Theory

Modernization theory is a Eurocentric view on development that emphasizes economic growth and views development from an economic perspective. The modernization theory argues that, as societies industrialize their economy grows and the growth of the economy influences the social and other characteristics of that society. Hence the theory equates development with economic growth. Elliot,[32] Myers,[33] Peet and Hartwick,[34] all argue that modernization theory is Eurocentric because it assumes that Western forms of development and the processes that were applied in Europe after the devastating effects on European economy caused by the Second World War could be repeated unmodified in other geopolitical locations or nations. Historically,

---

31. Vanhoozer, "Reader's Guide," 7–8.
32. Elliot, *Introduction to Sustainable Development*, 26.
33. Myers, *Walking with the Poor*, 27.
34. Peet and Hartwick, *Theories of Development*, 104, 131.

the primary target for the application of the modernization theory was nation states considered to be economically improvised and backward.[35] Most of these nation states were emerging from colonization in the 1950s and 1960s. Elliot states that in the 1950s and 1960s development thinking assumed that the gaps in development between the Western nations and the non-Western nations could be gradually overcome through imitating the experience of the Western nations.[36] J. Samuel Valenzuela and Arturo Valenzuela similarly argue that modernization theory assumes that underdeveloped nations can rapidly develop by adopting modernization methods and abandoning their national values and belief.[37] Elliott states that the modernization thesis assumes that

> underdevelopment was due to constraints that were internal to these countries and could be solved quickly through the transfer of finance, technology and experience from the developed countries and through spatial diffusion of modernity from the West and from urban centres to rural areas.[38]

Myers also notes the basic assumption of the modernization theory is that the traditional culture and values of poor societies needed to be changed through a modernization process[39]; a "mechanical process of shedding the old and embracing the new."[40] Therefore it is argued that the modernization theory is a biased Eurocentric perspective of development.

At its core, modernization theory posits that economic growth occurs along five linear evolutionary stages leading to the goal of modernity, mass consumption, and temporal socio-economic well-being.[41] Development in the modernization theory schema is measurable in economic terms.[42] Therefore, the measure of development of a nation was the size of its economy.[43] Modernization theory also posits that external factors can be introduced

---

35. Herath, "Development Discourse," 819–834.

36. Elliot, *Introduction to Sustainable Development*, 26.

37. Valenzuela and Valenzuela, "Modernization and Dependency," 211.

38. Elliot, *Introduction to Sustainable Development*, 28.

39. Myers, *Walking with the Poor*, 27.

40. Gow, *Countering Development*, 4.

41. Crewe and Axelby, *Anthropology and Development*, 6.

42. Jacobsen, "Revisiting the Modernization Hypothesis," 174–185.

43. Myers, *Walking with the Poor*, 27.

to stimulate economic growth in a nation. Industrialization, national governments, and market systems are considered as external factors responsible for stimulating economic growth in nations.[44] Walt Whitman Rostow is considered the chief proponent of the concept of evolutionary economic growth.[45] Gilbert Rist summarizes Rostow's five-stage evolutionary economic framework as follows.

The first stage is "traditional society," and it is characterized by limited subsistence agriculture, primitive technology, and a static society with traditions and social practices, such as collective social relationships and feudal political system, which are not favorable for the process of development to occur. Rist adds that Rostow's traditional society "seen from the special viewpoint of industrial society, its distinguishing feature is a low level of productivity due to ignorance of the modern technology that allows nature to be rationally exploited."[46] In this schema societies at the traditional stage are bound by traditional modes of production and modes of social organization that resist change. Development efforts at this stage therefore concentrate on re-orienting conservative norms and values aimed at freedom from customary beliefs and practices believed to be constraining economic growth and social transformation.

The second stage is the "pre-conditions for take-off," and is a stage during which a nation previously lacking financial capital and technology is provided for through foreign aid schemes and foreign investment deals secured from the "Western" societies. This resonates with Truman's proposed United States policy in the late 1940s, as quoted by Rist, to "embark on a bold new program for making the benefits of our scientific advances and industrial progress available for the improvement and growth of underdeveloped areas."[47] The aim of introducing foreign investment and aid was to introduce improved technology and scientific knowledge.

The "take-off" is the third stage. The take-off stage is characterized by a cultural conversion as "old" practices are abandoned for more beneficial activities of development such as the establishment of more manufacturing

---

44. Crewe and Axelby, *Anthropology and Development*, 6, 7.

45. Peet and Hartwick, *Theories of Development*, 21, 22; Elliot, *Introduction to Sustainable Development*, 27.

46. Rist, *History of Development*, 95.

47. Rist, 71.

industries and the development of additional infrastructure. Therefore, there is an increase in the agricultural production and the introduction of new technologies results in high production for the market. At this stage investment in the manufacturing industry exceeds ten percent of the national income.

The fourth stage is the "drive to maturity." At this stage there is a high diversification in the economy. Investment in manufacturing leads to the exportation manufactured goods as the country establishes itself in position of comparative advantage in international trade. The fifth and final stage is the "age of high mass consumption." The age of high mass consumption stage is characterized by urbanization and high social welfare.[48] Therefore, according to Rist, one of Rostow's objective was to show "how the recently decolonized countries might in turn promote growth leading to development" by reference to European economic history.[49] Before reviewing some of the criticism of the modernization theory a brief evaluation of its approach is necessary.

Modernization theory does not consider development from a holistic perspective. While it cannot be denied that the application of science and technology has enhanced increase in the economy of nations, it can be argued that it does not consider development from a holistic perspective. Development goes beyond economic growth, though both development and economic growth are interrelated. Peet and Hartwick differentiate economic growth from development. For Peet and Hartwick "Economic growth means achieving a more massive economy" that produces goods and services in a nation whereas "development is interested not so much in the growth of an economy but rather the condition under which production occurs and the result that flow from it."[50] This implies that development is concerned about both the well-being of the environment and the well-being of people who are engaged in activities that generate economic growth. Therefore, Peet's and Hartwick's understanding of development points to an expansion of the scope of development to go beyond mindless economic growth to include sensitivity to the environmental and the human contexts in which economic growth is pursued.

---

48. Rist, 94; Elliot, *Introduction to Sustainable Development*, 27; Crewe and Axelby, *Anthropology and Development*, 6, 7; Dhlamini, "Modernization Theory Versus Dependency."

49. Rist, *History of Development*, 94.

50. Peet and Hartwick, *Theories of Development*, 2.

Holistic development does include, but is not defined by, economic growth. Holistic development aims for human communities to be "endowed with intensive knowledge and perpetual well-being."[51] A holistic perspective of development, unlike the modernization perspective, should aim at cultivating requisite knowledge that will perpetuate the well-being of people that includes the spiritual, physical, psychological, and social aspects of their lives, either as individual members or as a community. Myers writes that no explanation of the cause and nature of "poverty is complete without a holistic view of the spiritual and material at the level and the social systems within which the individual lives."[52] Likewise no approach to development is adequate without a holistic view of the spiritual, physical, psychological, and social aspects of individuals in their sociocultural context.

Exploitation rather than cultivation and conservation of nature and its resources is the emphasis of the modernization approach to development. Human beings through the application of scientific knowledge and technology exploit natural resources to provide the economic base for mass consumption or consumerism, which is considered to be the state of being developed. R. Warren Flint describes this perception of development as "a certain material standard of living based on economic consumerism of centralized industrialization."[53] Borrowing from Flint's illustration it can be said that development from a modernization perspective has mass consumption as the destination in a journey, economic growth as the vehicle that conveys the travelers, while the exploitation of the ecological base of nature is the roadway or means of arriving at that destination.[54] Hence, from the perspective of modernization, development is simply economic growth to promote human consumption that is always focused on squandering resources without deliberate effort to conserve or reinvest resources. Looking at this approach from a biblical perspective the approach goes counter to God's cultural mandate at creation. At creation God commanded human beings to cultivate and take care of nature, though taking some of it for physical nourishment.[55] Arthur

---

51. De Rivero, *Myth of Development*, 72. De Rivero, indicates this to be the goal of development theorists but limited to the temporal situation of human communities.

52. Myers, *Walking with the Poor*, 118.

53. Flint, *Practice of Sustainable Community*, 6.

54. Flint, 15.

55. Gen 2:15–16.

F. Glasser states that "these commands mark the beginning of a stream of obligations – a mandate for family and community, law and order, culture and civilization, and ecological concern that widens and deepens as it courses through Scripture."[56] Flint, captures the task of human beings caring for planet earth, the natural infrastructure for supporting life, well by describing it as a "biological living trust."[57] Hence, acts of development on the natural infrastructure for supporting life should "do as little harm as possible to the productive capacity of nature, which constitutes our community self-support system . . . now and in the future."[58]

Instead of cultivating natural infrastructure that supports life, the modernization approach to development is exploitative and always squandering. The effect of the exploitation, rather than cultivation, of the environment for the purpose of mass production in the name of development is today acknowledged to be primarily pollution. Rist argues that economic processes entail destruction. The destruction takes place as a result of the conversion of available natural resources into objects or products "whose recycling is either problematic . . . or impossible – with the result that the destruction of the natural environment becomes worse still (pollution)."[59] Elliot writes that environmentalists began to raise concern about "the undesirable effects of industrialization and economic development" in the 1960s. These environmentalists considered development and conservation to be incompatible.[60] The modernization emphasis on exploitation of nature for mass economic growth, rather than the biblical notion of the cultivation and care of nature shows the incompatibility of modernization theory with the biblical concept of development.

People are rational beings created with the ability to independently make decisions and make choices. Modernization theory does not consider the development from the perspective of the people directly affected by the development it proposes. Rather, the modernization approach conceptualizes development from a Western perspective based on the experiences of Western

---

56. Glasser, *Announcing the Kingdom*, 38.

57. Flint, *Practice of Sustainable Community*, 3.

58. Flint, 3

59. Rist, *History of Development*, 13–14. The parenthesis is in the original quotation.

60. Elliot, *Introduction to Sustainable Development*, 40, 42.

nations. Modernization assumes that the mental models of the West, its institutions, and its goals are the norm to be attained by non-Western nations. Consequently, the application of the modernization approach to development is a top-down approach. The promoter of development, Western nations, at the top determining the agent for development, science and technology, based on the philosophical guideline of industrialization for economic growth, and for the goal of mass consumption in the life of the recipient at the bottom, underdeveloped nations. Examining this approach from a biblical perspective the non-involvement of the people in the context where development is supposed to take place does not resonate with God's approach. Considering the cultural mandate God gave Adam, God involved human beings in the process of the development of the natural habitat of human beings (Gen 2:15–20).

The goal of the modernization approach is to attain a level of mass consumption. This means that the indicator of development is determined by the level of goods and services provided for human consumption. The utopian goal that the modernization approach aims to achieve is contrary to the ultimate goal of development from a biblical perspective which is the kingdom of God as earlier discussed on Myers's framework. The Bible, according to the Christian faith, is the inspired word of God that serves as a guide for the whole of life (2 Tim 3:16; Titus 2:12–13).

The explicit expression of the modernization theory is no longer in the forefront of development discourse in the twenty-first century, yet its basic principle of economic growth as essential for development still persists. Crewe and Axelby argue that though the explicit expression of the modernization theory has disappeared from the front burner of current intellectual discourse on development the principles of the theory still persist in subtler forms.[61] Myers demonstrates that the modernization theory was reconceptualized by the development of other theories that proposed different means of economic growth. Myers used the dependency theory, which proposes an alternative approach to economic growth, as an example.[62] Crewe and Axelby outline some of the historical shifts that have taken place from the 1970s to the present: (1) from the earlier prioritization of industrialization and economic growth to a focus on poverty reduction; (2) from the initial ideas

---

61. Crewe and Axelby, *Anthropology and Development*, 7.
62. Myers, *Walking with the Poor*, 28.

of political independence, industrial progress, and urban expansion to the notion of integration into capitalist market system; (3) from the primacy of the state as provider of development to an emphasis on market as the driver of progress;[63] and (4) more recently the "Washington Consensus" of a mix of economic liberalism and good governance. Crewe and Axelby conclude that, "despite variations in the way development is conceived, the means of delivery through particular institutions and approaches have remained remarkably resilient."[64] This can be understood to mean that there may be different definitions of development but the basic principle of economic growth as a means of development has remained virtually the same. Has this been the case in the approaches of the CRDOs? The response to this question is found in the review on the approaches of CRDOs reviewed in the latter part of this chapter. For now a review of some criticism of the modernization approach and the implication for this study is next.

Modernization approaches to development have been criticized by several scholars. Carlos A. Martinez-Vela,[65] Cosma Sorinal,[66] and Theda Skocpol[67] summarize these criticisms to include: (1) reifying the nation-state as the sole unit of analysis; (2) assuming that all countries can potentially follow a single path (or parallel and converging paths) of evolutionary development from "tradition" to "modernity"; (3) concomitantly, for disregarding the world-historical development of transnational structures that constrain and prompt national and local developments along diverse as well as parallel paths; and (4) explaining in terms of ahistorical ideals types "tradition" versus "modernity," which are elaborated and applied to national cases.

For the purpose of this study the analysis of the modernization theory here includes promoter, goal, agents, and philosophical guidelines for development. Therefore, based on the modernization theory, the promoters of

---

63. Structural Adjustment Programs (SAP) were introduced as blueprint solutions for taming macro-economic imbalances, dismantling barriers to trade, and re-orientating production towards export markets. The central objective of SAP according to Elliott, citing Reed, is to modify the structure of the economy of a nation in debt so that it can maintain its growth rate while at the same time being able to repay its debts. Elliot, *Introduction to Sustainable Development*, 34.

64. Crewe and Axelby, *Anthropology and Development*, 7.

65. Martínez-Vela, "World System Theory."

66. Sorinal, "Immanuel Wallerstein's World System."

67. Skocpol, "Wallerstein's World Capitalist System," 231–232.

development are the Western nations. David D. Gow argues that modernization is a process that is "standardized according to terms and conditions, and criteria mandated by those in power."[68] Those in power were the Western nations who were therefore the promoters of development. The Western nations as promoters of development determine the goal of development, the role of agents the promoter considers essential, and the philosophy that serves as a guide for the implementation of the processes aimed at achieving the predetermined goal. The goal of development is economic growth, social transformation, and modernization. Economic resources are secondarily for the physical well-being of the members of the society in question, and primarily for the economic prosperity and security of the West. Social transformation in this case is to transform the society to mirror the characteristics of Western societies. The agents of development are technology, education, and national governments of nations that serve as catalysts for promoting modernization through policy implementation. Technology, through industrialization, increases economic resources for higher standard of living. Education is a means of re-orienting the society to be open to societal restructuring. National governments are means to steer citizens along the path predetermined by the West. The philosophical guideline for economic growth is contained in the predetermined path prescribed by the West. The predetermined path is spelled out in the conditions the West lays for the nations in need of development to adhere to. These predetermined conditions inform the development policies drawn by the nations. The application of the principles and methods prescribed by the modernization theory has not proved effective both at national macro-levels and at community micro-levels of societies. The foregoing analysis points to a number of implications of interest in this study.

First, the primary focus of the modernization theory is to attain a level of mass consumption not just the sustenance of life or just meeting basic human needs. Flint observes that the human "focus on consumption and economic growth amplifies human impacts above and beyond our simple requirements for survival."[69] Hence the modernization approach extends the need for the sustenance of life through meeting basic needs, which is intrinsically inherent in human beings to mass consumption. The primary

---

68. Gow, *Countering Development*, 4.
69. Flint, *Practice of Sustainable Community*, 15.

concern of rural communities is not mass production for mass consumption but the sustenance of life and the meeting of the basic needs for life in a sociocultural context of harmonious relationships.[70] The application of the modernization theory has laid the foundation for increasing economic gap between nations with capacity for mass production through science and technology and those that do not have the capacity. Dhammika Herath argues that the modernization paradigm does not follow the expected path of economic growth or development instead there are nations that are still more or less underdeveloped, and the gap between economically rich and economically poor countries steadily increases.[71] So, considering the history of its application, the modernization theory has not in any significant way proved to be effective in bringing about increase in the well-being or welfare of the majority. The application of the modernization theory has rather increased the exploitative abilities of one set of nations privileged to have and to determine how to distribute scientific and technological capabilities for mass production leaving another set still underdeveloped. Therefore, the goal of the modernization approach to development is detrimental to the well-being of rural communities, especially in Nigerian and Africa in general.

Second, problem-solving is the concern of the modernization theory. Solving the problem of material poverty provides the motivation for the modernization theory. It has been mentioned earlier that historically, the primary target for the application of the modernization theory was to enhance the economic growth of nations considered to be economically improvised and backward.[72] Thus the modernization theory is a welfare-based development approach to help economically backward (by Western standards) nations to grow more rapidly economically.

Third, the modernization theory demonstrates that the people at the grassroots, in rural communities, who are directly affected by the development efforts are not directly, or even indirectly, involved in determining what well-being is for them, and what the goal and the process of development in their immediate context should be. The people are neither involved as promoters nor as goal setters, neither as agents nor as philosophers of the development

---

70. The characteristics of rural communities are discussed later in the chapter.

71. Herath, "Development Discourse," 819–834.

72. Herath, 819–834.

that should affect them. The failure to involve the people impacted directly in the process is not unconnected with the then European sense of ethnocentric superiority over other cultures. In Eurocentric perception, the traditions, customs, and social practices of rural communities were considered to be restrictive therefore needed to be eradicated and replaced with the methodology that leads to modernization. This explains the lack of involvement of non-Western nations in the fashioning of the concept and process of development in the modernization approach. The non-involvement of the people that are the direct beneficiary of the modernization approach in the envisioning, the planning, the implementation, and evaluation of development does not resonate with the sociocultural sense of community and communal participation.

Fourth, development is about the exploitative use of natural resources since the focus of modernization is the use of technology for mass production to promote high consumption. This negates the divinely delegated responsibility of cultivating nature with a sense of stewardship as prescribed in the biblical metanarrative. The biblical metanarrative show that human beings are supposed to be stewards of God's creation not exploiters. Human beings should make use of the environment for the sustenance of life but staying in harmonious relationships with God, self, others, and nature.

Fifth, modernization theory implies that the West only has the monopoly of defining development. This is contrary to the biblical mandate given to humans by God. The approach therefore ignores the sovereignty of God over human reasoning and human capabilities.

Sixth, the spiritual dimension of human life and the relationship between human beings and God as described in the biblical metanarrative is not considered nor addressed as a concern. Instead the goal of modernization is limited to the temporal material and social well-being of human beings. It does not regard the spiritual dimension of human nature nor the future eternal state of shalom described in the biblical metanarrative. Therefore, modernization theory does not address the issue of development holistically and it is limited to a vision of an assumed utopian state in a temporal world. In addition to these limitations the prescribed methodology for development from the modernization perspective cannot lead, nor is it aimed at leading, to the application of biblical shalom. The term biblical shalom describes God's shalom therefore it is used interchangeably in this study. The concern of this study is to determine how effective a participatory appreciative dialogue approach could be for the application of biblical shalom in a sustainable transformational development process in rural communities in Nigeria.

Dependency Theory

Non-Western countries did not adopt or adapt to the progressive development path modernization theory proposed, instead, they remained more or less "underdeveloped." The economic gap between the rich Western nations and the poor non-Western countries steadily increased instead. Dependency theory offers explanations that account for the continued failure of non-Western nations to develop along the proposed modernization path.[73] According to Dhammika Herath, dependency theory is the product of a convergence of two intellectual traditions, neo-Marxism and the doctrine of the United Nations Economic Commission for Latin America (ECLA). On the one hand, Neo-Marxists proposed solutions to underdevelopment along the line of social revolution. On the other hand, the ECLA preferred a reformation approach that aims at reforming the international economic system.[74]

Dependency theory describes Western industrialized nations, Europe and America as core or metropolis, or dominant nations. Non-Western nations are described as dependent, periphery or satellite nations. Nations in Latin America, Asia, and Africa are the periphery or satellite nations. Thus, as stated above, J. Timmons Roberts and Amy Hite write that dependency theory presents the world as consisting of two economic poles, wealthy nations that are at the center of the global capitalist system and poorer nations that are satellite or periphery.[75] Raul Prebisch, according to Peet and Hartwick, see the world "as two distinct areas, a center of economic power in Europe and the United States, and a periphery of weaker countries in Latin America, Africa, and Asia."[76] How can this socio-political dichotomy be explained? Emma Crewe and Richard Axelby write that the dismantling of European colonialism led to the birth of new independent nation states across much of Africa and Asia, followed by concern for the economic and

---

73. Herath, 819–834.

74. Herath, 820.

75. Roberts and Hite, 12.

76. Peet and Hartwick, *Theories of Development*, 65–66.

political development of the new nation states.[77] After this brief mention of the economic and political dichotomy dependency theory uses to analyze nations we turn to its basic argument.

Theotonio Dos Santos and Elliot, both posit that the basic argument of the various kinds of dependency theory is that the economy of certain nations, particularly Western nations, is conditioned by the development and expansion of another economy, to which the former, non-Western nations, is subjected rather than any presumed inadequacies in economic, social, or environmental conditions within those non-Western nations.[78] The modernization theories, conceptualized in the socio-political context of Western nations, argue that inadequacies in economic, social, or environmental conditions within non-Western, post-colonial nations are responsible for their underdevelopment.[79] Dependency theory, conceptualized in a non-Western socio-political context, reacts against the presuppositions upon which the modernization theory was drawn. Richard Peet writes that dependency theory, as it originated in Latin America, is "a reaction against the failure of earlier theories to adequately explain economic backwardness in Latin America."[80] The economies of both Western and non-Western nations are integrated into one global economic system. Therefore, development and underdevelopment are interdependent structures in the global economic system.[81]

According to Roberts and Hite, "For dependency theorists the underdevelopment in the periphery is the direct result of the development in the center, and vice versa."[82] Dependency theorists therefore argue that the application of the modernization theory through the global economic system makes it possible for the "developed" nations to in fact "under develop" the underdeveloped nations.[83] Therefore, development and underdevelopment are considered to be two sides of the same coin.[84] Note here that both modernization

---

77. Crewe and Axelby, *Anthropology and Development*, 6.

78. Dos Santos, "Structure of Dependence," 194; Elliot, *Introduction to Sustainable Development*, 29.

79. Hettne, *Development Theory*, 3.

80. Peet, *Global Capitalism*, 43.

81. Peet, 45.

82. Roberts and Hite, "Editor's Introduction," 12.

83. Dos Santos, "Structure of Dependence," 194.

84. Elliot, *Introduction to Sustainable Development*, 29.

theory and dependency theory focus primarily on economic growth as a means of development in the "under developed" nations.

Dos Santos summarizes the historic forms of dependency into three types of dependencies. The first type is "colonial dependence" and the second type is "financial-industrial dependence." In both types of dependencies production is geared towards those products for export therefore production is dependent on demand from industrial nations. Hence, dependent nations' development is characterized by exportation. The growth of the internal markets in the export economies is restricted. National income is derived from export and the income is used to import inputs like machineries required for the production of raw materials for export or the import of luxury goods consumed by a few rich people. Another restriction is that the available manpower in the export economy is subject to "very arduous forms of super-exploitation" that do not allow them to benefit sufficiently for their consumption; instead they have to depend on their "subsistence economy" to complement their income or to survive in periods of economic depression. A final form of restriction is found where accumulated surplus, due to the activities of foreign investors, is sent abroad in the form of profits rather than making it available for internal consumption or for reinvestment. The third type of dependency, "technological-industrial dependence," is characterized by investments by multinational corporations who invest in industries to address internal markets of underdeveloped nations.[85]

Dependency theory claims that through the process of modernization politically emerging "Majority World"[86] nations in the 1950s and 1960s were incorporated by Western industrialized nations, through political maneuvers, into an exploitative world economic system in subordinate positions.[87] Dos Santos argues that an analysis of the process that integrates the economies of different nations into "a world market of commodities, capital, and even of labor power" shows that the relationships between the different economies are unequal because some economies develop at the expense of others.[88]

---

85. Dos Santos, "Structure of Dependence," 195–196.

86. Majority World will be used throughout meaning "third world" or "global south."

87. Elliot, *Introduction to Sustainable Development*, 29.

88. Dos Santos, "Structure of Development," 194.

Dependency theorists, Alvin Y. So,[89] Paul Baran,[90] and Roberts and Hite,[91] tie the characteristics of development, which is underdevelopment, in Majority World nations to political and economic inequalities. On his part So describes the unequal relationships between Western nations and Majority World nations, in strong language, as "imposed, exploitative, dependent, economic relationships which was incompatible with development."[92] Dependency theory thus describes historical conditions that shaped the structure of a world economic system that favors the economic development of some dominant countries to the detriment of other dependent countries. The theory implicates, from a historical perspective, the global political and economic structure as a structure that limits the possibilities of positive development in the economies of the dependent nations. According to Roberts and Hite, "For dependency theorists the underdevelopment in the periphery is the direct result of the development in the center, and vice versa."[93] Dependency theory therefore is first and foremost an explanation because the modernization theory did not provide an explanation for underdevelopment.[94]

In addition to being an alternative explanation for the underdevelopment of the non-Western nations dependency theory proposes an alternative plan of action to overcome underdevelopment. Patrice Franko reports that Presbich viewed development from a Latin American perspective to be a "need to promote growth in the face of an international system controlled by the center countries."[95]

The reformist version of the dependency theory offers an approach that favors reforms in international economy but neo-Marxist version favors a socialist revolutionary approach. The dependency theory proposed an alternative approach to the economic and social development of peripheral dependent nations. The approach aims to place peripheral nations in a trade relation that is not dependent on the type of exploitative relationships that exists between Western (core) and non-Western (peripheral) nations. The ECLA

---

89. So, "Dependency and World Systems."

90. Baran, *Political Economy of Growth*, 16.

91. Roberts and Hite, "Editor's Introduction," 12.

92. So, "Dependency and World Systems."

93. Roberts and Hite, "Editor's Introduction," 12.

94. Rist, *History of Development*, 116.

95. Franko, *Puzzle of Latin American*, 52

development strategy was industrialization through import substitution. The Import Substitution Industrialization (ISI) strategy purports the restriction of the importation of finished goods into the nation. Elliot describes ISI as "a strategy to enable peripheral countries to industrialize through looking inward (setting up domestic industry and supplying markets previously served by imports)."[96] Elliot further states that the ISI approach depends on the state protecting new industries through import tariffs, quotas, and controlling access to foreign exchange.[97] An analysis of the propositions of the dependency theory provides a clearer understanding of the alternative approach to economic and social development in dependent nations because "dependency theory focuses on understanding the periphery by looking at core-periphery relations."[98] Herath,[99] describes six major propositions of dependency theory as follows.

First, nations in Latin America, Asia, and Africa do not exist in isolation. Relations between these nations and the industrial nations (core) are asymmetrical. The flow of power and control is from the industrial nations of the West to the non-Western nations (periphery). Thus, political and economic events in the core nations have huge impact on the politics and economies of the periphery nations, whereas political and economic events in periphery nations have little impact on the core nations.

Second, interactions among the nations are skewed in a manner that makes periphery nations remain weak. Interaction among core nations is tremendous. There is also much interaction between core and periphery nations. However, there is little interaction between periphery nations. Because of the poor interaction between periphery nations these nations are not able to form a united and formidable alliance to be in a better position to stand up to the exploitative economic control the core nations have over the periphery nations.

The economic ties and relationships between core nations and periphery nations are not equitable. This third proposition posits that these relationships are advantageous for the core nations and disadvantageous for the periphery

---

96. Elliot, *Introduction to Sustainable Development*, 29.
97. Elliot, 29.
98. Martínez-Vela, "World Systems Theory."
99. Herath, "Development Discourse," 819–834.

nations. Because of this imbalance there is a continual widening of the economic gap between the richer core nations and the poorer peripheral nations. Hence, there is no likelihood of narrowing the economic gap between these two categories of nations.

The fourth proposition is that underdevelopment in peripheral nations is not a natural state but a condition caused by core nations. The core nations are actively under developing the peripheral nations.

Fifth, the underdevelopment of the weak peripheral nations is directly related to the development of the powerful core nations. Both core and peripheral nations are part of, and interdependent, even in asymmetrical ways, of the world economic system. Therefore, the continuous application of capitalism, the dominant world economic system, is sustaining the economic system responsible for the underdevelopment of non-Western nations.

Finally, the kind of relationship between core nations and peripheral nations is duplicated within individual peripheral nations. There are core or metropolitan centers, urban centers, which dominate and exploit periphery areas, rural centers.[100]

Basically, dependency theorists demonstrate a critical attitude toward the principles of the modernization theory. Lisa Zuchell writes that theorists in the dependency school of thought primarily allege that the modernization theory introduced and applied by Western nations had negative social, technological, and economic advancement of non-Western nations.[101] How has the application of the dependency theory affected the development of peripheral nations?

The unit of analysis in studying underdevelopment is the national society. J. Samuel Valenzuela and Arturo Valenzuela argue that the dependency perspective assumes that the development of any nation is best understood in connection with the historic integration of dependent nations into the global "political-economic system which emerged in the wave of European colonization of the world."[102] Harrison concurs by arguing that the theory shows that the interdependence between the economies of non-Western nations and those of Western nations in the context of world trade has resulted in a

---

100. Herath, "Development Discourse," 819–834.

101. Zuchell, "Theory of International Development."

102. Valenzuela and Valenzuela, "Modernization and Dependency," 204.

form of dependency that brings about the underdevelopment of non-Western nations.[103] Rural communities are not considered as direct stakeholders in the approach to development from the dependency theoretical approach.

The goal of the dependency theory therefore, like that of the modernization theory, is economic growth. The difference between both is the means of achieving development. Myers argues that "the goal of development for both theories was still economic growth, but the means of development was now a choice between Marxist and capitalist economics."[104]

The motivation for the dependency theory does not consider the spiritual needs of the people in the nations. Its motivation is to solve social, political, and economic problems. Although dependency theory developed as a critical reaction to the modernization theory it also towed the line of being a problem-solving approach to the problem of material poverty. The dependency theory like the modernization theory did not discern nor link a relationship between the problem of material poverty and the spiritual aspect of life.

World-System Theory

The world-system theory posits that there is a world economic system in which some sociocultural areas benefit while others are exploited due to unequal exchange in the global market. The history of the development of the world-system theory is closely associated with Immanuel Wallerstein, a sociologist. Wallerstein argues that, as early as the sixteenth century, an economic system that integrates different nations into a unified economic system not bound by any unitary political, social, or cultural structure developed and expanded; a unified economic system that is characterized by a bound system of divided labor that gives rise to significant exchange of essential goods and capital.[105] Scott Applerouth and Laura Desfor Edles state that Wallerstein contends that the process of unifying the global economic system was the result of European nations racing "to establish colonies and an international network of economic trade relations."[106]

---

103. Harrison, *Sociology of Modernization*, x.

104. Myers, *Walking with the Poor*, 28.

105. Wallerstein, *World-Systems Analysis*, x, 23; Peet and Hartwick, *Theories of Development*, 173.

106. Applerouth and Desfor Edles, *Sociological Theory*, 559.

There are four underlying principles for the world-system theory. First, the global economic system is the objective context within which the economies of nations are to be evaluated. Second, the global economic system is characterized by an international division of labor connected through a structured set of relations between three types of economic zones. Third, the economic zones are dynamic in the sense that they are constantly evolving new ways to grow. Finally, economic zones can be mobile moving either upwardly or downwardly in the global economic system.[107] These principles make the world-system theory coherent and give meaning to the global structure of the complex relations of interdependence of economic processes which is organized by the division of labor and not governed by any overarching single political structure.[108]

Ivan Eckhardt argues that Wallerstein's world-system theory is a holistic and macroscopic point of view "to critically study both the reality and the history of the modern world."[109] Remy Herrera also describes Wallerstein's world-system theory as "a holistic explanatory model, a structural analysis, a combination of history and theory"[110] that provides a comprehensive representation of phenomena that attempt to combine the economic, the social, and the political. Sorinal describes the world-system theory as a political and intellectual endeavor that falls into the fields of historical sociology and economic history but because of its emphasis on development and unequal opportunities across nations it has been embraced by development theorists and practitioners.[111] Carlos A. Martinez-Vela and Sorinal both define the world-system theory as "a macro sociological perspective that seeks to explain the dynamics of the capitalist world economy as a total system."[112] Hence the world-system theory explains the historical dynamics that created the global economic system. It is a theory that provides a theoretical framework that makes it possible to understand the historical development of the

---

107. Thompson, "World Systems Theory."
108. Herrera, "Theories of Capitalist World-System," 209.
109. Eckhardt, "Immanuel Wallerstein," 95–98.
110. Herrera, "Theories of Capitalist World-System," 210.
111. Sorinal, "Immanuel Wallerstein's World System."
112. Martínez-Vela, "World System Theory"; Sorinal, "Immanuel Wallerstein's World System."

existing capitalist economic system and the dynamics of its division of labor in a systemic economic structure that has no overarching political structure.[113]

The world-system theory posits that there is a single world market that is characterized by a drive for profit.[114] Appelrouth and Edles state that the capitalist world economy is characterized by a never-ending drive for profit, therefore the central objective for participating in production of goods or services "is determined not by their use, but rather by the potential value of their sale in the market."[115] Hence in the capitalist world economic system production is for profits and production is constantly expanded to make profit. The theory argues that the world is connected by a complex network of economic exchange relationship characterized by mechanisms that promote a redistribution of resources from periphery areas to core areas.[116] Therefore the driving force or motivating factor in the capitalist world economy is profit.

Though not controlled by any one political center, the capitalist world economy is characterized by the division of a hierarchy of labor or economic tasks among functionally defined and geographically distinct member states with one world market.[117] The labor is divided among functionally defined and geographically distinct membership groups, different nations, and different cultures, in a hierarchy of economic tasks. The world-system theory categorizes the distinct groups in three spatial and temporal categories or units of analysis. Each unit of analysis is described based on its relative position of production and exchange of basic goods and raw materials within the global market system.[118] The dependency theory categorizes the structure of the global economic system to consist of core and periphery nations. The world-system theory categorizes the nations into three economic, not necessarily geopolitical, zones: core, semi-periphery, and periphery.[119] Eckhardt,

113. Herrera, "Theories of Capitalist World-System," 218.

114. Peet and Hartwick, *Theories of Development*, 173.

115. Appelrouth and Edles, *Sociological Theory*, 568.

116. Sorinal, "Immanuel Wallerstein's World System."

117. Wallerstein, *Modern World System*, 229. See also, Martínez-Vela, "World Systems Theory."

118. Martínez-Vela, "World Systems Theory."

119. Roberts and Hite, "Editor's Introduction," 15; Edelman and Haugerud, "Introduction," 13, 14.

states that Wallerstein's core-periphery is an economic, not a geographical phenomenon.[120]

There are identifiable socio-political areas that are characteristically in the core zone. The core zone benefits most from the capitalist world economy. Nations of the core zone creatively produce goods and services to be sold on the world market for profit. These nations benefit the most profits from the exchange because of industrialization, political, and military advantages. These nations are described as the core nations in the world economic order. Core nations use these advantages to manipulate and exploit nations in peripheral zones for cheap labor and cheap raw materials. In addition, these core nations promote capital accumulation internally and within the world economic system.[121]

Nations that are defined as nations in the periphery zones are nations that provide the raw materials for the industrialized core zone nations. Periphery zone nations also provide the core zone nations the markets in which to market their manufactured goods for profit. Periphery zone nations lack strong central governments, may be controlled by other nations, and are dependent on core zone nations for capital to industrialize and have underdeveloped industries. Labor intensive production through low-skilled labor is also a characteristic of the periphery zone nations. Foreign investors from core zone nations promote the extraction of raw materials for export to core nations. The exchange of peripheral raw materials against core manufacturers on the global market is skewed to the advantage of the core nations. Therefore, when peripheral products, which attract cheap and unfair value, are exchanged with products from core nations, products that are over-valued, there is an unequal exchange. This results in the transfer of surplus value from the periphery nations to core nations.[122]

Semi-periphery zones are the socio-political areas "with strong enterprises that export products to peripheral zones, but that also relates to core zones as importers of more advance products."[123] Christopher Chase-Dunn describes semi-periphery zones as polities that are in the middle of a core/periphery

---

120. Eckhardt, "Immanuel Wallerstein."
121. Elwell, "Wallerstein's World Systems."
122. Wallerstein, *World-System Analysis*, 98.
123. Wallerstein, 30.

hierarchy of the world-system.[124] Semi-peripheral zones are characterized by the struggle to implement organizational and ideological forms that facilitate mobility toward core zone characteristics and the struggle to avoid characteristics of peripheral zones.

According to Marc Edelman and Angelique Haugerud,[125] the world-system theory posits that the development of a nation is subsumed into an existing capitalist world economic system. The driving force of the capitalist economy is profit making through competition. Therefore, the unit of evaluating the development of any nation based on the world-system theory is the level of the nation's participation in the world market or global economy. Hence core nations promote global capitalist economy to achieve the goal of capital accumulation and consumption of goods and services for luxurious living. The market is the primary agent for the development and sustenance of the global capitalist economic system through the strategy of unequal exchange in a so-called free market. The global capitalist economic system as a macro-system does not directly engage rural communities directly in the process of facilitating economic, or even holistic, development.

This review of the world-system theory reveals the global quest for exploiting nature and the ecological context of human existence to gratify insatiable human quest for material comfort. The exploitative nature of the world economic system as defined by the world-system theory negates the divine mandate for human beings to cultivate nature. The world-system theory also reveals that the effort to universalize consumption demonstrates insensitivity to the diversity of human needs in different socio-political and ecological contexts. Hence, the theory explains the reason for competition rather than cooperation for the common good of human beings regardless of their social, cultural, political, economic, and ecological context. The theory also reveals the insensitivity of the core nations to the actual needs of the peripheral nations hence the core nations impose their perceived human needs on the peripheral nations while the semi-peripheral nations strive to mimic the core nations. Therefore, the peripheral nations are pressured into engaging in misplaced priority and purpose of human labor. These global characteristics defined by the world-system theory do have their impact even

---

124. Christopher Chase-Dunn, "Contemporary Semiperipheral Development."

125. Edelman and Haugerud, "Introduction," 14.

in rural communities because of the inter-connectivity of nations through information technology, different media of communication, and ease of travel and migration.

The world-system theory has been described from philosophical, political, historical, intellectual, sociological, and economic perspectives by different scholars. A theological perspective can be added. From a Christian theological perspective, the world-system theory reveals the focus of development on, and near worship of, the "other god" of the global economic system for the glory of the greatest profit maker(s). God the Creator is not the center of nor the object of worship and devotion but economic and material gains. The focus is not on the welfare and development of people in economically and technologically weaker nations rather it is on the increasing development and pleasure of people in the economically and technologically stronger nations at the expense of the weaker nations. The process of development is therefore exploitation rather than cultivation. The theory ignores God therefore it does not view development in the light of cultivating or sustaining spiritual relationship with God nor the biblical cultural mandate to cultivate rather than to exploit the resources, both human and ecological relationships. And since the theory considers and explains the focus and process of development at the international and global level it gives no attention to rural communities therefore it makes no provision for the holistic development of people at the micro-rural community level. Therefore, the world-system theory does not provide for holistic transformational development for the application of biblical shalom.

Conclusion on Development Theories

The review of literatures in this section sought to determine the adequacy or inadequacy of the three global theories of development for the purpose of facilitating holistic transformational development in rural communities, particularly in Nigeria and generally in Africa. The review shows that the theories attempt to describe and develop frameworks for economic growth and its consequent impact on the socio-political well-being of nations. However, the theories have ignored the impact of religious and spiritual well-being of human beings in any development process. For example, the Christian faith as a religion posits that at creation human beings were created to have a spiritual relationship with God. The nature and state of the spiritual relationship between God and humans affects the responses of human beings in their psychological relationship with themselves, their social relationship with other human beings, and their relationship with nature. The Christian belief is that the distortion of the spiritual relationship with God has negative impact on the other relationships. Hence, the religious and spiritual aspects of human societies have impact on the way development is perceived and promoted. Therefore, the global theories do not facilitate holistic development since they ignore the religious and spiritual aspect of human existence. The goal of each of these approaches is a temporal utopian experience of economic, physical, social, and political life. Thus, the frameworks for each of these theories prescribe the application of pragmatic methods and tools to enhance economic growth. The methods and tools applied by each of them promote the exploitation of creation or environment for human pleasure. The exploitation of creation for human pleasure is opposed to biblical description of God intending human beings cultivating creation as co-regents and stewards for the glory of God. The exploitation of creation for human pleasure has an impact in promoting competition rather than cooperation for the common good of human beings. National or political or commercial institutions, rather than God, are the frame of reference for the formulation of policies and for the application of methodology proposed for each of the theories reviewed. These theories therefore do not have a framework of reference that is supreme or supra-human to humanly established institutions. They view development to be facilitated by stronger nations or organizations with economic, political, and technological superiority for weaker nations and communities as beneficiaries. In view of the foregoing critique it can be concluded that these theories are: (1) not holistic; (2) exploiting rather than cultivating creation; (3) non-participatory for the recipients of development who are seen as objects rather than subjects. Although the International Bank for Reconstruction and Development (the World Bank) has now recognized the value of engaging people as participators who share their values and perspectives to allow "policy makers to draw on all perspective so that change becomes inclusive,"[126] more needs to be done; (4) macroscopic rather than microscopic in scope; and (5) dependent on human rationality without reference to the supreme creator. The application of the frameworks of these theories in rural communities has

---

126. Johnson, "Introduction," vii.

proven inadequate because rural communities in Nigeria, for instance, have remained in states of abject socio-economic poverty.

The following also provide additional reasons why the application of the frameworks of these theories are found to be inadequate for rural communities and from a biblical perspective: (1) these theories do not treat recipients of development as human beings with the dignity of being creatures created in God's image, rather recipients of development are considered as objects rather than subjects of development; (2) the methods applied do not engage recipients of development as participants in the process of their development; (3) the frameworks of the theories do not conform to the plan of God. God's plan is for human beings to cultivate creation as co-regents and to be stewards of God's creation for the glory of God and Creator rather than the exploiters of God's creation primarily for human consumption; and (4) The framework and methods of these theories are inadequate for application in rural community contexts where life is viewed holistically, in a similar fashion as the biblical view of life, rather than in parts.

It has been stated in chapter 1 that this study is concerned with how effective a participatory appreciative dialogue approach could be for the application of biblical shalom in the process of sustainable holistic transformational development in Nigeria. The theories reviewed in this section do not make provision for the possibility of applying biblical shalom and for sustainable holistic transformational development in rural communities. There are at least three reasons for this claim. First, the theories do not address the general human religious practices or spiritual relationship with the divine for the purpose of development in different religions, nor specifically the biblical perspective of development. The theories do not address the beliefs and understanding people have about their relationship, responsibility, and obligations to the divine. By not paying adequate attention to the spiritual needs of human beings, the theories are not holistic in perspective. And for not considering the biblical perspective of development, the theories are inadequate for the application of biblical shalom. Second, since the theories are not holistic in perspective, their application has not led to the achievement of the goal of a holistic utopian state and do not show a promise of doing so in the future. Third, the theories do not engage rural communities in the process of envisioning, planning, execution, and evaluation of development that is contextually relevant to the people living in their specific sociocultural milieu. Consequently, they have overlooked the importance of context in the life of a people. Therefore, it can be argued that the application of these theories in rural communities, particularly in Nigeria and more broadly in other African nations which share common characteristics, have failed to yield the needed results. A supplementary approach is needed which is what this study proposes, and since the study is focused on rural communities the next section is a review on related literature on community development.

Community Development

Community development (CD) is concerned with the promotion of communal coherence that enables communities to relate to one another peacefully in order to make collective decisions and take collective actions to promote the community's well-being on issues of social, economic, political, vocational, religious, and other interests. R. Warren Flint describes a community as a group of people in a lively, self-reinforcing resonance of ever-changing, interactive, interdependent, reciprocal, and trusting relationship with one another.[127] A community can be place-based or interest-based.[128] As people interact with one another, they develop both formal and informal relationships that generate and manifest either good or conflict experiences.[129] Social interaction in the present global reality is no longer limited to spatial or chronological proximity. This collapse of space and time is due to advance in technology that has made inconsequential separation of time and space because of speed of travel and digital communication. Therefore, there are "post-place" communities, communities that are interest-based where its members interact with one another in either formal or non-formal relationships on issues of common interest without the limitations of time and space. People living and interacting with one another in a particular geographical location are a place-based community. The focus of this study is on place-based communities.

The practice of place-based community development originates probably with the establishment of the first human community in the garden of Eden based on the biblical account of creation. The act of Adam categorizing God's

---

127. Flint, *Practice of Sustainable Community*, 5.

128. Phillips and Pittman, "Framework for Community," 5.

129. Gilchrist, *Well-Connected Community*, 1.

creation and cultivating the natural habitat, at God's command, in which Adam and Eve were created and placed is an act of development. However, community development as a concept has been developed over time to become a complex interdisciplinary field of study as well as a practiced profession.[130] According to Paul Hoggett, Marjorie Mayo, and Chris Miller, the origin of the concept of community development can be traced to "work with the urban poor of industrializing nations at the beginning of the twentieth century."[131] Hoggett, Mayo, and Miller, further, state that the focus expanded to include disadvantaged communities in both rural and urban areas. Rhonda Phillips and Robert H. Pittman, point to the post-Second World War reconstruction efforts to improve the lot of less developed countries as the origin of interest in modern CD.[132] Community development has become a major post-colonial intervention strategy in developing countries.[133]

Definition of Community Development

Community development (CD) is defined by different scholars as either a process or an outcome of a process or both a process and an outcome of a process.[134] Phillips and Pittman define CD as a process and as an outcome that includes the community taking collective action with a resultant improvement in the community in any or all realms: physical, environmental, cultural, social, political, economic, etc.[135] Michael Pitchford defines CD as a process undertaken by a community to resolve problems in the community, identified by the community, and to promote changes that facilitate greater equality, justice, and respect within the community, a process that "can be done by volunteers and activists as well as paid professionals."[136] David Matarrita-Cascante and Mark A. Brennan propose a definition of CD that emphasizes both process and outcome:

---

130. Phillips and Pittman, "Editors' Introduction," xxv.

131. Hoggett, Mayo, and Miller, *Dilemma of Development*, 1.

132. Phillips and Pittman, "Framework for Community ," 3.

133. Hogget, Mayo, and Miller, *Dilemma of Development*, 1.

134. Phillips and Pittman, "Framework for Community," 3.

135. Phillips and Pittman, 6.

136. Pitchford, *Making Space for Community*, 32–33. Pitchford, cites the definitions of Henderson and Thomas, of Community Development Exchange, and of The Federation of Community Development Learning, to draw his definition.

Community development is a process that entails organization, facilitation, and action, which allows people to establish ways to create the community they want to live in. It is a process that provides vision, planning, direction, and coordinated action towards desired goals associated with the promotion of efforts aimed at improving the conditions in which local resources operate. As a result, community developers harness local economic, human, and physical resources to secure daily requirements and respond to changing needs and conditions.[137]

This definition highlights people, in a given geographical location, as stakeholders in structural relationships through which they interact and collectively harness economic and physical resources to facilitate their well-being. The people create or possess the vision of "the community they want to live in." The people plan, direct, and coordinate the activities that will lead to the development of the kind of "community they want to live in."[138] However, the mention of "community developers" in this definition implies that there are CD facilitators (who may be professionals) who act by harnessing "local economic, human, and physical resources to secure daily requirements and respond to changing needs and conditions."[139] Community developers, professionals or non-professionals who might or might not be "outsiders," engaged in the process with members of a community serve as facilitators to empower the "insider" members to harness all the requisite resources available to them in a process that facilitates the realization of the vision or the kind of community they want to live in. This definition does not limit the resources to social, economic, physical, and natural resources but allows room for the supernatural spiritual resource made available by God through the spiritual relationship between God and human beings. The supernatural resource, which is presupposed from a biblical perspective, can be accessible to the community.

Central to these definitions is the role of people in the community and the fact that the focus is not limited to problem-solving it simply states "improving the conditions in which local resources operate." It is people in a

---

137. Matarrita-Cascante and Brennan, "Conceptualizing Community Development," 297.

138. Matarrita-Cascante and Brennan, 297.

139. Matarrita-Cascante and Brennan, 297.

community acting on the basis of communal cohesion to collectively identify what needs to be improved in the community, to collectively identify resources needed for improving the local condition, to make collective decisions and to take collective action for improving the well-being of the community. Communal cohesion is achieved through healthy and harmonious interpersonal relationships. Cohesion implies the existence of interrelated resources or assets in a system of relationships.

Resources in Community Development

Communities need a wide range of resources for subsistence and improvement of the holistic well-being of the communities. The resources are the building blocks for community life. Phillips and Pittman summarize, from different CD literatures, five community resources or assets that are interrelated and thus enhance cohesion in a community. They are social capital, human capital, physical capital, financial capital, and environmental capital.[140] Anna Haines adds two other resources these are cultural capital and political capital.[141]

Social capital is the most basic resource in any community because it consists of the people in the community and the social networks that connect the people. Haines describes social capital as "the social relationships within a community" characterized by trust, norms, and social networks.[142] Paul W. Mattessich notes that these social relationships provide the structural interconnections among people that enables the flow of information, ideas, products, and services in the community. The interconnections provide the framework for the people's cognitive sense of shared purpose, which promotes increased commitment and mutual trust and strengthens norms of reciprocity in the community.[143] Alison Gilchrist, citing Woolcock, posits that there are three types of social capital that promote cohesion in a community. They are bonding capital, bridging capital, and linking capital. Bonding capital consists of the social ties within a homogeneous group. Bridging capital consists of the interest ties among different groups. Linking capital is derived from links

---

140. Phillips and Pittman, "Framework for Community," 6–7.
141. Haines, "Asset-based Community Development," 41.
142. Haines, 41.
143. Mattessich, "Social Capital and Community," 51.

between different groups beyond peer boundaries. The links make it possible for "people to gain influence and resources outside their normal circles."[144] The social capital in rural communities in the Nigerian context, which are characterized by people with sociocultural and religious homogeneity, can be developed through intentional actions and strategies employed by facilitators of holistic transformational development.

Human capital as a community resource include, among other things, labor, skill, capabilities, and experience. Susan Saegert indicates that skills acquired in group processes, knowledge of community resources, and competence in specific tasks constitute the human capital in a community.[145] Cultivating and improving the quality of human capital in a community is essential because it is vital for the management of other resources to produce progress, change, or transformation.

The physical capital of a community includes built infrastructures and natural assets. Physical capital facilitates means of subsistence, pleasurable environment, and providing the community with a sense of identity.[146] Financial capital refers to access to funds and credit markets. And environmental capital includes natural resources, land, weather, etc. Haines describes political capital as the capacity of a community to exert political influence.[147]

To the seven community resources, reviewed above, an eighth, which is spiritual capital, can be added. Spiritual capital is missing in Phillips's and Pittman's as well as Haines's summary of community resources in the CD literatures they reviewed. The spiritual capital is a resource, from a biblical perspective, obtained from the divine supernatural source, God. The spiritual resource includes divinely inspired guidelines revealed in the biblical metanarrative. It also includes the supernatural activities of the Holy Spirit to act and bring about changes that defy natural or scientific explanations.

Approaches to Community Development

A number of authors have proposed models or strategies to explain different approaches to community development. The models are intended to provide

---

144. Gilchrist, *Well-Connected Community*, 12; see also, Phillips and Pittman, "Framework for Community," 6.

145. Saegert, "Building Civic Capacity," 224.

146. Matarrita-Cascante and Brennan, "Conceptualizing Community Development," 295.

147. Haines, "Asset-based Community Development," 41.

explanation for the ways essential resources for CD can be integrated in a process that makes it possible for a community to work together in order to produce desirable outcome or outcomes. For example, Rothman's model of community change differentiates between four different ways in which community changes can occur. The four ways are: (1) Social planning, which aims at solving specific problems in a community. In this approach the program is designed, initiated, and implemented by and through experts. The approach is applied through policies and laws imposed on the community. (2) Community action, which is based on the initiation of a strong community leadership that identifies resources the community lacks and organizes members of the community to source for external resources. (3) Community development, this is initiated within the community to mobilize members of to use internal resources to initiate changes. In this approach the community, not the facilitator, is in control and the solutions to problems in the community. The solutions are based on indigenous knowledge and traditions. (4) Finally, community mobilization, which mobilizes or encourages members of a community to participate in activities aimed at solving their problems. The solutions are designed by experts and the members of the community are expected to contribute internal resources to the activities designed to solve the problems identified.[148]

Dirk Booy and Sarone Ole Sena state that, historically, education and development interventions have had three approaches: banking approach, problem-solving approach, and strength-based approach.[149] (1) The banking approach assumes that communities that require development intervention are empty, lacking capacities, skills, hope, spirit, and resources to build on. The banking approach dominated from the 1950s wherein development was done to the people by investment and transferring capital and technical resources to the communities. In the 1960s development was done for the people. In both the banking and problem-solving approaches communities were recipients of development but not active participants. In the 1970s the approaches involved communities in the process for achieving development but all the activities were orchestrated by experts from outside the community who had blueprint strategies for community capacity building and development. The

---

148. Hyman, "Six Models of Community," 32–47.
149. Booy and Sena, "Capacity Building," 38.

culture and institutions of the communities were viewed to be obstacles to development and should be eliminated completely. Thus, development was done with the participation of the people. (2) The problem-solving approach assumes that the communities are weak, with many problems. In this approach development is done with the people. Members of the communities were engaged to actively participate in the problem-solving process. Members of the communities were treated as persons with thinking, reflective, and acting capacities therefore development planners engaged the communities in "social construction of knowledge" by identifying problems, finding root causes of these problems, and working out practical ways to work towards changing the situation. Development practitioners created situations in which genuine dialogues take place for both members of the community and the development practitioners and for them both to share experiences, listen to, and learn from each other. In the problem-solving approach the communities develop the capacity to identify problems, plan with the development practitioners or partners, and link knowledge with action. (3) The strength-based approach, which has been adopted for this study, assumes the communities have capacities and strengths they can build on. The strength-based approach is an appreciative approach that celebrates past successes and builds upon the best of the past and the successes of the present.[150]

Matarrita-Cascante and Brennan have proposed a community development typology that synthesizes different approaches to CD in different contexts in modern times. Matarrita-Cascante and Brennan's typology is based on people-centered approach forms of CD.[151] This typology is adopted to provide a conceptual framework for understanding the approaches of the three CRDOs reviewed in a later section of this chapter. This typology is also a useful tool for analyzing the primary data collected and collated in this study which applies a people-centered approach to CD.

In Matarrita-Cascante and Brennan's typology there are three forms or models in a continuum. At one extreme is the imposed model and at the other extreme is the self-help model. In between these two extreme models is the directed model, which combines elements from the two extreme models

---

150. Booy and Sena, 38–41.

151. Matarrita-Cascante and Brennan, "Conceptualizing Community Development," 297–300.

in the continuum. Before the three models are reviewed it should be noted that Matarrita-Cascante and Brennan state that the models are not mutually exclusive because multiple approaches to development often coexist in the same place, and all the different approaches are critical for achieving goals considered necessary for the improvement of a community's living condition. The categories help in identifying and understanding the ways in which they tackle the basic needs of the community.

Imposed model of community development

Development efforts in the imposed form or model of CD seek to improve the living conditions of a community through physical and economic development by developing infrastructural facilities and technology. This model corresponds with the banking approach described earlier. Therefore, the focus is on a process of applying technological, financial, physical, and material resources to achieve a specific purpose in the community. The CD processes in the imposed models are guided by the expertise and judgment of professional and technical facilitators. Professional and technical facilitators are the primary actors involved in the imposed model. These primary actors do not require, and may not seek, the community members' input or involvement in the process. Hence there is little or even no learning outcome for the large majority of the community members. The imposed model provides the infrastructural facilities that the community lacks the technology, funds, and skills to develop. The professional and technical facilitators provide these infrastructures in a timely and efficient manner. However, members of the community are not provided the opportunity to be involved in the decision-making process. Negative consequences that arise from this non-involvement of members of the community include high dependency, feelings of alienation, opposition from members of the community, non-sustainability of the effort because members of the community do not have a sense of ownership, lack of empowerment of community members, and a failure to build a sense of communality.

Self-help model of community development

Members of a community are often the leading or primary actors promoting CD activities in their community in the self-help approaches to CD. The focus of the self-help model is on the establishment of mechanisms that will enhance the human resources of the community through capacity building. The capacity building process is achieved through interaction by members of the community. Members of the community are empowered with the capacities necessary for them to chart the course they are to follow to bring about holistic and progressive change in their locality. The mechanism developed in the process in the self-help model promotes the development of skills and know-how for a wider population in the community. Innovation, sustainable outcomes, sense of ownership, and the nurturing of the sense of community are some of the benefits of the self-help model of CD. An example of the self-help model is the application of Appreciative Inquiry (AI) approach to encourage communities to celebrate successes, as well as analyze critically the cause of mistakes and failures in order to find solutions to problems, and build upon those successes.[152] However, there are CD projects that may require the input of professional and technical personnel. Therefore, the self-help model encounters limitations in such situations because the communities may lack the technology, the time, the funds, and the expertise to design, implement, and maintain such projects.

Directed model of community development

The directed model of CD is characteristically a combination of elements of both the imposed and the self-help models of CD. Like the imposed model, in the directed model the primary actors are the professional and technical experts but unlike the imposed model the directed model engages members of the community, either out of interest or as a requirement, in the process. The model applies a problem-solving approach. In this model members of the community are often involved in the CD activities but based on predetermined options by the experts from which a group of stakeholders within the community may choose which to focus on. The CD project may be modified based on the input of members of the community. Matarrita-Cascante and Brennan cite Botes and van Rensburg as describing the directed model as an approach that attempts "to convince beneficiaries what is best for them."[153] Members of the community have the opportunity to collaborate and add

---

152. Booy and Sena, "Capacity Building," 40.

153. Matarrita-Cascante and Brennan, "Conceptualizing Community Development," 299.

their voice to the process of CD in their community. The changes that occur in the community are very easily observed and appreciated by the members of the community. The directed model enhances the building of a sense of community among members of the community. The model, however, faces the risk of creating tension when the input of members that are considered very important to the community are not taken seriously and thus not incorporated in the process. The opportunities for creative and innovative ideas are limited because of the limited options available and the limited number of persons that have the opportunity to be involved in the decision-making process. However, members of the community have the opportunity to gain some level of information and to add their voice in the process.

The Matarrita-Cascante and Brennan community development typology is adopted as the conceptual framework for understanding the approaches of the three CRDOs reviewed in a later section of this chapter. The CRDOs are guided by biblical and theological hermeneutics of development. Therefore, before the literature review concerning the CRDOs is presented it is necessary to review literature on the theology of development as part of the essential backdrop for understanding the perspective of the CRDOs. This review is also valuable for the analysis and interpretation of the primary data in this study.

Community development is concerned with harnessing and integrating essential resources to facilitate the achievement of desired experiences for the well-being of human communities, either in place-based or interest-based contexts. The essential resources include, but are not limited to: social capital, which consists of people and their social networks; human capital, which consists of labor, skills, capabilities, and experience; and spiritual capital, which consists of revealed divine guidance in the biblical metanarrative and the supernatural activities of the divine, for example, the Holy Spirit. There are different approaches that explain the strategies applied to facilitate CD. Matarrita-Cascante and Bernnan's models, especially the directed and the self-help models are of particular interest in this study. These people-centered models of CD provide the conceptual model for analyzing the CRDOs reviewed in this study and for analyzing the primary data collected and collated in this study. CD from a Christian perspective is guided by a theology of development. The next section describes theology of development.

Theology of Development

The theology of development is a guiding principle in the approaches of CRDOs and is also a guiding principle in this study. It is therefore necessary to understand what a theology of development is. To get a clear grasp of the theology of development a definition of theology is the point of departure for this section.

A Working Definition of Theology

Theology is "an intellectual and spiritual search for answers to questions about divine revelation and the human condition"[154] and "an ongoing conversation by fallible human beings, under the guidance of the Holy Spirit."[155] From this intellectual quest theology is subdivided into various specializations such as biblical theology, systematic theology, practical theology, and others.

Theology is based on a number of theoretical presuppositions, which include the following. First, the biblical text or metanarrative is the infallible source of divine revelation in which the sovereign Creator of all things, the triune God, reveals himself and his will through his words and deeds. Netland states that the source of theology, properly constructed, is the "unchanging truths revealed by God, truths that apply to all peoples in all cultures."[156] Hence the biblical metanarrative is the recognized normative standard for theology though theological confessions may reflect the characteristics of the culture of those who engaged in the process of doing theology. Second, the subject of the biblical metanarrative is God and his gracious provision of redemption for God's fallen creation through the person and work of Jesus Christ, the Son of God, and the second person of the triune Godhead. Kevin J. Vanhoozer, writes that the subject matter of theology is the "theodrama, the words and acts of the Triune God that culminate in God's reconciling all things to Himself in Jesus Christ."[157] Wright also argues that

> all the great sections of the canon of Scripture, all the great
> episodes of the Bible story, all the great doctrines of the biblical

---

154. Kunhiyop, *African Christian Theology*, 2.
155. Netland, "Introduction," 14.
156. Netland, 14.
157. Vanhoozer, "One Rule," 92.

faith, cohere around the Bible's central character – the living
God and His grand plan and purpose for the whole creation.[158]

Hence one will agree with H. Jürgen Hendriks, who writes that theology is, among other things, about "the missional praxis of the Triune God, Creator, Redeemer, Sanctifier."[159]

Third, theology is not limited to theoretical and academic theorization of concepts drawn from mere academic reflections by academic scholars in academic institutions. Theology is done by the people of God in specific sociocultural and historical contexts. Let us briefly define who the people of God are. The concept of the people of God refers to three sets of people. In the past, God chose a people, in the present God is choosing a people, and in the future God will have a people all chosen to partner with God in his mission as revealed in the biblical metanarrative. These are the Old Testament people of the historic nation Israel beginning from Abraham, the New Testament believers in Christ, the church, beginning with the first disciples of Jesus Christ, and all the dead, the living, and the future believers in Christ from all nations. The people of God, regardless of their sociocultural and historical context have the task of seeking intellectual and spiritual explanations for different human experiences in the light of the biblical text.

Therefore, the presupposition here is that theology is contextual and also practical. Meaning that theology is formulated in specific sociocultural and historical context. Paul L. Allen,[160] Harold A. Netland,[161] and Stephen B. Bevans,[162] agree that contextual theology involves rational reflection on the biblical message with a deliberate attention to the immediate context of those involved in theologizing. Hence the presupposition contextual theology includes two interrelated mental actions. First, is rational reflection on unchanging and supra-cultural message of the Bible. And second, a striving to arrive at a meaningful understanding of the faith commitment that the biblical message generates in Christians in their prevailing circumstances or experiences. The answers drawn from the process of intellectual and spiritual

---

158. Wright, *Mission of God's People*, 17.
159. Hendriks, *Studying Congregations*, 24.
160. Allen, *Theological Method*, 97.
161. Netland, "Introduction," 16–18.
162. Bevans, *Models of Contextual Theology*, 3.

reflection express the theological confession of the people of God in their sociocultural and historical context. In other words, theology, while being drawn from the normative biblical metanarrative, is contextual and is for practical Christian living in the particular context.[163]

The working definition of theology in this study relates to the intellectual and spiritual quest for answers to contextual questions raised in the contextual experiences of a community in the light of biblical revelation. The next sub-section describes a working definition of the theology of development adopted in this study.

A Working Definition of the Theology of Development

The theology of development is the intellectual and spiritual explanation about the state of creation, in the past, present, and future, drawn from the biblical metanarrative. Theology of development, applied in this study, is defined as the intellectual and spiritual explanation of the God's will and works through the biblical metanarrative concerning holistic development in human experiences in the present state of God's creation and towards its future state of perfect shalom. Theology of development is a sub-division of practical theology concerned with a Christian understanding, from the biblical perspective, about the state of God's creation at the beginning, the present state of God's creation, and what God is actively doing to make his creation what it should be in the future. The concept of theology of development draws from the disciplines of both biblical theology and systematic theology. For instance, doctrines described from the field of systematic theology such as the doctrines of creation, fall, redemption, and shalom are integrated into the theology of development. Myers writes that creation, incarnation, redemption, the kingdom of God, and power are theological ideas that seem to be useful for Christians working for transformational development.[164] Therefore theology of development is the theological description of what Christians can discern from the biblical perspective about what God intended his creation to be, the present state of God's creation, and what God is actively doing to make his creation what it should be according to his plan. The theology of development is the theological framework for this study that aims at the

---

163. Hendriks, *Studying Congregations*, 33; Kunhiyop, *African Christian Theology*, 2.

164. Myers, *Walking with the Poor*, 86.

application of biblical shalom in the process of facilitating holistic transformational development in rural communities. The theology of development, which can be contextual theology in rural communities, provides the intellectual and spiritual explanation of God's will and works through the biblical metanarrative concerning holistic transformational development in human experiences in the present state of God's creation and towards its future state of perfect shalom. The source of the theology of development is the biblical metanarrative, the subject is *missio Dei*, the context is God's creation, and the eschatological end is the new heavens and new earth. These elements of the theology of development are discussed in the following four sub-sections. These elements are the biblical metanarrative, *missio Dei*, the goodness of creation, and the eschatological goal of the *missio Dei*. Thus, a contextual theology of development is the expressed contextual understanding of the nature of spiritual, psychological, social, and environmental experiences that promote the holistic well-being of a particular community in the light of biblical revelation.

Biblical Metanarrative

The overarching biblical story of God's acts in creation from its original state through its present state and up to its future state constitutes the biblical metanarrative recorded in the sixty-six books of the Bible. Myers captures it well in his description of the biblical metanarrative as

> a whole story that begins with creation and continues with the call of Israel, the exile, Jesus and His death and resurrection, the church, and the end of history with the second coming . . . the story of a world in which the material and spiritual are seamlessly related, a world of persons and social systems.[165]

Glasser, also writes that the whole Bible, both Old and New Testaments, is the revelation of God's purpose and action in human history.[166] Joy Alvarez, Elnora Avarientos, and Thomas H. McAlpine write that, "the creation account in Genesis portrays a blueprint of God's intention for life as it should

---

165. Myers, 200.
166. Glasser, *Announcing the Kingdom*, 17.

be: harmony between God and human beings, harmony within each person, harmony among persons, and harmony between human beings and nature."[167] In other words the triune God, created all things that exist in interrelated, interdependent, and harmonious relationships within creation and in relation to God, in a state of shalom. Bruce Riley Ashford writes that everything God created was good and "man was in right relationship with God, with the world, with others, and with himself."[168] However, Wayne Grudem states, "the history of the human race as presented in Scripture is primarily a history of man in a state of sin and rebellion against God and God's plan of redemption to bring man back to Himself."[169] The biblical narrative does not begin with the history of the fall of man. Rather, it begins with creation and ends with new creation.[170]

So, the biblical metanarrative first reveals that the state of shalom into which all creation was established, it continues with how the state of shalom became disrupted due to the disruption of the harmonious relationships between God and human beings and between human beings within themselves and between human beings and other of God's creation. It further reveals how God planned and executes his plan to redeem and regenerate all of creation to end in perfect state of shalom.[171] Douglas Coleman writes that from Genesis 3 to Revelation 21 "Scripture narrates the story of God's plan for redemption," a story that contains "both explicit and implicit testimony of human's role in the process."[172] Wright describes the effect of human disobedience and rebellion against God to include human beings (1) being subjected to physical decay and death, and "living within a physical environment that is itself under the curse of God"; (2) intellectually rationalizing to "explain, excuse, and normalize" evil; (3) having fractured and disrupted social relationships; and (4) being spiritually alienated from God.[173] Ashford, states it cogently that

---

167. Alvarez, Avarientos, and McAlpine, "Our Experience," 56.

168. Ashford and Nelson, "The Story of Mission," 10.

169. Grudem, *Systematic Theology*, 415.

170. Wright, *Mission of God's People*, 40.

171. Gen 3:1–24.

172. Coleman, "Agents of Mission," 41.

173. Wright, *Mission of God's People*, 40.

"the harmony and holistic flourishing of God's good creation was broken" so that man's relationships were broken and distorted.[174]

In spite of the disruption of the state of shalom God has a design and acts based on that design to reinstate all of his creation into a new state of perfect shalom in the future. The biblical metanarrative presents in a diachronic fashion the design and acts of God, "within history through persons and events that run from the call of Abraham to the return of Christ," to redeem, transform, and regenerate all of God's creation into a future new state of perfect shalom.[175] To sum it all, biblical metanarrative describes God's mission, the *missio Dei*. *Missio Dei* is the subject matter of the theology of development.

Missio Dei

Eddie Arthur writes that the concept of *missio Dei* "has a long history and the origin of the use of the phrase can be traced as far back as (Saint) Augustine."[176] Tormod Engesviken also credits Augustine for the early use of the phrase *missio Dei*.[177] However, Karl Barth, Karl Hertenstein, and the Willingen International Mission Council are credited with popularizing the concept.[178] David Bosch, and others mentioned above, state that Barth articulated the *missio Dei* concept in a paper he presented at the Brandenburg Missionary Conference in 1932; that Barth, argued that mission is an activity of God himself.[179] Timothy C. Tennet and Keith Whitfield both write that German missiologist Karl Hartenstein in 1934 coined the phrase *missio Dei* in its contemporary usage.[180] The *missio Dei* is a concept that evolved from being exclusively applied to the doctrine of the Trinity, until the sixteenth century, describing "the sending of the Son by the Father and the sending of the Holy Spirit by the Father and the Son" to its wide use from the twentieth century

---

174. Ashford and Nelson, "Story of Mission," 10.

175. Wright, *Mission of God's People*, 41; Bartholomew and Goheen, *Drama of Scripture*, 13.

176. Arthur, "Missio Dei."

177. Engelsviken, "*Missio Dei*", 481–497.

178. Bosch, *Transforming Mission*, 389–393; Arthur, "Missio Dei"; McKinzie, "Abbreviated Introduction," 10–11.

179. Bosch, *Transforming Mission*, 389–393.

180. Tennet, *Invitation to World Missions*, 55; Whitfield, "Triune God," 19.

in relation to the missionary enterprise.[181] God's mission is to redeem and transform his creation into a new heavens and earth and in a new relationship wherein God dwells in the midst of his creation. Ashford posits that

> God's mission is to redeem for Himself a people who will be a kingdom of priests to the praise of His glory, who will bear witness to His gospel and advance His church, and who will dwell with Him forever on a new heavens and earth.[182]

Wright describes God's mission as fundamentally the mission that involves the participation of "God's people, at God's invitation and command, in God's own mission within the history of God's world for the redemption of God's creation."[183] So *missio Dei* is a concept that describes the mission of God as "primarily and ultimately, the work of the Triune God, Creator, Redeemer, and Sanctifier, for the sake of the world, a ministry the church is privileged to participate."[184]

There are different conceptual frameworks that provide explanation for the *missio Dei*. Keith Whitfield summarizes four of these conceptual frameworks of the *missio Dei*.[185] (1) An eschatological cosmocentric vision that emphasizes the goal of God's mission to be the redemption and reconstruction of the world to return shalom into the world. This view is attractive for application in efforts at holistic development however the goal is focused on the eschatological benefit of God's mission for the world. (2) A Christocentric model that emphasizes the God sending aspect of God's mission. "God the Father sends the Son into the world; the Father and the Son send the Holy Spirit into the world; the Father, Son, and the Spirit send the church into the world."[186] (3) A soteriological model emphasizes the salvation of individuals as the aim of God's mission not social structures. The model is Christocentric because Christ is placed at the very core of God's soteriological mission. Lesslie Newbigin also describes this approach as one that places exclusive emphasis on winning individuals to conversion and numerical growth of

---

181. Whitfield, "Triune God," 18.
182. Ashford, "Introduction," 2.
183. Wright, *Mission of God*, 23.
184. Bosch, *Transforming Mission*, 392.
185. Whitfield, "Triune God," 20–23.
186. Whitfield, 20.

the church as its central goal.[187] This perspective, like the eschatological approach under-emphasizes the mighty work of God in the *missio Dei*. (4) Eschatological-Christocentric-Trinitarian approach that conceives God's mission as encompassing all of history from creation. Newbigin, Wright, and Timothy C. Tennent[188] subscribe to this perspective. Newbigin writes that this model "offers people the possibility of understanding what God is doing in history."[189] Wright describes the *missio Dei* as "God's own mission within the history of God's world for the redemption of God's creation."[190] Tennet considers this model as a model that reveals God's redemptive action in the world to fulfil God's redemptive purposes and initiatives in the world to bring about political revolution, change in economic trend or social movements.[191] In the Eschatological-Christocentric-Trinitarian model, the mission of God is said to be God making himself known to his creation as the Lord. The eschatological kingdom of God to be established at the end of human history has been the ontological priority of the work of Christ. Christ brought the kingdom into being and the Holy Spirit has provided a foretaste of it in the present.[192] So *missio Dei* from the perspective of the Eschatological-Christocentric-Trinitarian approach, Newbigin posits, includes "the total life of a community enabled by the Holy Spirit to live in Christ, sharing His passion and the power of His resurrection" in both words and acts.[193] Wright posits in his missional hermeneutics that *missio Dei* "proceeds from the assumption that the whole Bible renders to us the story of God's mission through God's people in their engagement with God's world for the sake of the whole creation."[194] *Missio Dei* is the idea of the triune God to establish an eschatological kingdom executed through the person and work of Christ for the redemption and reconciliation of a people belonging to God and is being extended by the person of the Holy Spirit to all humanity regardless

---

187. Newbigin, *Gospel in a Pluralist Society*, 135.

188. Newbigin, *Gospel in a Pluralist Society*; Wright, *Mission of God*; and Tennent, *Invitation to World Missions*, 55.

189. Newbigin, *Gospel in a Pluralist Society*, 128–129.

190. Wright, *Mission of God*, 23.

191. Tennent, *Invitation to World Missions*, 55, 56.

192. Newbigin, *Gospel in a Pluralist Society*, 135–136.

193. Newbigin, 137.

194. Wright, *Mission of God*, 51.

of their physical, economic, and sociocultural context. The next sub-section discusses the context in which the *missio Dei* takes place.

The Goodness of Creation

God's creation is essentially good even though it has been marred by the effects of human sin and rebellion. The *missio Dei* (mission of God) takes place in the context of the present state of God's creation. Ashford argues that the goodness of creation is a fundamental teaching of the Scriptures as repeatedly affirmed in the creation narrative as well as in the teaching of the apostle Paul that "everything created by God is good."[195] Ashford goes on to state that though the world is in a bad state due to human sin yet God, in his common grace toward man, has restrained the world from being useless.[196]

The entirety of creation is under the sovereign rule of God, therefore, all of creation is, metaphorically, the kingdom of the sovereign God and God alone is its king. God created human beings as special creatures on earth. Human beings are special creatures in that God created them in his image and likeness and established them in a special relationship with himself. This special relationship is "stunningly evoked in Genesis 3:8," which records that God is in the habit of meeting with the man and woman and speaking with them.[197] In the kingdom he created, God assigned to human beings a special role to serve as vice-regents and stewards. Human beings are, under God, to rule over the nonhuman parts of creation. And the creation narrative "tells us that God gives man stewardship over the whole of the created order . . . so that they may flourish in their mutual interdependence."[198] In executing their stewardship responsibility human beings were to organize and to tend and care for God's creation.[199] This is God's mandate to human beings to cultivate/develop not exploit God's creation. It is in the context of the sin-marred good creation of God that the *missio Dei* takes place

---

195. Ashford and Nelson, "Story of Mission," 8.

196. Ashford and Nelson, 10.

197. Bartholomew and Goheen, *Drama of Scripture*, 36.

198. Ashford and Nelson, "Story of Mission," 10.

199. Genesis 2:15, 19.

The Eschatological Goal of the *Missio Dei*

It has been stated earlier that the theology of development is focused on what God intended his creation to be, the present state of God's creation, and what God is actively doing to make his creation what it should be according to his plan. According to Stanley J. Grenz,

> the final goal of the work of the triune God in salvation history is the establishment of the eschatological community – a redeemed people dwelling in a renewed earth, enjoying reconciliation with their God, fellowship with each other, and in harmony with all creation.[200]

The acts of God in the present state of creation have been described as the *missio Dei*. The purpose of the *missio Dei* is expressed in the eschatological vision of the biblical metanarrative which, upon the return of Jesus Christ, will usher in right harmonious relationships between God's people as human beings between themselves, between God's people and nature, and between God's people and the triune God. The people that did not respond to God's invitation to become his people will not enjoy the kind of relationships Jesus Christ ushers in upon his second coming. Grenz describes the eschatological goal of the *missio Dei* aptly by stating that "God is directing His actions toward an all-encompassing goal, the transformation of the entire cosmos into the glorious eternal community of the new creation."[201] Myers, describes this eschatological end as the "best human future" and that best human future is the kingdom of God, which consists of transformed people who in a state of just and peaceful relationships.[202] The best human future is the "eschatological community which will be characterized by harmonious human existence on the new earth."[203] The best human future is described by the theological concept of God's shalom, which is reviewed in the next section.

Theology of development attempts to explain the design of the triune God for all of God's creation from its beginning through its present state to its future state as revealed in the biblical metanarrative. God's design includes engaging all of God's people, regardless of their sociocultural, historical, and

---

200. Grenz, *Theology for the Community*, 151.

201. Grenz, 813.

202. Myers, *Walking with the Poor*, 202.

203. Grenz, *Theology for the Community*, 148.

geographical location, to participate with him in the divine process of redeeming and transforming all distorted relationships in order to apply biblical shalom progressively until it is fully realized upon the return of Jesus Christ. The theology of development must be contextual in order for it to provide the intellectual and spiritual answers to contextual questions, in the light of biblical revelation. The ultimate goal of theology of development is the establishment of biblical shalom. This is the subject of review in the next section.

Biblical Shalom

Biblical shalom and the kingdom of God are interrelated concepts in the biblical metanarrative. Alvarez, Avarientos, and McAlpine write that God's vision for the world is the reign of right relationships characterized by sustainable peace and harmony within diversity as God rules over the created order.[204] Biblical shalom and the kingdom of God are concepts that describe the ultimate goal of the *missio Dei* as revealed in the biblical metanarrative. In this section the concepts are reviewed and their relationship is considered.

Definition of Biblical Shalom

Biblical scholars and theologians define and describe biblical shalom as a state of harmonious interrelatedness of all of creation within itself and with its Creator. A few examples are presented here. Craig G. Bartholomew and Michael W. Goheen write that shalom is "the Old Testament word for peace, meaning the rich, integrated, relational wholeness God intends for His creation."[205] Terry McGonigal writes that "the way God designed the universe to be," is to be in a state of "order, relationships, stewardship, beauty and rhythm."[206] Myers's definition of biblical shalom is that it is a state of "just, peaceful, harmonious and enjoyable relationships with each other, ourselves, our environment, and God."[207] Whitfield describes it as "a universal human flourishing, a right ordering of things, a divine peace."[208] Shalom can thus

---

204. Alvarez, Avarientos, and McAlpine, "Our Experience," 56.

205. Bartholomew and Goheen, *Drama of Scripture*, 42.

206. McGonigal, "If You Only Knew," McGonigal is Dean of Spiritual Life, Whitworth University.

207. Myers, *Walking with the Poor*, 175.

208. Whitfield, "Triune God," 20.

be described as the state of equilibrium in creation and human society that exists based on the operation of the interconnected, interdependent, and harmonious relationships God designed for all creation within itself according to God's sovereign will and with God who is the Creator of all creation. The components in biblical shalom are: God as the sovereign source of all creation, human beings in relationship with God, with selves and with one another. Furthermore, it includes human beings in relationship with other non-human creation like animals, vegetation, land, in accord with God's revealed divine will. God designed creation to exist and operate in a state of shalom. However, this state was disrupted by the introduction of sin by the first human beings. In spite of the disruption God is still in it.

Biblical Shalom in Human History

McGonigal has made a panoramic survey of the Bible based on broad historic time frames or periods: the period of creation and the creation of community, the period of kings and prophets, the period of Jesus's ministry, and the period of the early church in Acts, Pauline epistles, and Revelation.[209] McGonigal's overview of the Bible serves as the framework for the review of the concept of shalom in this section.

The biblical account of creation in Genesis 1 and 2, and many other biblical passages, declare that God created all that exists. God as the sovereign creator determines the means and the way creation operates. God determines creation to have order. Because God determines creation to have order, life flourishes on earth in all its abundance. The independent parts of creation are to be in a web of harmonious relationships. The web of relationships God put in place in creation included spiritual, psychological, social, and ecological relationships for human beings. To establish spiritual relationship with his creation, God created a man and a woman, Adam and Eve, in his image and likeness. Hence human beings possess spiritual relationship with God. God established social relationships of love and joyful partnership between Adam and Eve.[210] This relationship reflects the nature of God. In God's providence at creation God created human beings with a sense of personal contentment within themselves. Adam's response upon the receiving the gift of a partner,

---

209. McGonigal, "If You Only Knew."
210. Gill, "Christian Social Ethics," 629.

Eve, as recorded in Genesis 2:23 indicates a sense of personal or psychologi-cal contentment.

God established the principle of stewardship by placing Adam and Eve in the garden of Eden to serve as stewards in partnership with God to care for the earth. In this way God created human beings into a spiritual, psy-chological, social, and ecological relationships in a state of organizational unity and well-being, a state best described by the term shalom. In God's sovereign order, creation is to be cared for by human beings. The principle of stewardship established a relationship between human beings with the rest of God's creation in the world. All of creation is to be a beautiful reflection of the majesty of the Creator. The beauty of creation is in the distinct yet connected and interdependent and beautiful relationships of unique parts of creation. Creation operates through a divinely predetermined rhythm. Robert W. Jenson and Bruce Riley Ashford agree that the beauty of creation point continually to beauty and glory of God's triune nature.[211] God also es-tablished, at creation, a time-bound rhythm of day and night and of seasons. This analysis of the creation narrative demonstrates that the doctrine of cre-ation serves as a foundation for understanding God's shalom. God's shalom is seen in the state of harmonious interrelated, interdepended, relationships of unique components of creation into which God created the world and all that exists in it. Hence, God's shalom established at creation (even though short lived) is "the starting point, trajectory, and parameter" for understand-ing the theme of God's shalom in this study.

God's shalom became distorted due to pollution by the willful disobedi-ence of Adam and Eve. Adam and Eve violated God's prescribed way of life for them in the garden as stewards. God's prescription was simply for human beings to cultivate nature and to take some of the produce of nature to sustain life.[212] God set a limitation by commanding Adam and Eve not to eat from one of the trees, the tree of the knowledge of good and evil in the middle of the garden of Eden.[213] However, Adam and Eve violated God's command by succumbing to the temptation of the serpent in the garden of Eden to eat the forbidden fruit. Adam and Eve ate the forbidden fruit of the tree of the

---

211. Jensen, *Systematic Theology*, 129; Ashford and Nelson, "Story of Mission," 6.

212. Gen 2:15–16.

213. Gen 2:17; 3:3.

knowledge of good and evil.[214] Therefore due to the violation of God's command, things no longer operate the way God designed them to function. The corruption of God's shalom brought about the alienation of human beings from God in their spiritual relationship. The alienation extended to psychological alienation within themselves, social alienation from each other, and alienation from their ecological environment.[215] Therefore, God's shalom for creation is marred as a consequence of the sin of human beings.

Re-Instatement of God's Shalom

Following the distortion of God's shalom God initiated his divine plan to reinstate it. Alvarez, Avarientos, and McAlpine argue that "If *shalom* is life as God made it, then *shalom* is life as God still intends it to be (and because of this) Yahweh embarked on a grand mission, stretching across the ages to restore that original vision."[216] First, in his mission God began with one particular family, Abraham's family. Though God started with a specific family, God's vision is universal. The history of Abraham's descendants includes the enslavement in Egypt that ends with the exodus. The exodus is the event of God's deliverance and liberation of Abraham's descendants, Israel, from the bondage of slavery in Egypt. The exodus story demonstrates spiritual and physical redemption from the domination of the Egyptian gods, socio-political redemption from oppression, redemption from serving the economic interests of the Egyptians, and psychological redemption so that the people of Israel can learn their true identity as people created to prosper in the land God provided for them. During a period of forty years of wilderness sojourn, God prescribes through the provision of the Decalogue and other related laws, simply described as the Torah, how the Israelites as God's redeemed people should live. In the Torah God describes the salvation he offers as acts of grace and prescribes Israel's communal life as a trajectory of his shalom, not only for Israel but for all people and creation. After Israel took possession of the promised land and settled, the biblical account of the period of kings and prophets follow.

---

214. Gen 3:6.

215. Ashford and Nelson, "Story of Mission," 6.

216. Alvarez, Avarientos, and McAlpine, "Our Experience," 56.

Second, God promised a future messiah during the biblical period of kings and prophets. During this period Israel willfully refused to live by God's pre-scribed principles of shalom and the Torah. Israel's rebellion against God led to chaos. Israel began to long for communal prosperity that seems to come through political stability in surrounding nations. Israel demanded a human king, a human monarchy, which Samuel warned against (1 Samuel 8:10–19). The kings enslaved the Israelites by using the power allotted to them to serve personal interests, conscript forced labor, impose taxation, and mislead the people. God dealt with the situation by raising prophets, men and women, with burning passion in their hearts to speak and to live by the Torah. The prophets called Israel to rectify its circumstances by recommitting to live according to the Torah. The prophets emphasize that shalom "can only be re-ceived from God, not manufactured by human effort" because shalom always comes as a gift from God based on God's covenant.[217] The persistent rejection of the messages of the prophets eventually leads to the Babylonian captivity.[218] The prophets continued to envision shalom attainable through God's gracious creative action through the ministry of a "Servant-Messiah."[219] The promised "Servant-Messiah" will, through his vicarious suffering, provide atonement for the sins of the people and this will result in shalom, therefore through the atoning suffering of the servant-messiah shalom for creation is restored.[220]

Third, the gospels in the New Testament describe Jesus's ministry. McGonigal states that in the gospels, Mark focuses on the restoration of order through Jesus's miracles. Matthew asserts how stewardship responsibility is restored through Jesus's teaching. John highlights beauty and glory through Jesus's incarnation and suffering. And Luke demonstrates the priority of re-lationships in community as Jesus refused to be bound by the restrictions inspired by Jewish culture and reached out to the religious, cultural, and socio-economic outcasts. All people are created in the image and likeness of God, therefore all people are welcome in Jesus's shalom community. Jesus, the promised servant-messiah, is crucified to provide for the redemption of

---

217. Ashford and Nelson, "Story of Mission."
218. 2 Chron 36:15–20.
219. Isa 42:1.
220. Isa 53:1–12.

people to be restored into God's shalom. McGonigal shows how the actors in the death and resurrection event of Jesus Christ were inclusive. It included an African in the crowd, Roman soldiers, members of the Sanhedrin, and some of Jesus's disciples, including women.

Finally, in Acts, the Pauline epistles, and Revelation, McGonigal shows how the small Jewish group of Jesus's disciples transform into a global movement that encompassed every known people group within the sphere of the Roman Empire. Jesus envisioned his disciples with a mission of proclaiming the good news of the reign of God and the blessings it brings to people. The New Testament emphasizes that the wall separating humanity and God and the wall separating people from each other have both been destroyed by God through the atoning death of Jesus Christ resulting in both God reconciling humanity to himself and reconciliation between human beings. In Revelation, the apostle John emphatically asserts that God incarnate in Jesus Christ is the only one who can redeem and unite all peoples. Shalom as a biblical theme is interrelated with the biblical theme of the kingdom of God, Matthew calls it in his gospel, the kingdom of heaven.

Relationship between God's Shalom and the Kingdom of God

There is a relationship between the biblical concept of God's shalom and the biblical concept of the kingdom of God. God's shalom is also referred to, and used interchangeably, as biblical shalom in this study. An understanding of the inseparable interrelatedness of these concepts is beneficial for the purpose of this study. An extensive analysis of the concept of the kingdom of God does not serve the purpose of the study; however it is necessary to describe its relationship to the concept of God's shalom for the purpose of clarifying the use of God's shalom in this study rather than the kingdom of God, even though both concepts have an inseparable interrelationship. The historical development of the idea of the kingdom of God can be traced from its first significant mention in the Old Testament. Wright states that the first significant time the kingdom of God is mentioned in the Bible is in Moses's triumphant acclamation after the exodus from Egypt that "The Lord will reign for ever and ever" (Exod 15:18). It was an acclamation that can be interpreted to mean that the Lord "has now demonstrated that He is king, He is now reigning, and He will go on reigning forever."[221] Jedidiah Coppenger states that, "Although the 'kingdom of God' phraseology is not present in the Old Testament as it is in Jesus's ministry, the kingdom is present."[222] Jacob Chinitz also states that the Torah does not emphasize the kingship of God whereas it is prominent in the Prophets and Writings.[223] During the inter-testament period H. N. Ridderbos posits that there was an emphasis of Jewish expectation of a future decisive intervention of God to liberate the Jews from their enemies and oppressors. This Jewish expectation was based on Old Testament prophecies in the Prophets and Writings.[224] Judaism, which became more rooted in the inter-testament period, also promoted the concept. Chinitz writes that in Judaism one of the Rabbinic morning prayers[225] has three phrases drawn from three different biblical verses[226] that speak of the eternal kingship of God: "God reigns, God who has reigned, God shall reign for all eternity."[227] God as Creator of all that exists is the sovereign ruler of everything that exists. All that God has sovereignty over is God's kingdom therefore God determines how all that he created functions. Wright writes that through God's actions and words in the Old Testament God reveals his sovereignty over history, over all nations, and over all creation.[228] God's shalom is the state or condition, in all the relationships God has placed human beings in, that the kingdom of God generates. In the New Testament the kingdom of God is a central theme in Jesus's teaching and ministry.

In the New Testament, beginning with the central theme of Jesus's preaching and teaching it is clearer that the concept of the kingdom of God is a concept that expresses the sovereignty of God. Lesslie Newbigin interprets Jesus's words "the kingdom of God has come near" as recorded in the gospels to mean that, "The reign of God is now confronting you as a present reality. It

---

221. Wright, *Mission of God*, 78.

222. Coppenger, "Community of Mission," 63.

223. Chinitz, "Three Tenses," 255.

224. Ridderbos, "Kingdom of God," 656. Some of the biblical passages that the prophecies can be found include Ps 2; 110; Isa 2:1–4; 11:1–10; Jer 23:5–8; 31:31–44; 32:37–33:26; Ezek 34:23–31; 37:24–28; Dan 2:44; 7:14, 27; 9:25–27, and Mic 4:1–13.

225. Chinitz makes reference to the "*Pesukei de-Zimra* section of the prayer service," Chinitz, "Three Tenses," 255.

226. Ps 10:16; 93:1; Exod 15:18.

227. Chinitz, "Three Tenses," 255.

228. Wright, *Mission of God*, 75–104.

is 'among you.' Its powers are now at work in your midst."[229] So God reveals his sovereignty in the life and ministry of Jesus Christ by making God's "kingly power" manifest in "the man Jesus."[230] Wright argues that the New Testament unequivocally puts Jesus alongside God in God's activity of the creation of the universe and the exercise of universal governance that belong uniquely to God.[231] In both the Old Testament and the New Testament the concept of kingdom of God expresses the sovereignty of God over all of creation. God, by his sovereign will, spoke and acted to create and establish all he created in a state of shalom, which is evident in the harmonious interrelated and interdependent relationships of the unique entities of God's creation.

The foregoing shows that the kingdom of God establishes God's shalom, therefore God's shalom is the consequence of God's kingdom. Creation is the will and act of the sovereign God and the sustenance of creation is in accord with the will and words of the sovereign God. God's act of creation and words that guide the sustenance of all creation established the foundation of the state of God's shalom. The state of God's original creation demonstrates God's shalom by the harmonious relationship that existed between the interrelated and interdependent unique entities of creation. The goal of development from a biblical perspective is to re-establish God's shalom for all creation in partnership with God according to God's divine plan.

The preceding three sections reviewed literatures on community development, theology of development, and biblical shalom. These concepts are foundational for understanding approaches to transformational development from a biblical or Christian perspective. The next section reviews the practices of three selected CRDOs engaged providing services aimed at facilitating transformational development in rural communities in Nigeria.

---

229. Newbigin, *Gospel in a Pluralist Society*, 105.
230. Newbigin, 105.
231. Wright, *Mission of God*, 113, 115.

The Practice of Holistic Development by Three Selected Christian Relief and Development Organizations in Nigeria

There are different Christian relief and development organizations (CRDOs) that are providing services aimed at facilitating holistic development in rural and urban communities. CRDOs operate based on CD principles, in the light of the theology of development, and with the goal of achieving biblical shalom. This section reviews the practice of transformational development by three selected CRDOs serving in Nigeria. The three selected CRDOs are the People's Oriented Development (POD) of Evangelical Church Winning All (ECWA), Christian Rural and Urban Development Association of Nigeria (CRUDAN), and the Rural Development Counsellors for Christian Churches in Africa (RURCON). The review is drawn from different types of literature namely books, unpublished official reports, and newsletters. The selected CRDOs are a part of many faith-based organizations (FBOs) in the global scene that are non-governmental organizations (NGOs) providing services to facilitate development in different contexts. Each of these NGOs, FBOs, and CRDOs approach its development work from its unique perspective. CRDOs provide services to facilitate development based on their understanding of development from a Christian perspective. Matarrita-Cascante and Brennan's typology is applied in this review as a framework to classify the selected CRDO. The view guiding the approach of each CRDO, the process each CRDO applies in its approach, the primary actors in the process and the benefits of the approach for the community are presented.

Myers argues that a Christian's vision of and how the Christian works to facilitate development are grounded in the Christian theology and understanding of God's acts recorded in the biblical metanarrative.[232] Myers further states that there is a misconception concerning the relationship between development and theology. Some think that development is a practical activity in the real material world as it affects human life whereas theology concerns itself only with thinking about God and about otherworldly and spiritual things.[233] This may be so for practitioners of development activities who do not have God as their starting point nor God's purposes and goal as

---

232. Myers, *Walking with the Poor*, 47.
233. Myers, 47.

their ultimate goal. Practicing development from a Christian perspective has God as the starting point. This means God's purposes, God's goal, and God's plan are supposed to be the framework for practicing development from a Christian perspective. Hence theology has a modifying role in the practice of development from a Christian perspective. POD, CRUDAN, and RURCON are organizations established by God's people to participate with God in his acts aimed at re-establishing God's shalom to all of God's creation. These CRDOs are engaged in a process of development in human communities. How do each of these organizations participate with God in their respective development practices?

People Oriented Development (POD)

The People Oriented Development (POD) is a holistic community-based development missional ministry of the Evangelical Church Winning All (ECWA). ECWA is an indigenous church in Nigeria that has "to glorify God" as its goal, and ECWA has various ministries through which it pursues its goal which is "to glorify God." POD is one of such ECWA ministries. POD was established in 1988 from a merger of two previously separate ministries of ECWA. The two ministries are the Extension services of the Rural Development program, and the Preventive Health Care unit of ECWA Community Health program. Joshua D. Kasai writes that,

> Prior to the formation of POD in 1989, ECWA Rural Development and ECWA Community Health Programme were ministering especially to the rural poor through the diffusion theory of innovation. By the mid-1980s a number of evaluations revealed that these two departments were not really meeting the numerous needs of these rural poor. This was due to the ineffectiveness of their strategy and the down turn of the Nigeria economy. These departments agreed to change their approach, which led to a series of reorientation on community-based development. A decision to merge the Extension Section of ECWA Rural Development and the Preventive Health Care Unit of ECWA Community Health Programme was then taken to form POD.[234]

234. Kasai, "Evangelical Church," 1. Kasai, was then the Director of POD. Also, the Evangelical Church Winning All was previously named Evangelical Church of West Africa.

At its inception the POD had clear statements of mandate, mission, vision and goal, and values. POD also had clearly defined target group, strategy, programs, monitoring and evaluation methods, and organizational management structure.

Kasai provides a broad overview of POD which is summarized here. Later the methodologies POD applies to facilitate holistic development in its target communities are reviewed. Kasai's overview includes the following descriptions of POD. First, the mandate of POD is to be "involved in wholistic community-based development as an act of demonstration of God's love to mankind." Second, the goal and vision of POD is "Nigerian communities attaining wholistic development," as POD "envisions improved and sustained living conditions of Nigerian communities." Third, POD aims at achieving its goal and vision through "effective community development." Fourth, POD's target group is the rural poor and underprivileged communities in Nigeria. Fifth, there is a two-pronged strategy of Participatory Learning and Action (PLA) and Capacity Building. POD staff facilitate the development process using these two broad strategies. They do this by coaching target communities to implement projects the community decide to embark upon. POD seems to have a predetermined list of what it identifies as the major needs in rural communities. These needs are centered on need for sufficient and healthy potable water, agricultural needs, health needs, income generation, and inaccessible roads during rainy seasons. POD also operates from a project-based perspective. The projects are implemented in ways that are relevant to the community's situation and using locally available resources.

Sixth, POD has seven programs. Six programs focus on the target communities and one focuses on POD as an institution. The community focused programs are: (i) community mobilization that guides each community to identify its priority needs; (ii) community-based health care aimed at providing health education, training voluntary health workers and traditional birth attendants, and advocacy on HIV/AIDS prevention and home care; (iii) food security/sustainable agriculture to reorient the communities on organic farming and advocacy on the dangers of deforestation; (iv) sustainable water supply to enable communities to dig concrete lined wells with covering facilities to provide clean and safe drinking water and to reduce water borne diseases; (v) economic empowerment to improve the economic well-being of the target communities. This is done through advocacy, training for skills acquisitions, provision of "seed money" (soft loans); and (vi) peace building to promote harmonious relationship in the target communities through advocacy, training, and media programs (radio), etc.

The seventh, institution focused, program focuses on strengthening POD and networking with other organizations, cooperating with other agencies to learn from each other, and to assist and collaborate with each other. The cooperation is done with NGOs, government agencies, and sister CRDOs like CRUDAN and RURCON. POD monitors and evaluates its work. The monitoring and evaluating activities are carried out to assess progress and for the growth of POD as an organization. Monitoring is done through field visits and reports. Evaluations are carried out at least once in three years. Other important matters in the operations of the POD include the management style of the organization, its funding and partnership pattern, and its financial sustainability strategy. For the management style, Kasai writes that, policies are made by the board and handed to management who implement based on ECWA constitution and bye-laws and operates a participatory management style of governance. In the area of funding and partnership most of the financial resources had been from external donors as partners. These external partners/donors include EZE/EED Germany, Inter-Church Action Canada, and Inter-Church Organization for Development Cooperation, Netherlands. To raise internal financial support ECWA instituted the observance of an annual POD week observed by all its local churches. Collections and offerings made through the week provide for some of the financial needs of POD. In addition, POD embarks on investments to raise funds by purchasing lands to build conference facilities, guest houses, plant orchards, and establish integrated fish farms. POD has also considered the building of a head office complex and the construction of staff housing estate.[235]

A number of observations from Kasai's document include: (1) POD's ultimate goal is to demonstrate God's love. This is an emphasis on deeds as a testimony to God's love. (2) POD's primary objective is to help target rural and underprivileged communities to consciously delineate, prioritize, and work together towards meeting the communities' physical and social needs. However, POD limits itself to specific predetermined needs. From Kasai's document the spiritual needs of the people in the communities are

---

235. Kasai, "Evangelical Church," 3–7.

not mentioned nor is there mention of how the activities of POD are directly linked with the content of the gospel of God's love. (3) The communities are engaged as participants through the PLA approaches.

Willi Ehret, a Coordinator of POD, also states that the development philosophy of POD is to facilitate "villagers to take more charge for themselves and in doing so, they should be empowered to influence their situation by themselves to a greater extent."[236] The objective of this philosophy according to Ehret, is to animate the people so that "out of the animation process the villagers will discover their different needs in technical areas."[237] The application of this philosophy leads the people to gain self-esteem and to realize that they can improve on the quality of their livelihood by themselves.[238] Thus the focus of POD's program is the development of people by building their capacity to be self-reliant.[239] (4) POD follows a top-bottom and a project approach. This means that the projects to be considered are predetermined by the board that may not have a first-hand knowledge of the situation in the target rural communities. The board may therefore be drawing up policies based on a theory or theories that are universalistic in character and not particularistic to address the actual questions of the target communities. The communities may have concerns that are outside the POD predetermined interests or concerns. The top-bottom approach limits the community's scope of expression to POD's predetermined concerns whereas the community may have given another concern priority attention. A review of the methodologies POD uses follows.

POD applies a project approach to development. The projects are drawn in three-year phases. The first phase was extended to five years. The first phase was started September 1989 and ended December 1994.[240] Projects in any specific location may be determined by the target community but the choice of project is limited to options predetermined by the donors and the board. David Abidan writes that the projects are to be in three major sectors: water supply, health care, and agriculture.[241] The target community is guided

236. Ehret, "Training and Capacity Building," 1

237. Ehret, 1.

238. Ehret, "Brief Sketch."

239. POD of ECWA, "Know More About POD of ECWA."

240. POD of ECWA, "People Oriented Development of ECWA Internal Evaluation."

241. Abidan, "People Oriented Development," 6.

through one or more participatory process, described below, to identify and prioritize the community's needs. Development projects are designed to meet the identified and prioritized developmental needs of the target community from the three major interest of POD.

POD selects a number of villages for each phase of its community development program. According to Abidan, villages are selected by a team that include ECWA District Church Council (DCC) leaders, the Evangelical Missionary Society (EMS) Coordinator in the DCC, the Medical Supervisor in the DCC, and the Community Development Officer (CDO) of POD. The guidelines for the section of villages include (1) 50 percent of the villages selected are to have ECWA local churches, (2) 30 percent of the villages to have EMS mission stations, and (3) the remaining 20 percent are to be villages without a church base. In addition, the villages should be in clusters of three or more villages.[242]

A two-pronged strategy of Participatory Learning and Action (PLA) and Capacity Building is the strategy POD applies. The PLA consists of a variety of participatory approaches to facilitate community development. Some of these participatory approaches include: (1) Group of research and support for self-help activities of farmers, a method that is best known by the French acronym GRAAP. The main element of the methodology is to "see," to "reflect," and to "act." The methodology is based on adult learning principles, learning through self-discovery and visualization, with great emphases on visualization. Ehret states that the GRAAP pedagogy is a very suitable method for community development.[243] The GRAAP process is applied to lead the people to first see their situation in a broader context, and then reflect about possible ways of improving their situation based on their strengths and resources, and finally the people apply their choice of action to improve their situation. (2) Rapid Rural Appraisal (RRA), introduced to POD in June 1991. It is a method that appraises a community's space within a time frame. The approach profiles the geographical environment of the community, the history of the community, the seasonal calendar of the community and the trends in the communities. The appraisals are done through a process of interaction between the CDO and the villagers. Closely related to the RRA is (3) the Participatory Rural

---

242. Abidan, 6.

243. Ehret, "Training and Capacity Building."

Appraisal (PRA) approach. This approach is geared towards meeting identified prioritized need in a community. The major role of the facilitator of the approach is to create awareness and not to impose solutions on the people. In the process the people see the community's situation, analyze the situation, discuss and decide among potential solutions, act according to their priorities, and evaluate the outcome.[244] (4) Songs, drama, role plays, stories, etc. are used to pose the problems of a community in a Learners-centered, Problem-solving, Self-discovery, and Action oriented (LePSA) approach. The people reflect on the problem and then act based on their chosen course of action. (5) The community organizing approach is a problem-solving approach that aims at empowering a community to identify and prioritize their needs for a collective action. According to Joel Lamingo, the goals of community organizing are to empower a community for sustainability, liberation from poverty, justice, freedom, and equity in the distribution of resources and power, better life, and leadership development.[245] (6) Participatory Monitoring and Ongoing Evaluation, a method that is applied to record and periodically analyze the information that the community or the beneficiary has determined to be important. This approach provides information to help make decisions.[246] (7) POD Animation Technique (PAT) is a methodology being developed by POD. The methodology is based on the concept of Appreciative Inquiry (AI). AI builds more on the positive experiences of people. The AI concept uses the positive experiences of the people involved to envision a future for their community through a process of dialogue. The PAT approach gives the communities an opportunity to reflect on their past experiences to forecast the future and work towards it. The approach causes the people to focus on potentials and not problems and needs.[247]

Collaboration with Local Churches. POD proposed and adopted a program, Church and Community Mobilization Process (CCMP) for its sixth project phase scheduled for the period 2007–2009. The CCMP approach was started in Kenya, adopted by Tearfund UK, and adopted in Nigeria by POD.[248] A pilot

244. Kidd, "Participatory Rural Appraisal."

245. Lamingo, "Community Organizing."

246. Musa, "Participatory Evaluation."

247. POD of ECWA, "People Oriented Development of ECWA Internal Evaluation."

248. POD of ECWA, "Workshop Report on CCMP."

phase to apply the approach was initiated in 2008. In a report on the CCMP model, Abidan states that the model is "considered to gradually form part of POD thinking, planning and working in order to meet up the increasing challenges of the integral mission of the church."[249] The objective of the CCMP is to "mobilize communities through the church to design, plan, implement, and evaluate their development process."[250] Therefore the "CCMP is designed to mobilize the community through the church to discover, design, implement and evaluate their development."[251]

The CCMP applies participatory evaluation process (PEP), a process that facilitates communities to discover who they are, their potential, and to envision their destiny. The PEP approach is an approach that facilitates the community through five stages: relationship building, community description, information gathering, analysis, and decision making. The objective of relationship building is to increase the level of trust between the church community, the community outside the church, and the facilitator. The community outside the church and the church community tell their own stories that indicate who they are and their perspectives in life. The aim of this stage is to lead to the stakeholders in the community to discuss the current situation in their community. The community description stage leads to information gathering where the community gathers specific information regarding the real issues affecting them. The next stage is to facilitate the community analyzing the information gathered and interpreting it to identify the causes and effects of the problems the community faces and the efforts the community makes to solve the problems. In the final stage the participants envision and formulate specific goals and objectives that will help them attain the vision. The process targets the church to help the church understand its biblical mandate for holistic ministry. Therefore, the process begins with awakening and mobilizing the church "through a series of Bible Studies." Then a second part of the process focuses on the community outside the church and the church community.[252]

---

249. Abidan, "Report of Church and Community."

250. POD of ECWA, "Evaluation Report of Sixth Project Phase."

251. ECWA People Oriented Development, "Church and Community Mobilization Process (CCMP)."

252. POD of ECWA, "Notes and Handouts," 5. A process under the support of Tearfund, UK.

The introduction of CCMP demonstrates an understanding of holistic development as combining Christian witness to meet spiritual needs with development practice to meet physical needs. This understanding, according to Myers, demonstrates captivity to the modern worldview that dichotomizes between the spiritual and the physical. So, holism is understood to "mean that Christian witness was something to be added to the development mission to make it complete."[253]

Outcomes and Challenges. A survey of the reports show the following as the outcomes and challenges POD has experienced over the years.[254] First the positive experiences. The approaches applied by POD are assessed as effective because to a large extent the goals, purpose, and objectives of POD are being achieved. This has been attributed to the strong element of community participation in the projects. The establishment of Community Development Committees in the rural communities has proven very effective in mobilizing community cooperation. The impact of POD's facilitations has positively resulted in transforming the quality of the lives of several less privileged communities. The program has proved relevant because it meets the needs and priorities of the local communities and the local churches situated in the communities. Concrete lined wells, health clinics, construction of improved stoves to reduce the amount of firewood use and water-filtering clay pots, and the reintroduction of communal farming and community farms are some of the concrete means by which the quality of people's lived was improved. POD programs are assessed as operating well within the resources and capacity available to it. The program is also sustainable because "some communities are now focused on conception and implementation of development projects."[255] In addition, the involvement of the ECWA denominational leaders at the DCC level in selecting the villages and target communities and the training of church leaders at the DCC level for integral mission have been found very helpful as it encourages the cooperation of local churches with the POD program. Also, the introduction of the CCMP approach increased the awareness of church leaders on their role in the community by envisioning them and the

---

253. Myers, "Setting the Table," xii.

254. The reports of both mid-term and final evaluative reports for all the seven project phases from 1989 to 2012 were considered for this summary.

255. POD of ECWA, "Evaluation Report of Sixth Project Phase," 13.

local churches for integral mission. This awareness has further enhanced the evangelistic role of the local churches and mission in the rural communities.

One of the negative challenges POD experience includes the abandonment of projects in some communities. Reasons attributed to this challenge are (1) poorly motivated communities, (2) poor management of the process by some of the CDOs due to either poor understanding or outright lack of competence for particular projects, (3) due to seasonal changes where farmers abandon projects to concentrate on their farm work in the rainy season, and (4) due to lack of financial resources for members of the community to make timely contributions. Another challenge is that due to a lack of a sustainable source and method of funding POD there is no long-term provision for funding. Instead POD has been over dependent on international donors whose funding is generally for short-term projects. For example, in the mid-term evaluation report of the fourth project phase it is noted that there is still a dependency of POD on outside donors after thirteen years and the recommendation made is that "the church (ECWA) should be made to totally own POD."[256] Collaboration, cooperation, and networking challenges include lack of adequate cooperation between POD and other departments of ECWA, limited fruitful outcome from cooperation with government related agencies unlike the good cooperation between POD and other NGOs. POD recommends a formalized program for cooperation between POD and other ECWA departments, and the introduction of community development as part of the curriculum for training in ECWA theological institutions. This calls for serious consideration for alternative long-term methods for sustainable funding of POD.

The foregoing description of POD and its methodologies for facilitating development in rural communities show great strength in the area of community mobilization and community empowerment. This strength ensures sustainability in communities well mobilized and empowered with skills to identify, plan for, and take action to address the community needs and problems within the capabilities and means of the community. It is evident that the POD program focuses primarily on the physical, ecological, economic, and social well-being of the communities. POD does not ignore the spiritual needs of the people. For example, it is stated in the fourth project

---

256. POD of ECWA, "Fourth Project Phase 2001–2003," 3.

phase end-term evaluation of POD that the work of POD is a means of reaching non-Christian communities by presenting the gospel not as bait but as partner to evangelism.[257] Also, in the evaluation of the sixth project phase the work of POD was described as "showing people what it means to be a part of God's kingdom such as showing love to others" and that "the process opens doors for proclamation of the gospel."[258] The introduction of the CCMP had as part of its objectives to help the church to "understand and apply her biblical mandate for holistic ministry to her immediate community and that truly become salt and light."[259] This approach, POD claims to be holistic in the sense that "Christian witness was something to be added to the development mix to make it complete."[260] This expresses the modern worldview of dichotomizing spiritual and physical needs instead of considering them as a seamless whole. The biblical worldview does not view the physical world as separate from the spiritual world but views both as a seamless whole under the sovereign rule of God.[261]

The POD model of CD can be classified, based on Matarrita-Cascante and Brennan's typology, as a directed model of CD. The ultimate goal of POD is to demonstrate God's love through the process of engaging the rural poor to participate in activities designed to improve and sustain living conditions. The goal of directed model of CD is the improvement of the living conditions of a community through physical and economic development by developing infrastructural facilities and technology. In the POD approach its goal is achieved through the choice of a priority area by a group of stakeholders in the target community from predetermined physical needs, determined by experts, in rural communities. Hence, both experts and a group of stakeholders in the community are the primary actors who mobilize the members of the community to participate in the drawn activities for the good of the community. The community is mobilized and coached by Community Development Officers (CDOs) to use locally available resources to execute the project. A paradigm shift beginning from the sixth project phase of POD from 2007

---

257. POD of ECWA, 3.

258. POD of ECWA, "Evaluation Report of the Sixth Project Phase."

259. POD of ECWA.

260. Myers, "Setting the Table," xii.

261. Myers, xiii.

introduced the application of the CCMP approach. The CCMP approach used the participatory evaluation process to mobilize communities through the local churches in rural communities. It was adding Christian witness to the relief and development efforts POD was primarily engaged in. This is why, POD states, that the CCMP further enhanced the evangelistic role of the local churches and mission in the communities. The engagement of local churches as facilitators of CD projects reduces the reliance on professionals and experts in the process of mobilizing and engaging members of the communities as active participants. The benefits from the approach applied by POD, in addition to the improvement of the living condition due to the development effort embarked upon, include: (1) the use of the communal lifestyle of rural communities, which the communities are familiar with, as a means to empower members of the community collectively with skills to facilitate development in their community; (2) the empowering local churches in the rural communities with cognitive understanding and vocational skills for applying their biblical mandate for holistic ministry through deeds, to be salt and light in their immediate communities, to show "what it means to be a part of God's kingdom"; and (3) the opening of doors for proclamation of the gospel.

The POD approach has not always been successful as reported in the reviewed cases in the evaluative reports. Cases of non-commitment and lack of continuity to complete projects have been reported. This is not unconnected with tensions created by the limitation of the areas of POD projects. From the limited options of POD projects there may not be a project that addresses the priority need of the community. There is tension therefore between the project options available to the community through POD and the actual priority needs of the community that are not offered in the options. Therefore, this limitation of options limits the community's input in the choice of their priority need to be addressed. Opportunities for creative and innovative ideas are limited even though members of the community have the opportunity to gain some knowledge and to add their voice in the process.

The POD approach assumes by its deeds the organization demonstrates the love of God – but do they explain the gospel message? Deeds alone do not provide verbal explanation of the message of the gospel. While deeds may provide possible opportunities for the proclamation of the gospel it is worth raising if they guarantee the elicitation of the questions that provide opportunity for the verbal explanation of the gospel message. Do these deeds engage the beneficiaries of the deeds in a direct dialogical interaction with the biblical metanarrative on their place in the *missio Dei*? The deeds are focused on the activities of POD and the activities of the engaged communities without providing for a clear integration of the activities of God who is revealed in the biblical metanarrative.

The outcomes of the deeds in the process of POD to facilitate holistic development in the communities may be considered as "signs" of the power of the gospel but are these signs adequately pointing to the *missio Dei*? Do the signs point primarily to the power of science and technology or to the wisdom of POD that facilitates the participation of the communities that lead to the identifiable outcomes? In what ways are these signs or outcomes directly linked with the *missio Dei*? The POD approach does not provide for a direct explanation, in words, for the gospel message of the *missio Dei* nor to the progressive application of biblical shalom in the communities and to the biblical shalom as the ultimate eschatological goal of the *missio Dei*.

Therefore, the POD approach to CD does not provide for a direct dialogical interaction of the biblical metanarrative in the process of facilitating holistic development. Hence the approach of POD is considered inadequate. This then suggests the need for a Christian approach to CD that integrates words that explain the gospel message in a seamless process for facilitating holistic transformational development. It suggests a need for an approach that provides a target community the opportunity to identify and appreciate their community worldview on development. It also suggests the need for a community worldview that can be engaged in a direct dialogical interaction with the biblical worldview on holistic transformational development. The approach needed is an approach that demonstrates, explains, and generates the progressive application of biblical shalom in target communities.

Rural Development Counsellors for Christian Churches in Africa (RURCON)

Rural Development Counsellors for Christian Churches in Africa (RURCON) is a Christian organization that was established with the main objective to work with churches at all levels to promote holistic development based on the biblical theology of development as reflected in the biblical theme of the kingdom of God.[262] The objective of RURCON is pursued through empowering churches in different parts of Africa to be more effective in their efforts to transform whole communities through holistic development. RURCON is described as "an enabling organization which believes in local self-reliance, sustainable lifestyles and livelihoods based on good Christian stewardship focusing on the poor."[263] The historical account of the establishment of RURCON as presented in its official website states that RURCON was established in 1971 out of a merger of two other Christian organizations, Faith and Farm, and Christian Rural Advisory Council (CRAC). Faith and Farm, now Action Partners, was an international organization established in 1958 by Peter Batchelor. Batchelor was a missionary with the Sudan United Mission (SUM). Faith and Farm was established to help churches meet their material needs and to help raise the living standard of its people without compromising the spiritual stand of the church. The CRAC, headed by Pa Barnaba Dusu, was established in Nigeria in 1965, based on insight gained from the ministry of the Faith and Farm, to help churches in Northern Nigeria in their development efforts.[264]

RURCON observes the following: (1) there is a rapid growth of the church and Christianity in Africa, yet the socio-economic and political situation in Africa suggests that in spite of this rapid growth the church and Christianity have not made the requisite impact they should. The church and Christianity in Africa have not brought about significant transformation in the African continent, which is burdened by a multitude of problems. Some of these problems include "social injustice, poverty, high incidence of HIV/AIDS, high infant and maternal mortality, inadequate portable water supply, poor environmental hygiene, etc." This myriad of problems are caused, in addition to other factors, by corruption and mismanagement of the economic and social resources in Africa. The church has the biblical responsibility and mandate to be "salt and light" and so has a role to play in responding to these problems, though the church in Africa has often times failed in regard to corruption and mismanagement of its resources. The church as a community

---

262. RURCON, "RURCON Long-Range Strategic Plan," 11.

263. RURCON, "RURCON: A Brief History"; See also, RURCON, "RURCON Long-Range Strategic Plan," 10; Nehemiah Wuyep, "Introducing RURCON." Wuyep, is the Monitoring and Evaluation Officer of RURCON.

264. RURCON, "RURCON Long-Range Strategic Plan," 10.

of the body of Christ is a forum through which holistic development can be effectively facilitated. The spread of the church as different denominations and in different locations provides a natural context through which holistic development in African communities can take place.

(2) The cause for the failure of the church in Africa to make significant impact in transformation is "due to inadequate theology of development" therefore many churches take "wrong steps in addressing social issues." RURCON posits that the theological training of church leaders in Africa still emphasize the dichotomy of physical and spiritual issues with emphasis on the spiritual at the expense of the physical. The direct consequence of this lack of integration of the relationship between the spiritual and the physical in the theological training of church leaders is that the church leaders are not adequately equipped to respond to the holistic need of the society. (3) Churches establish development projects through parastatals of the church instead of being an integral part of the church's ministry. Development projects are established to generate income for the church instead of raising the standard of living and improving the well-being of its people through holistic ministry. (4) "A lack of understanding of wholism by most Church leaders has resulted in dichotomy of the spiritual and physical development."[265] (5) There is a general lack of responsible stewardship and accountability to God and the people in most of our churches today. Church leaders are allegedly more interested in power and prestige rather than being relevant to the people and so they fail to mobilize people towards holistic ministry. (6) Social action is still considered as a means of evangelism instead of an integral part of the church's ministry.[266] Therefore RURCON provides Christian development education "to help the churches with a vision to see the African Church transformed as God intends."[267] The local church provides the forum through which holistic development can be facilitated.

RURCON has the vision of establishing transformed African communities to reflect how God intends them to be. RURCON therefore provides services with the aim of facilitating the holistic development of people through

---

265. RURCON, 8–9, 13.

266. RURCON, 8–9, 13; A brochure for RURCON, "International Wholistic Development Course," scheduled and conducted at the RURCON Headquarters, 7–18 September 2015.

267. A brochure for RURCON, "International Development Management Course," scheduled and conducted at the RURCON Headquarters, 6–17 March 2017.

Christian churches and organizations in Africa. In its brochure, RURCON describes its four core ministry programs as follows.

(1) Conflict transformation and peace building. The goal of this program is to "work with churches, Christian Development agencies and partners towards building their strategic capacity, enabling them to prevent, manage and monitor conflict."[268]

(2) Wholistic development education. RURCON observes that there is a lack of vision in many of the churches towards holistic ministry. Because of this lack of vision on holistic ministry the churches have approached their ministry in rural communities with a dichotomy of the spiritual and physical development. The result of this dichotomous approach is that members of the church are not able to connect their faith and their work in a seamless manner to model biblical values in proactive and positive ways and to effectively influence society. Hence, members of the church are not able to make a connection between the transformation of their society and the Great Commission. To address this problem of lack of vision for holistic ministry, RURCON provides "Wholistic development education" to enable churches in Africa "understand holistic ministry and rightly interpret and apply Scriptures so as to equip members and communities for improved livelihood."[269] RURCON posits that equipping Christians not only with spiritual vigor but also with the responsibility to be light and salt to a "bleeding" continent is a big challenge to the church in Africa. The appropriate response to this challenge, according to RURCON's position, is for the church in Africa to look beyond evangelism to awareness of and capacity to take social action. Therefore, RURCON posits that the church in Africa should focus more on ways to empower peoples and societies in the process of transformation.[270] RURCON aims at equipping Christian institutions and churches in Africa to be able to work towards the transformation of African communities.

(3) Governance advocacy. This ministry focuses on helping the churches and Christian development organizations in Africa to build the capacity to "lobby and advocate for good governance and sustainable development."[271]

---

268. Zasha, "2016 Evaluative Report 2011–2016," 10, 16.

269. Zasha, 10, 16.

270. RURCON, "RURCON Long-Range Strategic Plan," 10.

271. Zasha, "2016 Evaluative Report 2011–2016," 10, 16.

RURCON strives for the establishment of "an African society where every citizen has access to livelong security and is free from all forms of discrimination."[272]

(4) Partnership and networking. This ministry promotes "partnership and networking between Christian and other Development Organizations in order to address key development issues."[273] RURCON views optimal collaboration as essential for achieving the goal of the transformation of African communities. RURCON believes that the active pooling of ideas, talents, and experiences promotes mutual learning and implementation of action plans.[274]

RURCON conducts its ministries mainly through participatory training workshops for development facilitators and organizational leaders. James Zasha, in the 2011–2016 Evaluative Report on RURCON, states that all RURCON workshops are participatory and because of that approach, participants in the training flow with the training.[275] After this general description of RURCON and its services, a review of RURCON's approach through churches to promote holistic development follows.

RURCON as an enabling organization (which believes in local self-reliance, sustainable lifestyles, and livelihoods based on good Christian stewardship) focuses on equipping pastors and church leaders, Christian development workers/facilitators, leaders of para-church organizations, theologians, missionaries, lecturers and tutors, and other interested persons to facilitate participatory approach to development as the means whereby it works through churches to address the needs of the poor. The pastors and church leaders, Christian development workers/facilitators, leaders of para-church organizations, theologians, missionaries, and the like are simply referred to hereafter in this sub-section as church leaders. Participatory Rural Appraisal (PRA), and Appreciative Inquiry (AI) are among several participatory approaches RURCON applies.[276]

---

272. Zasha, 10, 16.

273. Zasha, 10, 16.

274. RURCON, "RURCON Long-Range Strategic Plan," 11. Wuyep, "Introducing RURCON," 7–18 September 2015.

275. Zasha, "2016 Evaluative Report 2011–2016," 10, 16.

276. Choji, "Development Aids and Relief," 13; Also see Report of RURCON "International Wholistic Development Course," 17.

Though RURCON services are not limited to training workshops for church leaders the review here is limited to its ministry through the church because this is of immediate value for the purpose of this study. RURCON describes the role of the church in society and development as a task of enhancing growth, advancement, or enrichment of the people of the world or of a given culture in which the church has been established. The church is to impact society for good and to be a good model in development work for society's growth and enrichment holistically. The church executes its task as "partners with God in making the world a better and conducive place for everyone to live, irrespective of who he or she is."[277] RURCON views the processes of holistic development to include improved living conditions, looking beyond evangelism to awareness and having the capacity to take social action, being involved in politics by way of advocating good governance, and partnership and networking to share ideas, talents, and experiences to promote mutual learning and complementary action. RURCON's approach of conducting training workshops for church leaders is aimed at providing services for the "wholistic development of people through Christian churches and organizations in Africa"[278] based on the assumption that promoting authentic African Christian communities through discipleship development can empower churches to be more effective in their efforts to transform whole communities through holistic development.

The RURCON approach fits Matarrita-Cascante and Brennan's directed model of CD. The focus of RURCON is to empower churches in Africa, through the church leaders, with the knowledge and skills to engage in facilitating processes of holistic development in the communities they serve. The RURCON approach empowers church leaders with the knowledge and skills to serve as the "professional and technical" experts to navigate the members of the churches in the process of problem-solving as guided by the church leaders work. A sample of some of the objectives of the training workshops illustrates this. Some of the objectives include: (1) to introduce participants to the concept of Christian wholistic development/integral mission; (2) to increase participants' understanding of having community involvement and ownership of development projects; (3) to increase the understanding of

277. Yamsat, "Role of the Church."
278. Zasha, "2016 Evaluative Report 2011–2016," 10.

participants on Christian holistic development with a view to equipping them with knowledge, practical skills, and changed attitudes towards community transformation for wholeness in Christ; (4) to enable participants to incorporate holistic development into their work in order to empower the poor for improved livelihood, and more.[279]

Through the training workshops the church leaders learn how to facilitate networking and partnership. The approach therefore results in a cognitive reorientation of the church leaders concerning holistic development without making provision for equipping them with skills to engage the communities in a direct dialogical interaction with the biblical metanarrative. Also, by aiming to enable participants in the training workshops to incorporate holistic development into their work, it implies that holistic development is not considered as a seamless part of the church leaders work. This suggests a dichotomous view of holistic development being different from the work the church leaders are engaged in.

It is observed here that while the vision of RURCON is to establish transformed African communities to reflect how God intends them to be, its application is inadequate. The RURCON approach does not provide a direct dialogical interaction between the worldview of the target community and the biblical worldview on the issue(s) addressed for holistic transformation.

The wholistic development education may help church members to be able to cognitively connect the need to their faith and their vocations but the approach does not provide for a direct dialogical interaction between the worldviews of communities and the biblical worldview. Dialogical interaction facilitates worldview transformation. Paul G. Hiebert argues that if the worldview of a community is not transformed then the gospel message communicated in that community "is subverted and the result is a syncretistic Christo-paganism, which has the form of Christianity but not its essence."[280] Joy Alvarez, Elnora Avarientos, and Thomas H. McAlpine argue that God creates and recreates by his powerful word therefore the Bible is a source that mediates the creative power of God and by reflecting upon the Scripture it

---

279. RURCON, "International Wholistic Development Course," 7–18 September 2015; "International Development Management Course" 6–17 March 2017.

280. Hiebert, *Transforming Worldviews*, 11.

results to human transformation.[281] Applying Hiebert's argument and the argument of Alvarez, Elnora, and McAlpine to RURCON's approach shows that the lack of demonstrable effort to facilitate the engagement of the worldviews of communities in dialogical interaction with the biblical worldview on issues of concern, for the purpose of eliciting the transformation of the worldviews of the communities, is an inadequacy that needs to be addressed. However, the focus on equipping church leaders with the capacity to facilitate efforts at holistic development in communities through the church is a strategic approach and a good starting point.

Christian Rural and Urban Development Association of Nigeria (CRUDAN)

Danladi Musa writes in a historical overview of Christian Rural and Urban Development Association of Nigeria (CRUDAN)[282] that CRUDAN was inaugurated and established in 1990. CRUDAN is the outcome of an amalgamation of two Christian organizations concerned with development in rural areas of Nigeria, Christian Rural Fellowship (CRFN) and Christian Rural Advisory Council (CRAC). CRFN was established in 1953 and was focused on rural communities in Southern Nigeria. CRAC was established in 1965 to reach out to rural communities in Northern Nigeria. These two organizations worked with and through church denominations. Both were focused on sharing knowledge and concern as they share experiences and information on rural development work as well as in the publication of leaflets on related subject matter.

Musa further writes that CRUDAN has reviewed its operations and strategy plans four times between 1990 and 2007. Out of its reviews and evaluation CRUDAN concludes that: (1) churches dichotomize "the spiritual from the physical, evangelism from social action and words from deeds."[283] (2) Churches involved in rural development efforts applied approaches that did not involve the active participation of the people for whom development projects were instituted for. The approaches were institution-based and

---

281. Alvarez, Avarientos, and McAlpine, "Our Experience," 56.

282. Musa, *Promoting Christian*. Musa is a pioneer member and the first Executive Secretary of CRUDAN.

283. Musa, 25.

project-centered instead of being community-based and people oriented. (3) "It was noted that even in areas where churches had been carrying out development work for a number of years, poverty was still prevalent."[284] These insights led CRUDAN to make three major shifts in its approaches. First, the shift from dichotomous to holistic approach. Second, the shift from project-centered development to people-centered approach to development. Third, the shift from institution-based to community-based approach to development.

CRUDAN is a Christian inter-denominational, not for profit, non-governmental organization that has as its main goal the promotion of the growth of the church in Nigeria. CRUDAN aims at achieving its main goal through assisting in the church in Nigeria in rural/urban development work as part of the church's witness. Therefore CRUDAN has as its vision statement, "a dynamic self-sustained Christian organization facilitating (w)holistic community transformation with the church as agent of change, manifesting the kingdom of God on earth."[285] CRUDAN mission statement also reads that they aim, "to promote sustainable development in Nigeria in partnership with the church, members and other organizations through capacity building, (W)holistic Development Education, Advocacy, Mobilization, and Peace Building for poverty reduction and good governance."[286]

CRUDAN, states in its constitution,[287] as part of its objectives (1) motivating and training "leaders and members, Christian development workers, community-based organizations and theological institutions, on Christian Wholistic Development"[288] to equip them with knowledge, practical skills, and changed attitudes to enable communities to develop themselves toward wholeness in Christ; (2) promoting "community-based and people-centered development approaches through participatory training and development management counselling of member organizations and other development organisations"[289]; (3) promoting "cooperation, collaboration and partnership among Christian development practitioners, Christian development agencies

---

284. Musa, 29.

285. CRUDAN, "2015 Annual Report," 4. The parenthesis is in the original.

286. CRUDAN, 4; Musa. *Promoting Christian (W)holistic Development*, 16. The parenthesis is in the original.

287. CRUDAN, "Constitution and Bye-Laws," 7.

288. CRUDAN, 7.

289. CRUDAN, 7.

and other bodies"[290]; (4) working "to actively promote social justice, through raising awareness and sensitization of the church, equipping her to speak on behalf of and with the community involved, to cause sustainable and good governance."[291] CRUDAN engages Christian development organizations, public and private institutions, and government and non-government organizations through the application of different participatory learning methods as a means of enhancing their capacities for development.

CRUDAN applies participatory learning tools like participatory evaluation process (PEP), Participatory Learning and Action (PLA)/Participatory Rural Appraisal (PRA), community resource planning and management, and others. The participatory learning methods are applied in small groups' discussions, brainstorming, case studies, plenary sessions, role playing, experiential exercises, and arts. It is through these capacity enhancement methodologies that CRUDAN expects participants to acquire knowledge, skills, attitudes, and abilities to empower the poor. The training is conducted by "highly experienced capacity building facilitators, industry experts, policy research analysts and organizational development practitioners."[292] The CRUDAN trainers work with the trainees to identify capacity needs, skills sets, and tools required to adequately address specific issues that challenge effectiveness. In addition, the trainers collaborate with institutions, organizations, and the church in Nigeria to remodel, re-tool, and upscale skills-mix, program approaches, and articulate strategic processes for them to achieve positive resource efficiency and effectiveness.[293]

CURDAN's approach falls into the directed model of CD and, like RURCON, empowers participants in its capacity enhancement trainings with knowledge and skills with which to facilitate self-help model approaches in target communities. Experts and professionals engage trainees in a process aimed at acquiring knowledge and skills to organize and promote self-help models to facilitate holistic development in target communities. The approach helps participants to address the problem of non-involvement of target communities in the process of their development and attempts "to convince

---

290. CRUDAN, 7.

291. CRUDAN, 7.

292. CRUDAN, "CRUDAN Services." See also www.crudan.org

293. CRUDAN, "CRUDAN Services."

beneficiaries what is best for them"[294] so as to promote higher chances of sustainability in the development effort.

CRUDAN in its approach seeks to support the church as a primary agent of development through being a model of the kingdom of God community; a community that teaches and preaches the gospel message and work for the holistic well-being of the community. This makes the church a visible sign that points to the wonders of God's work. Modelling does not amount to verbal explanation of the gospel message to watching non-Christian members of the community. The modelling approach does not aim at facilitating a direct dialogical interaction of the community's worldview on development with the biblical worldview on holistic transformational development. The approach may indeed demonstrate the wonders of the gospel, the approach may also raise interest in the church and what the church represents for the unchurched members of a community, yet the approach does not guarantee the kind of interest that leads to raising questions the gospel message can explain. The approach does not guarantee that a direct dialogical interaction between the between the community and the biblical metanarrative.

Strengths and Weaknesses of the Approaches of the Christian Relief and Development Organizations

The review of the three major global theories and approaches to development and the review of the approaches applied by the three CRDOs in the process of facilitating development in rural communities demonstrated the strengths and weaknesses of the theories and approaches. The review also demonstrated how the theories and approaches relate to the issue of holistic development in rural communities. In the light of the foregoing review the strengths and weaknesses the approaches are highlighted.

The literatures review demonstrated that the theoretical or philosophical principles that guided major global approaches to development (1) are not holistic in focus, (2) are dependent on the application of science and technology as the most essential tool for development, (3) are aimed at achieving economic prosperity as a means to experience physical, social, and political state of utopia, and (4) are not aimed at a direct engagement of rural communities who are at the grassroots in the process of development. Instead these

---

294. Matarrita-Cascante and Brennan, "Conceptualizing Community Development," 299.

major theories aimed at engaging national or political structures of individual countries to formulate and implement policies based on the global theories.

The approaches of the CRDOs reviewed are all aimed to (1) be holistic, (2) directly engage rural communities in the process, (3) integrate community-based knowledge and technology, (4) improve the economic, physical, social, and political well-being of the rural communities, and (5) to demonstrate the love of God and to be a visible model of the kingdom of God community in words, deeds, and signs. The approaches of the CRDOs do not reject the approaches of the global theories whose goal is to improve the well-being of human beings primarily from physical, economic, political, social, and psychological but go beyond these to seek a holistic well-being that includes the spiritual aspect of human needs from a Christian or biblical perspective.

However, the literature review reveals that the CRDOs do not facilitate a direct dialogical interaction between the worldviews of target communities and the biblical worldview on issues for holistic and transformational development. As stated earlier the CRDOs approaches are problem-solving approaches that fit Matarrita-Cascante and Brennan's directed model approach to CD. The approach of this study applied a strength-based appreciative approach to CD. It is an approach that applies a direct dialogical interaction of both biblical worldview on transformational development and the study communities' worldview on development. The dialogical interaction is applied as a seamless part of a process necessary for authentic, sustainable, and contextually meaningful holistic transformational development. The approach transforms attitudes and practices for holistic development that progressively applies biblical shalom in the selected homogeneous rural communities in this study. What then are the characteristics of homogeneous rural communities?

Homogeneous Rural Communities

The literature review in this section aims at drawing insights from the fields of sociology and cultural anthropology to provide a panoramic understanding of the characteristics of a homogeneous rural community. The fields of sociology and cultural anthropology have, through different methods, helped to provide explanations concerning human beings in their social and cultural contexts. The focus of the study is on homogeneous communities bound in common geographical and environmental locations described as rural. People live in different geographical or spatial locations and they are interrelated in varying ways for both their survival and well-being. Historically, human beings are always in the process of finding and providing explanation for their experiences and looking for ways to improve on their living conditions.[295] In other words, human beings have always sought to understand themselves and their environment. This quest for understanding, which should help improve the well-being of the individual and community, has led to the development of different fields of academic inquiries. Interest in the physical, psychological, emotional, social, and spiritual well-being has given rise to different academic fields like biology, education, anthropology, sociology, theology, and many more academic disciplines.

The term community provides the mental picture of an interdependent relationship of a group of human beings who relate and participate in various activities aimed at promoting the well-being of members of the group. The biblical account of human history from creation to the close of the biblical canon indicate that people live and relate on both common and diverse, but related, interests and concerns regardless of their geographical residency. Sociologists describe how people interrelate, interact, collaborate, and work in interdependent relationships regardless of where they live. Jeffrey C. Bridger, A. E. Luloff, and Richard S. Krannich write that social anthropologists describe the community as a system of interaction between members of a unit.[296] Rhonda Phillips and Robert H. Pittman, and John W. (Jack) Vincent II, agree that the concept of community can refer to either people defined by geographical boundaries or defined by common interest regardless of residency.[297] The basic goal of a group of people relating, interacting, collaborating, and working in interdependent relationships is to promote or sustain the well-being of the individual and collective members of the group. Thus, a community consists of people interacting with each other on issues of common interest such as social, economic, political, vocational, religious, or other interests regardless of their spatial proximity.

---

295. Haviland, *Cultural Anthropology*, 30. Haviland, explains that traditionally myths and legends were the means by which human societies explained their experiences.

296. Bridger, Luloff, and Krannich, "Community Change," 9.

297. Phillips and Pittman, "Framework for Community," 5; Vincent II, "Community Development Practice," 58.

Each human community, spatially or non-spatially relating, interacting, and acting, has homogeneous characteristics. The term homogeneous is an adjective that qualifies that which is common or similar to certain things or certain people. Characteristics that are homogeneous in a community include social and cultural relationships and cultural interests, vocational or professional interests, or political interests, or religious interests.[298] Studies in anthropology describe the characteristics of homogeneous to communities. For instance, William A. Haviland[299] analyzes some of the characteristics that can be found in communities resident in a common geographical area. They may include common language, common cultural values, common cultural and historical heritage, and common religious affinities. Other homogeneous characteristics are a shared economics system, a common family and kinship system, a socio-political structure, shared art, and other common interests.[300]

A rural community, as applied in this study, consists of a group of people with homogeneous characteristics and living in dynamic relationships in a geographical area described as rural. A geographical area described as rural is one that lacks social and infrastructural facilities that are in cities such as good roads, safe sources of potable water, hospitals, and the like.[301] Relationships are dynamic because they are prone to changes due to situations that may occur as a result of different factors such as increase in knowledge, changes in the economic status of the people, new experiences brought about by natural ecological changes or by encounter with new religious perceptions etc. Therefore, homogenous characteristics in rural communities are not static but dynamic due to both internal and external influences.

According to sociologists, such as Bridger, Luloff and Krannich, the rise of modernization, industrialization, and urbanization to address different facets of human lives since the mid-twentieth century had effects on the concept, nature, and social order of human communities.[302] That is to say that the demography, the social lives, the economic activities, the religious lives, and many aspects of human activities were changed by this development. One

---

298. Vincent II, "Community Development Practice," 58.
299. Haviland, *Cultural Anthropology*.
300. This is a summary drawn from Haviland's seminal work, *Cultural Anthropology*.
301. "Rural" in www.dictionary.reference.com/browse/community accessed May 26, 2015.
302. Luloff and Krannich, "Introduction," 1.

of the major demographic changes is the division of human settlements into rural and metropolitan or urban communities. New technologies have been developed and are continuously being developed to the present day. These new technologies have different effects on both rural and urban communities too.

The nature, social structures, economic activities, and many other aspects of rural communities, like urban communities, are prone to change. Bridger, Luloff and Krannich state that for "most of the twentieth century community theory was dominated by approaches that emphasized a stable and predictable aspects of life."[303] But with the development of different forms of mass media like the television, and the increasing ease of transportation and communication, cultural distinctions were being compromised even as different communities were now open to interaction with multiple communities.[304] Bridger, Luloff and Krannich, citing Roland Warren's Great Change thesis, argue that local communities tended to lose their autonomy and decision concerning local affairs were shifted to "people and places far removed from the local scene."[305] It can be conceded that ideas from other communities, due to the new possibilities of closer interactions, do have effects and influence the decision and actions of a local community.

It is however extreme to claim that local communities lose their autonomy due to such effects and influences. Haviland, argues that "change may be forced upon one group in the course of especially intense contact between two societies."[306] Historically such a situation occurred during the era of colonialism and still continues in other forms as argued by dependency theorists and world-system theorists in the arena of global economics. However, in practical terms, local communities do still have the autonomy to choose what it considers beneficial for its well-being and the general well-being of individuals in that local community. Haviland, further posits that the diffusion of ideas and other occurrences in a community like cultural loss and

---

303. Bridger, Luloff and Krannich, "Community Change," 9.

304. Bridger, Luloff and Krannich, 9–10.

305. Bridger, Luloff and Krannich, 10. Bridger, Luloff, and Krannich, reject Warren's conclusion that the community as a unit of social organization has become less important.

306. Haviland, *Cultural Anthropology*, 450.

innovation can be the mechanisms that influence the transformation of the community's lifestyle.[307]

It is worthy to note that some of the aspects or factors that were responsible for local solidarity in a community may become eroded or weakened due to new ideas that may promise a better form of well-being for the community. For example, Western curriculum and methods of formal education in schools weakened the apprenticeship curriculum and methods of non-formal on the job forms of education in Nigerian societies. However, in the present century the conscious or unconscious decision of a community to make transformational changes in its lifestyle is based on the autonomy of the community and not based on force from outside the community. Therefore, rural communities are no longer "stable and predictable" but dynamic and prone to change and transformation because of the interrelatedness of different human societies brought about by advances in communication via various technological platforms communities. The dynamic changes in a community occur first at the community's worldview.

A homogenous community consists of people interacting on issues of common interest in the context of interdependent relationships for the purpose of physical, emotional, psychological, social, and spiritual survival and well-being. A homogenous community could be a spatially placed people or a group with a common interest who may not have a common spatial location. In each type of community the people hold a common worldview related to their issues of common interest. The worldview of any community is prone to transformation. The two rural communities selected for this study have the characteristics of homogeneous communities. Therefore, since this study seeks to examine a deliberate approach to facilitate the transformation of the worldview of two rural communities on development it is imperative to examine how to analyze worldviews.

Analyzing a Worldview

Eugene Webb asserts that, "No human being lives without a worldview, but comparatively few ever give much thought to what worldviews are, how they

---

307. Haviland, 450.

come into being, how they change, and how they are held."[308] The transformation of the worldview of any homogenous community can be facilitated through a deliberate effort. Hiebert posits that worldviews are prone to transformation because they shape and integrate "various fields of knowledge: from theology, anthropology, and missions to physics and the culinary arts."[309] To successfully facilitate the transformation of any particular worldview requires an understanding of the characteristics of a worldview and the processes that can be applied to facilitate worldview transformation. In this study Hiebert's framework for analyzing worldviews serves as the framework for the review of the concept.[310] The starting point for analyzing a worldview is to define the concept.

Definition of Worldview

Kenneth Richard Samples points to the historical development of the concept of worldview. The word is derived from the German term *Weltanschauung*. A term that "refers to the cluster of beliefs a person holds about the most significant issues of life – such as God, the cosmos, knowledge, values, humanity and history."[311] Samples further states that a people's beliefs form the big picture, the mental structure, the general outlook or the grand perspective on life, and the world the people have.[312] Brian Baxter defines a worldview as that which "embodies a specific understanding of reality based on presuppositions."[313] Nicole Note et al. describe a worldview as subconscious explanations, developed and transmitted by and through generations of people, as explanations concerning "how the world ontologically is, becomes, or is experienced."[314]

The foregoing definitions imply that a worldview is the subconscious conceptual understanding of reality within the context of the person or community that hold the worldview. This means that a worldview is the subconscious conceptual understanding that people operate on, that guides their attitudes,

---

308. Webb, *Worldview and Mind*, 1.

309. Hiebert, *Anthropological Reflections*, 11.

310. Hiebert, *Transforming Worldviews* and *Gospel in Human Contexts* are the major sources for Hiebert's definition and worldview analysis framework applied in this review.

311. Samples, *World of Difference*, 20.

312. Samples, 20.

313. Baxter, *Darwinian Worldview*, 1.

314. Note, Fornet-Betancout, Eastermann, and Aerts, "Worldview and Cultures," 1.

values, interpretations, perspectives, decisions, and actions and not what they think about. Hiebert posits that a worldview consists of the foundational conceptual assumptions that guide the way people who share a common culture make sense of what they perceive as reality and determines how the people order their lives.[315] In his comprehensive philosophical analysis of the traditional African worldview, Yusufu Turaki argues that the traditional African worldview has four components: holism, which "governs man's relationship and integration with the world of nature and to some extent with the spirit world"; spiritualism, which "governs man's relationship and integration with the spirit world"; dynamism or power consciousness, "which governs man's relationship and integration with the mystical, mysterious and spirit powers and forces"; and communalism, which governs man's relationship and integration with the kinship community that values loyalty, affinity and obligations that "mould and shape man's moral responsibility and accountability in the community."[316] In view of the foregoing, the traditional African worldview can be described as the subconscious conceptual understanding of the human world, nature, and the spirit world being an integrated whole predominated and controlled or influenced by spiritual beings or forces in a dynamic state that can be controlled or manipulated to meet human needs and sustain life.[317]

Therefore, if a worldview is what people who share a common culture operate on then it determines: (1) the epistemological understanding of what they see and/or experience, (2) the affective response of the people to what they see or experience, and (3) the evaluative judgment of the people about what they see and experience. It means then that the worldview of a people who share a common culture has a firm grip on the choices and the decisions they make and also the actions they commit themselves to take. This is evident in the people's culture. A people's culture is an integrated system of beliefs, feelings, and values that set the pattern of behaviors guided by rules, norms, and sanctions that members of the community learn from parents

---

315. Hiebert, *Transforming Worldviews*, 15, and Hiebert, *Gospel in Human Contexts*, 158; Samples, *World of Difference*, 21.

316. Turaki, *Foundations*, 57–58.

317. Turaki, 57–58.

and peers and are communicated by means of stories, symbols, rituals, and other forms of pedagogical tools.[318]

Sherwood Lingenfelter argues that individuals or subsets of a community, for example Christians, are constantly under the powerful pressure of the "social games" the community live and participate by.[319] These "social games" are in reality the unwritten prescribed ways of living in a community's culture. Therefore, to live in a state of organic well-being and to avoid unpleasant tensions and crises, individual members and subsets of a community live according to the dictates of the community's culture guided by the community's worldview.

According to Turaki, traditional African religions and worldviews do not have creeds that have to be learned rather they are caught, passed on, and lived. Therefore, the African worldview has "a dominant and powerful influence on man in traditional Africa,"[320] and "the traditional African seeks to live in harmony and to balance his life in a harmonious and peaceful existence with his entire world and especially with the spirit world."[321] How then do worldviews function?

Functions of Worldviews

Worldviews have several functions but their primary function is that they provide each culture and its people "with a more or less coherent way of looking at the world."[322] In the following sub-section six functions of worldviews Hiebert posits[323] are reviewed and applied to the African worldview as it relates to the objective of this study.

First, worldviews provide the underlying conceptual blueprint that guides the cultural practices of a community. Drawing from Clifford Geertz and Brian Walsh, Hiebert writes that worldviews provide a community's plausible

---

318. The concept of culture has many definitions but the definition applied here is based on an integrated understanding of the concept from different anthropologists, for example, Hiebert, *Gospel in Human Contexts*, 150; Lingenfelter, *Transforming Culture*, 17.

319. Lingenfelter, *Transforming Culture*, 18, 23–24.

320. Turaki, *Foundations*, 41–42.

321. Turaki, 39–40.

322. Hiebert, *Transforming Worldviews*, 28.

323. Hiebert, 29–30.

answers to the ultimate questions of life.[324] Samples also argues that when a worldview elucidates reasonable answers to ultimate questions "life (and death) issues become much more comprehensible and easier to get through."[325] Toyin Falola states that increasing secularization and modernization in Africa have not diminished the impact of a worldview based in indigenous cultures.[326] Hence the African worldview, as Turaki, argues, has "a dominant and powerful influence on man in traditional Africa."[327]

Turaki posits that African Christians spirituality and practice are influenced by their African traditional beliefs and culture.[328] This is so because the traditional African conception of reality is deeply rooted and grounded in the understanding that reality goes beyond what is visible but also consists of "what lies behind and guides life phenomena."[329] This understanding provides a basis for aiming to engage the worldview of the study community in dialogical interaction of with the biblical worldview on holistic transformational development.

Second, according to Hiebert worldviews give emotional stability in the face of crises in life. Worldviews provides emotional reinforcement for the fundamental beliefs of a community.[330] African traditional beliefs and practices sustain the social and cultural harmony of African communities. According to Turaki, a combination of African psychological, philosophical, and moral and ethical beliefs, which are integrated in the African worldview, dominate African thinking.[331] Falola also posits that indigenous religions and worldview provide the foundation for understanding and critiquing the changing world around the people "partly in order to adapt to them and partly in order to create a defense mechanism."[332] This means that the traditional worldview of a community navigates the processes by which the community sustains its harmony. Therefore, a state of emotional disequilibrium is introduced when

---

324. Hiebert, 29.

325. Samples, *World of Difference*, 21, 22.

326. Falola, *Power of African Cultures*, 202.

327. Turaki, *Foundations*, 41–42.

328. Turaki, *Trinity of Sin*, 9.

329. Turaki, *Foundations*, 62.

330. Hiebert, *Transforming Worldviews*, 29.

331. Turaki, *Trinity of Sin*, 15–16, 21–22.

332. Fola, *Power of African Cultures*, 208.

these traditional beliefs and practices are threatened. This implies that the processes of this study should not threaten the stability of the study communities' relational harmony.

Third, worldviews provide the conceptual course of action a community takes in response to its experiences. This is so because worldviews validate the deepest cultural norms a community uses to evaluate its experiences. On the basis of such evaluation a community selects the course of action it takes in response.[333] The philosophical foundations of the traditional African worldview influence the foundational religious beliefs, practices, feelings, and behavior of Africans.[334] Therefore, the continuation of many indigenous practices amongst Africans means that they are still guided by their traditional worldview.

Fourth, worldviews organize the ideas, feelings, and values of a community into a more or less unified view of reality. Worldviews help communities to integrate their culture.[335] The African worldview is characteristically holistic. It holds the spirit world, the natural world, and the human world or society in a seamless interrelationship.[336] Turaki argues that cosmic harmony/order is a moral and ethical principle in traditional African worldview.[337] African traditional values are shaped by religious traditions therefore millions of Africans make decisions based on traditional beliefs.[338]

Fifth, drawing from Charles Kraft, Hiebert writes that worldviews help communities to accept or reject new ideas, new behavior, and/or new products from within or without communities. Any new ideas or behaviors, or products that are accepted, the worldviews reinterpret to fit the overall cultural patterns of the community.[339] The African worldview is holistic unlike Western thinking, which is dualistic. Traditional Africans see "all things as existing in a state of complex interdependency."[340] Contact with the Western world through trade, colonialism, and missionary activities introduced

---

333. Hiebert, *Transformaing Worldviews*, 29.

334. Turaki, *Foundations*, 36.

335. Hiebert, *Transforming Worldviews*, 29.

336. Turaki, *Trinity of Sin*, 22.

337. Turaki, *Foundations*, 75.

338. Falola, *Power of African Cultures*, 202.

339. Hiebert, *Transforming Worldviews*, 29–30.

340. Turaki, *Trinity of Sin*, 16.

Western dualistic worldview in the African context. Because of its holistic characteristic the African worldview resists any notion that presupposes the disruption of the status quo. The status quo means being in a harmonious and peaceful existence in the seamless and coherent world of the spiritual, the natural, and the human worlds. Hence the orientation of the African worldview is toward the past and less toward the unknown present and future. This study aims at facilitating the study communities' worldview on development through its dialogical interaction with the biblical worldview on holistic transformational development. Therefore, to transform the traditional worldview of rural African communities on development it has to be engaged in a dialogical interaction with the biblical worldview, which is holistic and has past, present, and future perspectives.

Finally, worldviews provide psychological equilibrium that reassures communities that the world is truly as they see it. Therefore, worldviews provide communities with a sense of peace and a sense of being at home in the contexts in which the communities live.[341] The study seeks to engage the biblical worldview on holistic transformational development without disrupting, yet transforming, the psychological equilibrium of the study communities. The next sub-section describes what a biblical worldview is.

Worldview Analysis Framework

The analysis of a worldview helps in identifying how worldviews come into being, how worldviews change, and how worldviews function as well as the value of worldviews in the lives of individuals and in the life of a community that share common cultures. Hiebert states that in missiology it is necessary to study the people served. He further states that

> The categories and theories of theology show what people are like as created in the image of God, fallen yet redeemable, objects of God's supreme love and sacrifice. The categories and theories of biblical theology show God's presence in the people's history . . . The categories and theories of anthropological theology show how the people's social and cultural systems expedite or impede their understanding of the Bible's message.[342]

---

341. Hiebert, *Transforming Worldviews*, 30.
342. Hiebert, *Anthropological Reflections*, 13.

Therefore, for the purpose of this study, there is need to understand a community's worldview. A framework is required to analyze worldviews, which is the focus of this sub-section.

The analysis of worldviews makes it possible to compare similarities and differences between worldviews, in addition, as in the case of this study, to show how a particular worldview can be transformed through dialogue with another worldview. In this study Hiebert's model of worldview analysis, which can be used to study specific worldviews, has been applied.[343] Hiebert integrates ideas from "Ferdinand Eisenstein, Alfred North Whitehead, Ludwig von Bertalanffy, and others"[344] to formulate and propose a model that combines synchronic and diachronic approaches for the analysis of worldviews. What follows is a review of Hiebert's model for worldview analysis.

Hiebert's model of worldview analysis situates the method in two broad approaches, synchronic and diachronic approaches.[345] A synchronic approach examines characteristics that provide structures by which to understand worldviews. A synchronic approach presents universal structures but does not fully explain particular worldviews. Conversely a diachronic approach makes it possible to discern how particular worldviews give meaning to life for the community that is governed by their particular worldview.

The synchronic characteristics of a worldview, according to Hiebert's model, consists of five universal structures, which are: (1) mental categories, (2) signs by which to determine realities in both objective and subjective ways, (3) logical systems by which to examine reality, (4) belief systems used to explain any given situation, themes, and counter themes that control or stimulate or keep behavior in check, and (5) epistemological assumptions that shape thoughts and actions. Hiebert further states that cultures are made up of three interacting dimensions that interact to provide people with a way of looking at the world that makes sense to them. The three dimensions are: a cognitive dimension, which consists of ideas shared by members of a group; an affective dimension, which consists of feelings that influence people's tastes;

---

343. Hiebert, *Transforming Worldviews*, 335, for a tabular presentation of Hiebert's model.

344. Hiebert, 31.

345. Hiebert describes a synchronic approach is an etic analysis which is analysis that applies philosophical categories of the West. Whereas a diachronic approach is an emic analysis that applies the philosophical categories of the community holding the worldview. Hiebert, *Anthropological Reflections*, 13.

and an evaluative dimension, which consists of values that give rise to the social and moral order in a culture. These three dimensions of a worldview together provide people with a structural way of looking at the world and making sense of it.

The diachronic approach in Hiebert's model helps identify meaning for a specific community embedded in its stories situated within a specific historical and ecological context. The stories of a community fuse scattered pieces of the community's experiences into a meaningful whole. The stories, or narrative, keep providing new insight in new situations hence stories shape the community's interpretation of the world around it. Hiebert writes that "We must realize that ultimate meaning in our lives is found not in an understanding of our human structures, but in our human stories."[346] The diachronic approach in Hiebert's model is applied to identify what makes experiential sense in a community's worldview.

A synchronic or etic analysis and a diachronic or emic analysis of a community's narrative are different approaches that complement one another as a means of looking at reality from two different points of view. The integration of both perspectives provides refined understanding of a community's worldview.

Methods of Analyzing Worldviews

There are several methods that can be applied in analyzing worldviews with none of the methods being considered the overarching method. Hiebert posits that "it is best to triangulate the findings of any one method with those produced by other methods."[347] He describes thirteen different methods. Out of these thirteen different methods, two are briefly described here because of their relevance in this study. The two are thick descriptions and narrative analysis methods of worldview.

A thick description method analyzes particular sociocultural events. It describes a sociocultural event from different perspectives and at different levels of a community's experiences. A thick description method, according to Heibert, can be a means by which "to build bridges of understanding that help translate and bring understanding between different cultures and

---

346. Hiebert, *Transforming Worldviews*, 31.
347. Hiebert, 91.

worldviews."[348] Kevin J. Vanhoozer applies a thick description method in his theory for interpreting cultural discourses and trends from a Christian theological perspective. Vanhoozer states that thick descriptions include multiperspectival and multilevel descriptions. To him multiperspectival considerations "uses a variety of academic disciplines to illumine what is going on in cultural discourses" and the multilevel considerations describe the same cultural phenomenon "on a variety of levels: historical, psychological, social, educational, economic" etc.[349] Hence a thick description method is a method that promotes a holistic examination of a community's narrative.

Hiebert's narrative analysis method seeks to make sense of the experiences a people have put into narrative form. Citing Riessman, Hiebert writes that "People create plots from disordered experiences and give them meaning by going beyond historical events into their deeper understanding of the world's story and their place in it."[350] The narrative conveys either explicit messages or implicit pictures of the world from the perspective of the people influenced by the community's history, its past and present experiences, and its projection of a desired experience.[351]

Triangulating the synchronic structure and the diachronic themes of a community provides a holistic understanding of the community's worldview on development. This study seeks to facilitate a biblical transformation of two selected homogeneous rural communities' worldview on development. It assumes that it is through the application of an appreciative dialogue between the communities' worldview on development and the biblical worldview on holistic transformational development. The next section reviews the concept of appreciative dialogue.

Appreciative Dialogue

The transformation of the worldview of any homogenous community can be facilitated through a deliberate effort. Appreciative dialogue is considered

---

348. Hiebert, 102.

349. Vanhoozer, "What Is Everyday Theology?," 45-47.

350. Hiebert, *Transforming Worldviews*, 100–101.

351. This idea is borrowed from Vanhoozer's three-dimensional framework for interpreting cultural texts which is "the world behind, of, and in front of the cultural text," Vanhoozer, "What Is Everyday Theology?," 48.

as a process through which the transformation of a community's worldview can be effectively and fruitfully undertaken. Appreciative dialogue is defined here as a dialogical interaction between people in the same community that is focused on the strengths, successes, values, hopes, and dreams of a community. Appreciative dialogue is applied as a dialogical interaction between the worldview of a community and the biblical worldview on the same issue(s). Appreciative dialogue applies the primary tool of Appreciative Inquiry (AI). At this point it is considered necessary to present a brief history of AI as a backdrop for understanding the appreciative dialogue approach.

Brief History of Appreciative Inquiry

The AI method was developed by David L. Cooperrider[352] in 1980. Cooperrider, in his doctoral research, examined factors that inspire people in an organization to be at their best and to bring about a lively and productive progress in the organization they belong to. Gervase R. Bushe writes that at its inception Cooperrider's proposed AI generated excitement and experimentation.[353] According to Diana Whitney and Amanda Trosten-Bloom, AI is characterized by appreciative interviews that apply appreciative questions to generate conversations focused on strengths, successes, values, hopes, and dreams of an organization.[354] Whitney and Trosten-Bloom further state that AI is improvisational, meaning that it can be approached in a variety of ways though it begins with a clear purpose.[355] There are however guiding principles for the application of AI that serve as a framework for appreciative dialogue. A review of the principles of AI is beneficial for understanding how appreciative dialogue can be creatively applied in different contexts.

Principles of Appreciative Inquiry

The AI approach is guided by four guiding principles that serve as its conceptual framework. AI scholars and practitioners describe the four principles as the 4-D Cycle. The 4-D Cycle includes Discovery, Dream, Design, and

---

352. David Cooperrider was then a doctoral student at the Case Western Reserve University. Cooperrider was guided in his study by Suresh Srivastra. See Cooperrider, Whitney, and Stavros, *Appreciative Inquiry*, xxvii.

353. Bushe, "Advances in Appreciative Inquiry," 14–22.

354. Whitney and Trosten-Bloom, *Power of Appreciative Inquiry*, 1, 6, 12.

355. Whitney and Trosten-Bloom, 13.

Delivery. The discovery principle is characterized by appreciation. According to Whitney and Trosten-Bloom, the discovery principle applied through one-on-one interviews, focus groups interviews, or large groups meeting, to guide stakeholders in an extensive, corporate search to understand the best of the present and the past of an organization. Whitney and Trosten-Bloom further state that purposeful affirmative conversations at the discovery stage of the 4-D Cycle produces "rich descriptions of the organizations positive core, stories of best practices and exemplary actions, enhanced organizational knowledge and collective wisdom."[356] The discovery principle deliberately brings to the fore in the minds of the people involved a conscious consideration of the things to be proud of. The dream principle stimulates imagination. When applied, the dream principle helps people to envision possibilities for a more valuable and vital future. Innovation is the characteristic of the design principle. The design principle draws on the insight gained from the application of the discovery and dream principles to select the best elements that can be put in place to design a plan of action. Finally, the application of innovative ideas towards the realization of the imagined better future characterizes the delivery principle.

Appreciative Inquiry seeks to promote innovation, confidence, and committed action to promote the progressive well-being of the participants based on reflections on the positive experiences of the research participants. The focus of AI according to David L. Cooperrider, Diana Whitney, and Jacqueline M. Stavros is on "a process for engaging people at any or all levels to produce effective positive change."[357] The AI approach is not focused on problem-solving rather it is an approach that seeks to further strengthen already existing progressive experiences in a given context. The traditional problem-solving approach to solve existing problems in specific contexts includes identifying problems, analyzing the causes of the problem, analyzing possible solutions, and developing an action plan to solve the problems.

According to Cooperrider and Whitney AI is guided by five basic principles. (1) The constructionist principle, which posits that human knowledge and organizational destiny are interconnected. This principle encourages holistic thinking. (2) The principle of spontaneity, which argues that inquiry

---

356. Whitney and Trosten-Bloom, 7–8.

357. Cooperrider, Whitney, and Stavros, *Appreciative Inquiry Handbook*, xv.

and change are simultaneous because the moment we question we create change of perception. (3) The poetic principle, which states that the story of an organization is co-authored by members of the organization based on what the members focus on. (4) The anticipatory principle, which involves the collective imagination and discourse about the future of the organization. It is the image of the future that stimulates the current behavior in an organization. (5) Finally, the positive principle, which involves the emotions serving as that which build and sustain the momentum for change.[358]

The AI process includes: (1) appreciating and valuing the best of what exists in an organization or community. This step is referred to as "Discovery" step. (2) Envisioning or dreaming about a more ideal situation, the "Dream" step. (3) Co-constructing what should be the ideal situation. This is the "Design" step. Finally, (4) the "Destiny" or "Delivery" step in the process which involves considering how to adjust and improve the present situation in a sustainable way

The guiding principles for the AI methodology are combined in a seamless whole process that engages stakeholders/participants in the inquiry process. The inquiry process provides the stakeholders/participants the opportunity to, through responses to questions raised, identify principles from their positive experiences. The identified principles can then serve as a springboard for and sustain the process in which the participants/stakeholders imagine, design an action plan, execute the action plan for the purpose of realizing a better future, and even evaluate the outcome. In other words, the participants appreciate, dream, design, and act towards a more fruitful and more satisfying experiences in their contexts. AI applies interactions through interview conversations that focus on strengths, resources, and capabilities of an organization or a community.[359]

Myers writes that Christian practitioners are concerned about an ongoing "struggle to find an authentically holistic practice of transformational development." The reason for this quest, Myers further posits, is because Christian development organizations are captivated by the modern worldview that separates or disconnects the physical world from the spiritual world. In addition the Christian development organizations express such captivity by

---

358. Cooperrider and Whitney, *Appreciative Inquiry*, 49–54.
359. Cooperrider, Whitney, and Stavros, *Appreciative Inquiry Handbook*, 5–7.

conceiving holistic ministry to mean combining Christian witness with relief and development. Therefore, the quest is for holistic development practice that integrates rather than separates the Christian gospel-as-word, as-deed, and as-sign in the process of facilitating holistic development.[360] The AI methodology has generative and sustainability building principles inherent in it, principles that facilitate dialogical engagement of stakeholders on issues of common concern. These principles that generate dialogical engagement of stakeholders, as co-designers, with the potential for sustainability in positive transformational process in organizations or communities have informed the choice of integrating AI principles in the development of the research tool applied in this study.

Appreciative dialogue does not discuss problems in a quest for a solution to the problems, rather the focus of discussion is on the potential and available resources that have enhanced the well-being of the community and considering ways to further develop the potential and available resources to further improve the well-being of the community. The aim of appreciative dialogue, in the case of people in the same community, is to unearth and to inspire a conscious deliberation on the positive potential in the community that can be further developed to strengthen and sustain processes of progressive development or improvement of life in the community. Also in the case of the dialogical interaction between a community's worldview and the biblical worldview, the aim is to bring about a transformation of a community's worldview as the community's worldview aligns with the biblical worldview. In other words, the aim of appreciative dialogue is to stimulate creativity through a process of worldview transformation.

Value of Appreciative Inquiry

David L. Cooperrider, Diana Whitney, and Jacqueline M. Stavros report that the AI is an action research methodology that has been found useful in other endeavors.[361] Action research emphasizes the involvement of stakeholders on an issue as co-researchers.[362] AI has been defined by different AI scholars and practitioners in different ways. AI has been defined either as a theory or as a

---

360. Myers, "Setting the Table," xii–xvii.

361. Cooperrider, Whitney, and Stavros, *Appreciative Inquiry Handbook*, xxvii.

362. Bushe, "Advances in Appreciative Inquiry," 14.

process or as a practice. Bushe, and Ulla Johansson and Jill Woodilla, describe AI as "a theory of intentional collective action by people that leads to change in their social systems."[363] Whitney and Trosten-Bloom, and Cooperrider, Whiteney, and Stavros describe AI as a process that inspires creative imagination in people for the transformation of the organization or community the people belong to.[364] Chris Laszlo and David Cooperrider describe AI as an "innovative and transformational methodology" that inspires change through engaging whole systems to tap into "its strengths, its assets, and its capacity to innovate."[365] Nadya Zhexembayeva points that the AI philosophy and method does not serve as a ready-made-fit-for-all method but serves as a framework, a structured approach, by which stakeholders in an organization or community co-create a vision of a better future for the organization or community.[366] Therefore AI as a philosophical or conceptual framework is applied to guide appreciative dialogue among stakeholders in organization or community. The AI approach provides all, or inclusive representatives of, stakeholders the opportunity to express their creative ideas through dialogues that lead to generating a normative vision, a collaborative design of action plans, and collective actions, to realize the organization's or community's articulated normative vision.

According to Whitney and Trosten-Bloom, four beliefs about the human nature inform the AI philosophy. First, the uniqueness and giftedness of people as individuals and as collective groups have to bring about dynamism in life. Second, people relate and interact through human social systems. Third, people related in a common social system articulate the vision that serves as a guide for individual and/or collective actions. Fourth, it is through inquiry and dialogue that people in an organization or community analyze their situation. Therefore, Whitney and Trosten-Bloom argue that the AI approach based on these beliefs about the human nature shifts the attention and actions of people away from problem-solving analysis to analyzing ideal and productive possibilities for the future.[367]

---

363. Bushe, 14; Johansson and Woodilla, "Bridging Design and Management," 69.

364. Whitney and Trosten-Bloom, *Power of Appreciative Inquiry*, 1; Cooperrider, Whiteney, and Stavros, *Appreciative Inquiry Handbook*, xi.

365. Laszlo and Cooperrider, "Creating Sustainable Value," 32.

366. Zhexembayeva, "Whole New Value," 87–88.

367. Whitney and Trosten-Bloom, *Power of Appreciative Inquiry*, 2.

The AI approach puts the people in an organization or community to be "the experts" concerning their situation and experiences. Traditional approaches towards improving situations placed the responsibility upon people that may not belong to the organization or community. Such people are "the experts" who collect, collate, analyze and interpret statistical data from the organization or community. The meaning the "experts" assume from the data they analyze prescribes the course of action to be taken and not the people directly involved with the organization. However, it is evident then that the AI approach is based on the assumption that when people in an organization or community are engaged in appreciative dialogue they can effectively analyze, interpret, evaluate, and take collaborative action to transform their organization or community into and towards a better context for positive life experiences. Therefore, the AI approach creates a context for, and grants opportunity for, inclusive representatives or all members of a community to be included in a process of discovery and cooperation. AI enables people to create together a vision, a plan, and strategy for a better future in their community.[368]

Application of Appreciative Dialogue

Appreciative dialogue applied in a process aimed at facilitating holistic transformational development engages the people in a community to craft together ideas, plans, and actions for a better future in their context. Instead of focusing discussions on looking for a best solution to a problem the focus of discussion is on looking for "the boldest dream of positive possibilities."[369] Johansson and Woodilla posit that the application of an AI approach engages stakeholders in an organization or community to reflect on successes, articulate a normative vision, design a plan, and implement the plan for a better future.[370]

Johansson and Woodilla describe four integrated phases in an appreciative dialogue process. (1) The first phase is focused on observing and reflecting on what has been as and is the best in the organization or community. When applied in the development context, appreciative dialogue begins with discussions on "an already existing, even if limited, life-giving,

---

368. Whitney and Trosten-Bloom, 5.

369. Whitney and Trosten-Bloom, 16.

370. Johansson and Woodilla, "Bridging Design and Management," 69.

cooperative social reality."[371] Zhexembayeva, and Whitney and Trosten-Bloom agree that the AI approach reframes the angle from which positive change is approached. Instead of inquiry into problems, the AI approach examines past successes to uncover, magnify, and spread possibilities.[372] (2) The second phase is characterized by a collaborate articulation of what stakeholders in an organization or community consider to be a possibility in their context. It provides opportunity for the people involved to express their creative ideas that can be integrated into a commonly held conceptual vision of possibilities by members of the community for the community's better future. The creative ideas are inspired by the affirmative approach in the first phase of the process. Zhexembayeva, and Whitney and Trosten-Bloom argue that the AI approach differs from other approaches to change in terms of focus. These scholars argue that other approaches are deficit based because they focus on problems and how to overcome them. This problem-solving approach, Zhexembayeva, and Whitney and Trosten-Bloom, further argue, allows little room for long-term visions, strategic reflection, and innovation but the AI approach offers tools that unite the creative minds of people to envision a better future.[373] Therefore appreciative dialogue stimulates imagination and creativity. (3) The third phase focuses on ensuring the consent of the people in the organization or community concerning the action to be taken. In this phase the people collectively design an action plan or action plans aimed at achieving an envisioned better future for the organization or community. The AI approach provides opportunity for all stakeholders to participate and to collectively design action plans to realize the vision. (4) Finally, stakeholders as individuals and as a group experimentally implement the organization's or community's action plans.

Appreciative Inquiry is a philosophy, a process, and a practical tool that can be used to improvise a theory from its process. The guiding principles of the AI approach provided the theoretical framework for drawing up the appreciative questions applied in this study. The appreciative questions guided the appreciative dialogue that took place in the empirical and primary data

---

371. Myers, *Walking with the Poor*, 259.

372. Zhexembayeva, "Whole New Value," 92; Whitney and Trosten-Bloom, *Power of Appreciative Inquiry*, 10.

373. Zhexembayeva, "Whole New Value," 93; Whitney and Trosten-Bloom, *Power of Appreciative Inquiry*, 15.

phase of this study. Thus, the already existing life-giving, cooperative social reality of the communities engaged in this study were interfaced, through an appreciative dialogue, with the biblical holistic transformational development mission for a better holistic reality.

God's revealed holistic transformational development mission is in effect the *missio Dei* discussed earlier in this chapter. The dialogical interaction aims to help each community consider the best option the community or group can apply in their immediate ecological, sociocultural, and spiritual context in the light of the *missio Dei*. Sulaiman Z. Jakonda writes that development realities from a biblical perspective are what God intended the world to be and what it should be.[374] Molefe Tsele writes that development is the work of God who is concerned about both the supernatural and the world as we know it and that God's power is active in the ordinary everyday life activities of human beings.[375] God's activity includes the role and responsibility God has designed for God's people to participate with God in his acts. Through the application of the appreciative dialogue approach a community can have the opportunity to consider options that generate positive designs for progress toward a better future for the community. Options that accelerate the process leading to a better future, and options that sustain progress toward a better future for the community. The appreciative dialogue approach applied in this study engages both a community's worldview on development and the biblical worldview on holistic transformational development expressed in the *misio Dei*.

Summary

This chapter reviews literature on modernization, dependency, and world systems global theories of development, community development, theology of development, biblical shalom, the practice of transformational development in Nigeria, homogeneous rural communities, worldview transformation, and appreciative dialogue.

The review indicates that the focus of the global theories is on economic growth, using different tools and methodologies, and its consequent impact

---

374. Jakonda, *Your Kingdom Come*, 7.

375. Tsele, "Role of the Christian Faith," 214.

on the socio-political well-being of societies at the macro-level or national level without paying attention to the micro-level of community life. The goal of the global theories is not holistic because each is focused on achieving temporal utopian experience of economic, physical, social, and political life but failing to include the spiritual aspect of human life. The review also shows that the Matarrita-Cascante and Brennan community development typology can be applied to analyze and evaluate approaches to community development.

The approaches of People Oriented Development (POD), Christian Rural and Urban Development Association of Nigeria (CRUDAN), and Rural Development Counsellors for Christian Churches in Africa (RURCON) all fall in the category of directed model of CD. In the directed model the primary actors in the model are professional and technical experts though a group of stakeholders are involved in planning some of the activities in the process of facilitating CD. The review of the practices of the selected CRDOs demonstrates that these CRDOs presuppose that the church, through the proclamation of the gospel in evangelism, demonstration of God's love by deeds of CD, and demonstrating miraculous signs, is a model of the kingdom of God. This presupposition answers the first of the three sub-research question: on what biblical foundations have CRDOs approached holistic transformational development in rural communities in Nigeria?

Biblical shalom, characterized by harmonious relationships between human beings and God and between human beings and other entities of creation, is the consequence of God's kingdom. Biblical shalom is a state that can be progressively applied in the process of holistic transformational development while anticipating its final and perfect consummation upon the second coming of Jesus Christ.

The worldview of any community is prone to transformation, therefore through deliberate strategies the worldview of a community can be effectively transformed. An appreciative dialogue can be applied to engage the worldview of a community on development and the biblical worldview on transformational development to bring about the transformation of the community's worldview. Based on this assumption the appreciative dialogue was developed as the theoretical framework for collecting the primary data in this study.

The outcome of the field study reported in the fourth chapter and analyzed in the fifth and sixth chapters of this study answer the second and third sub-research questions: in what way is the biblical shalom helpful in developing holistic transformational development in in Kurmin Gwaza and Kurmin Jatau? and how effective and contextual is the application of biblical shalom by means of an appreciative dialogue in Kurmin Gwaza and Kurmin Jatau?

CHAPTER 3

Methodology

Introduction

The research design for this study is a qualitative design. A qualitative re-search design is a system of inquiry that explores, primarily verbal data in a holistic manner.[1] The approach seeks to interpret, from the perspective of participants in the study, the meaning of a social or cultural phenomenon in their daily experiences. The research method is the focus group approach and the theological research framework is Osmer's method of doing prac-tical theology.[2] The research tool is developed based on the principles of Cooperrider's Appreciative Inquiry (AI). A focus group methodology is a means by which qualitative data is generated through planned small group discussions, facilitated by a moderator, to obtain perceptions about specific topics. Osmer's method of doing practical theology provides the theological framework for studying contextual and contemporary experiences in the light of biblical revelation. Cooperrider's AI is a means of collecting qualitative data through appreciative dialogues. This chapter describes and explains the methodology applied in the study.

The research design and the research methodology are adopted for this study because the objective of the study is to facilitate the engagement of the worldview of two rural communities in an appreciative dialogical interaction with the biblical worldview on transformational development. The theological

---

1. Hancock, *Introduction to Qualitative Research*, 2.
2. Osmer, *Practical Theology*.

framework is also adopted because the study involves examining a contextual and contemporary issue. The application of an appreciative qualitative data collection is, in addition, appropriate because the goal for facilitating the appreciative dialogical approach is to facilitate holistic transformational development for the progressive application of biblical shalom. Because this study is conducted from a theological perspective and guided by a theological framework, the description of the research methodology applied begins with a description of the theological framework and the data collection tool developed therefrom.

Theological Framework

Osmer's method of doing practical theology[3] provides the theological framework for the study. It informs the choice of tool applied in the study. Prior to the review of Osmer's method of doing practical theology, a definition of practical theology is necessary.

Practical theology can be described as a way of helping people to examine their contemporary experiences in the light of biblical revelation. That is the reason, Niel Darragh states, that the process of practical theology "begins from contemporary practice, then investigates the Christian sources in order to arrive at a transformative practice."[4] Kevin G. Smith also explains that practical theology "is a critical, constructive and grounded theological reflection by communities of faith, carried on consistently in the contexts of their 'praxis.'"[5] Smith further states that practical theology calls for critical reflection on various disciplines like theology, culture, sociology, organization, psychology. Hence it can be argued that practical theology provides a foundation for stimulating theological reflection on contextual problems holistically. The task of practical theology keeps the hermeneutical vision at its core, therefore Smith describes it as an "action-theological reflection-practical contemplation-action."[6]

---

3. Osmer, *Practical Theology*.
4. Darragh, "Practice of Practical Theology," 3.
5. Jaison, "Practical Theology," 4.
6. Smith, "Review of Richard Osmer," 99.

Osmer's practical theology method has been applied as the framework for engaging the communities' and the biblical worldviews on holistic transformational development in a hermeneutical process of conversation. The objective of the conversation is to help the communities make decisions that are ethically, theologically, and biblically correct. Osmer's framework consists of four primary tasks that guide researchers to undertake their research on issues from a biblical and theological perspective. The tasks are the descriptive-empirical task, the interpretative task, the normative task, and the pragmatic task.

The data collection tool used in this study is an interview protocol. Questions in the interview protocol integrated Osmer's four simultaneous and interrelated tasks and Cooperrider's AI principles. Osmer's model and Cooperrider's AI have points of integration, each complementing the other. The point of departure for both Osmer's model and Cooperrider's AI is the people's *actual lived experience or reality*. However, AI focuses primarily on strengths, resources, and capabilities rather than on problems or deficiencies. Both methodologies have interpretive functions. Hence the principles of AI narrow the discussion to that which is appreciated in the social and cultural context of the communities involved in the study.

Osmer's model grounds the process in a biblical and theological perspective, which is the normative for evangelical Christian interpretation. It is in the light of this understanding that the principles of the AI are drawn on in this study to design the open-ended questions that served as a guide for the focus groups interactions.

The following is a description of Osmer's four tasks. The consequent interview questions that were developed and applied are presented in the research tool section.

1. The descriptive-empirical task. This task is concerned with describing the experiences or situation of a particular social and historical context. In this study, the contexts are the two rural communities in which the empirical examination in this study took place. The task attempts to answer the question: "what is going on?" The function of this task is to engender listening to a community's stories. Osmer refers to that function as "priestly listening." Applied to this study the descriptive-empirical task is to tease the research participants to describe their experiences.

2. The interpretative task. The interpretative task is concerned with identifying the cause(s) of the experience(s) of the community in the particular social and historical situation being examined. "Why is it going on?" is the question the second task seeks to answer. Osmer describes this reflective task as having the function of "sagely wisdom." The interpretive task for this study is to answer the question: what explanations does each community give concerning its development?

3. The normative task. What the community should consider to be the ideal experience is the focus of this task. The normative task seeks to answer the question, "what ought to be going on?" The function of the normative task is to provide "prophetic discernment." The normative task is to guide each community to evaluate its worldview on its development through a dialogical engagement with the normative biblical and theological worldview on holistic transformational development.

4. The pragmatic task. This task aims at determining the choice of action that will be taken to move the community's present experience(s) towards the identified ideal or normative situation. This task leads to the functional practice of servant leadership.[7] The pragmatic task applied in this study is aimed at stimulating each community to design and apply strategic plans that will lead to the realization of the theologically transformed worldview brought about by the dialogue in the preceding step.

Research Design

This study is based on a qualitative research design because the objective of the study requires it. There are different types of approaches or methodologies within the qualitative research framework. Some of the qualitative research approaches include case studies, observation, and focus group techniques among others. In this study the focus group technique is applied. The focus group technique is used to generate primary data through the groups'

---

7. Smith. Note it has been stated in an earlier footnote that that the primary source, which is Osmer, *Practical Theology*, will be accessed later.

discussions. The data is then analyzed to identify the worldview of the two selected rural communities on development. The technique was also applied in the process to engage the communities' worldview on development in an appreciative dialogue with the biblical worldview on transformational development.

Research Methodology

The focus group methodology was applied to gather relevant data for the purpose of this study. The methodology is an approach that engages a small group of selected individuals, as research participants, in discussions designed to obtain the perceptions of the participants on specific topics.[8]

Monique M. Hennink describes focus group discussions as "a unique method of qualitative research that involves discussing a specific set of issues with a pre-determined people."[9] Hennink further states that the aim of focus group discussions is "to identify a range of different views around the research topic, and to gain an understanding of the issues from the perspective of the participants themselves."[10] Michael Bloor et al. write that the focus group discussions provide occasion and the stimulus to articulate "normative assumptions."[11] A moderator facilitates the discussions of the research participants.

The following informed the choice of the focus group discussion. First, focus group discussions enable an in-depth discussion of a relatively small number of people focused on a specific issue.[12] The range of responses in the discussions makes it possible to gain greater understanding of the perceptions, opinions, attitudes, and actions of the larger community the focus group is a sub-set of. The focus group discussions held in permissive, non-threatening, environments where the participants feel comfortable promises greater contributions. Secondly, focus group discussion is an approach appropriate for examining the stories, experiences, beliefs, concerns, and points of view of a

---

8. Smithson, "Using and Analysing," 103–119; Smith, *Academic Writing*, 161.

9. Hennink, *International Focus Group*, 4.

10. Hennink, 4.

11. Bloor, Frankland, Thomas, and Robson, *Focus Group*, 5.

12. Patton, *Qualitative Research*, 230.

community. The focus group discussion approach helps research participants to discern the meaning or implication of their life experiences.[13] Therefore, focus group discussion is an effective approach that centers on the people's actual lived experience or reality, that guides people to interpret their acts and activities, and that helps the people to discern the meaning or implication of the events in their lives.[14] Note that it is the people who are the main actors in the process not the researcher who does the exploration. In this study the main actors are the research participants.

The research participants in this study were organized into two focus groups consisting of ten participants in each group. They were selected individuals that are members of the communities. The research participants are the experts in the issues examined, they are the experts in matters concerning their cultural beliefs and practices, not the researcher.[15] The participants, through the discussions examine their actual lived experiences or reality and interpret their acts and activities. Focus groups are useful for people to deliberately explore and examine what the participants, and by extension the community, think and why they think the way they do about the issue they focus on. It is assumed that what the participants think represents what the community thinks still on the assumption that it is a shared perception and experiences in the community.

Study Area

Two rural communities, Kurmin Gwaza and Kurmin Jatau, of the Jaba people situated in Kaduna State, North Central Nigeria were the sites selected for this study. The population of the Jaba people, as at the 2006 Nigerian national census, is 155, 377.[16] Both communities have homogenous characteristics. In both communities there are local churches. There are a total of five denominations and nine local churches in both communities. The five denominations include Anglican, Baptist, Catholic, Deeper Life, and Evangelical Church Winning All. The aim of this study, is to propose an appreciative dialogue as

---

13. Stringer, *Action Research*, 37.

14. Stringer, 1; Swinton and Mowat, *Practical Theology*, 29.

15. Stringer, *Action Research*, 20.

16. "Jaba," *Joshua Project*.

a participatory approach, and as a missional tool, geared towards the application of biblical shalom in a process of sustainable holistic transformational development among communities.

Research Population

Two focus groups were selected in Kurmin Gwaza and Kurmin Jatau, in Kaduna State, North Central Nigeria to serve as the research population. According to the 2006 national census figure, the population of Kurmin Gwaza was 762 and projected to be 1,789 by 2016, and the population of Kurmin Jatau was 4,583 and projected to be 12,340 by 2016.[17] Each of these communities consists of aged and young people, married and single people, teenagers and children, literate and non-literate people, and people of different religious traditions. All these categories of people, except children below twelve, constitute the sample frame.[18] The method of selecting the research population to be sampled was agreed upon by the researcher along with the community leaders.

Each of the focus groups in the study consist of ten persons, an inclusive group of elderly women, elderly men, young married men, young married women, and male and female teenagers. Bloor et al. write that

> focus group texts have typically advised groups consisting of between six and eight participants as the optimum size for focus group discussion. However, groups have been reported that have ranged in size from as small as three participants to fourteen.[19]

For practical purposes and in order to provide equal opportunity for the different age group range and gender, the researcher proposed a representation of two participants for the different age range and different gender. However, adjustments were made in each of the communities in order to represent different sections of the respective communities. The adjustments were made

---

17. This information is yet to be gazetted, the record is in the office of the Kachia Local Government Area Population Officer.

18. Floyd J. Fowler, Jr, describes a sample frame as "the set of people that has a chance to be selected, given the sampling approach that is chosen." Fowler, *Survey Research Methods*, 19.

19. Bloor, Frankland, Thomas, and Robson, *Focus Group*, 26.

on the request of the community leaders the researcher consulted to select the groups.[20]

The composition of the focus groups provided for the expression of a range of views, meanings, and experiences. Hence a more robust understanding of the communities' worldview on development the study seeks to identify can be arrived at. It is the communities' worldview on development, analyzed from the data, that is engaged in dialogical interaction with the biblical worldview on transformational development. In Kurmin Jatau the ten persons that constituted the focus group were selected as representatives of three different sections of the community. The sections are: *Fhu-Kampani, Fhu-Ngarbyen,* and *Fhu-Angwan Tsauni.* The focus group selected included one elderly man, three married men, two married women, two unmarried youth, both males, and two teenagers, one male the other female. In Kurmin Gwaza the focus group consisted of two elderly women, two elderly men, two young married men, two young married women, and one male and one female teenager.

Data Collection Technique and Procedure

A focus group interview technique was used to study the ideas or perspectives of the research participants in each of the communities in the study sites. According to Marczyk, DeMatteo, and Festinger, a focus group is a formally organized group of individuals "brought together to discuss a topic or series of topics during a specific time period" to obtain the impressions and concerns individual members of the group have about certain issues.[21] The focus group technique was originally developed for use in marketing research to provide useful insight into how various procedures, systems, or products are viewed as well as the desires and concerns of a given population.[22]

A focus group is typically composed of between six and ten participants. Marczyk, DeMatteo, and Festinger posit that participants fewer than six may

---

20. While the researcher proposed the characteristics of those to be selected was based on scientific consideration the community leaders had the sociocultural structure of their communities as part of the criteria for the selection of the participants from their communities. The researcher respected the view of the communities' leaders.

21. Marczyk, DeMatteo, and Festinger, *Essentials of Research*, 154.

22. Marczyk, DeMatteo, and Festinger, 155.

restrict the diversity of opinion to be offered and that participants more than ten may make it difficult for everyone to express their opinion comprehensively.[23] Stringer states that focus group discussions provide each participant the opportunity "to describe their experience and present their perspective on the issues discussed."[24] Thus, the focus group technique allows for interaction between the researcher and the research participants and interaction among the participants themselves.

The focus group technique also provides research participants an open, fairly unrestricted forum for individual participants to discuss and to clarify each other's impressions and opinions. Though the focus group format may have benefits in terms of helping the participants to flesh out and distil the perceptions and concerns of the group, it is also very likely that opinions of individuals may be altered due to group influence. Responses to open-ended questions are difficult to quantify in focus group interactions because qualitative variables vary in kind. This is unlike quantitative variables that vary in amount. Therefore, a thematic approach, described in a later section, is applied to analyze the data.

Focus group dialogical interactions constituted the sampling design of this study. Anthony J. Onwuegbuzie et al., citing several social science researchers, explain that there are multiple benefits in using focus groups to collect qualitative data. The focus group approach (1) is economical, fast, and efficient; (2) provides interactions that can yield important data and create the possibility for more spontaneous responses; and (3) creates a sense of belonging that increases a sense of cohesiveness and a sense of safety to share information, among other benefits.[25]

It is through focus group discussions that the research facilitator drew up the primary data in this study. The participants were guided to build a picture of their experiences that leads to understanding what and how events occur, and gives clarity and insight on the issue(s) considered.[26] The research facilitator guided the research participants to discuss. It was through the

---

23. Marczyk, DeMatteo, and Festinger, 154.

24. Stringer, *Action Research*, 111.

25. Onwuegbuzie, Dikinson, Leeck, and Zoran, "Qualitative Framework," 1–21.

26. Stringer, *Action Research*, 133.

groups' interaction that the data and insights were generated.[27] An interview protocol, described in the research tool section, was applied to facilitate the focus groups discussions.

The researcher travelled at two different times to Kurmin Gwaza and Kurmin Jatau to discuss the plan to establish and work with a focus group in each of the two respective communities. The discussion in both communities was with the district head of each community and some other leaders. In Kurmin Jatau the other community leaders included a pastor, who is an indigene of Kurmin Jatau but not serving as a pastor in the community, and two other officials in the district head's palace. In Kurmin Gwaza the research facilitator met with the district head through the assistance of a political representative of the community in the Kaduna State government and with two other officials in the district head's palace. The district head and the other community leaders in attendance suggested the list of those to participate in the focus groups discussions in each of the communities.

There were four focus group discussions scheduled to hold in each of the communities over a successive period of three weeks. These did not hold as scheduled due to logistic challenges such as bereavement or non-attendance by some of the participants due to one sociocultural event or the other. This necessitated the research facilitator to travel for up to a total of thirteen times rather than the eight initially planned for. In all the meetings the process was video recorded for later transcription.

The research participants were given a period of twelve weeks to apply the process of discussions to plan, design, and implement their plan for a project they selected. After the twelve-week period, the research facilitator listened to feedback and received a written report of the processes the research participants followed.

The participants made their contributions in either of these three languages: the Ham language, the Hausa language, or the English language. The discussions held at each meeting have been transcribed in English with the assistance of a research assistant. The research assistant, who is Jaba by tribe, helped the research facilitator translate and transcribe contributions made by participants in the Ham language to the English language. The following section presents the interview protocol that was applied in the study.

---

27. Sillitoe, Dixon, and Barr, *Indigenous Knowledge Inquiries*, 177.

Research Tool

The research tool applied to generate primary data is an interview protocol. The following is the interview protocol that guided the focused group discussions of each community in the study sites. There were five different sessions in the process.

Session 1

The first session was aimed at facilitating the research participants to describe their individual experiences and perceptions.

Introduction

Every community desires to improve upon its present state of affairs to make life more functionally beneficial for the life and wholeness for each person, each family, and the entire community. I have invited you here to interact with you so that you can clearly define and understand the resources that are available in your community to enhance the acceleration of the improvement of the present state of affairs in your community. The goal therefore is for you to decide how to use those resources for accelerating and sustaining the process of progressively improving the state of affairs in your community. The ideas you will generate and use from this process are intended to promote qualitative progress of life and wholeness.

There will be a total of five sessions of discussion. This is the first of the five discussion sessions. The discussions will be held fortnightly at the venue and time you have chosen. Each session will be for approximately two hours. My role in these discussions is simply to facilitate your interactions and help you articulate the ideas you come up with. You that have agreed to participate in these discussions will later serve as the facilitators for the implementation of your plans for the progress of this community. The activities of each session will be video recorded, with your permission, so that all your discussions will be transcribed and summarized. The video recordings will be confidential and used only for the purpose of this research. The summary of each session will be presented to you at the beginning of the next session. You will select two or three stories/experiences that you will continue discussions on in the remaining sessions. The final session will be a summary and evaluation of the entire sessions. Thank you very much for agreeing to participate in these discussions.

Leading questions

1. How will you describe your community?
2. Each one of you may have has witnessed or learned of an event or events that occurred in this community which you or the community as a whole considers to have brought about and/or is bringing progressive development for the well-being of this community. I will request that each of you take as much as five minutes or less to describe such an event or events.

Session 2

The second session was aimed at guiding the research participants to interpret the phenomena they described in the first session. The goal was for the participants to understand those phenomena.

Introduction

Thank you for attending the second session of our interaction as you participate to articulate ideas and plans to enhance an accelerated and sustainable development process in your community. We will begin by presenting a summary of your discussions at the last session. After the presentation of the summary and the discussion that may arise, each participant will be given three minutes to share his or her ideas in response to the questions that will be asked. Only the two or three stories you selected at the end of last session will be the focus of these discussions in this session.

Leading questions

1. This is the summary of the discussions you had at the last sessions. Is there anything important that is not mentioned in the summary? Is there an additional information you would like to give before we proceed?
2. What were the benefits derived in your community from the events you described at the last session?
3. How did the events bring about progress and development for the well-being of the community?
4. Who in your opinion were responsible for the occurrence of the events?
5. What other factors do you think contributed to the realization of these benefits?

Session 3

The aim of the third session was to guide the research participants to evaluate their ideas on the issues discussed in the second session in the light of the biblical metanarrative. Prior to this session, the researcher had identified biblical narratives that are parallel to the narratives the research participants' narrative.

Introduction

Once again thank you for creating the time to participate in the third session of your group's discussion aimed at articulating ideas and plans for the development of this community. Again, we shall begin with the presentation of the summary of your discussions in the last session. Thereafter I will be presenting stories from the Bible that demonstrate similar experiences in the biblical times among different communities. After the presentation you will each be given opportunity to identify similarities and differences between those experiences. From these experiences you will identify lessons that can be learned. You will thereafter decide what to use and how to use the lessons to enhance the acceleration and sustenance of development in your community. Each participant will be given five minutes to share his or her ideas before you will collectively make your decision, plan of action, and means of evaluation.

Leading questions

1. The following is a summary of your discussions in the last session. You may wish to point out any omission or error in the summary.
2. What are the similarities between the experiences of the biblical story and the experiences of your community that we have focused our discussions on in the past two sessions?
3. What are the differences?
4. What lessons have you learned from these comparisons?

Session 4

The fourth session was dedicated to decision making and planning. The research participants were to decide the course of action they will take in light of the lessons drawn from the discussion in the last session.

Introduction

Welcome to the fourth session, which is the second to the last scheduled for our meeting in this project. Thank you for being active participants and making the sessions exhilarating. In this session you will make decisions on what actions to take in the light of the lessons you highlighted in our last session. You will also plan how to implement your decision and how you will evaluate the outcome. Once again I encourage each one to contribute his or her own idea freely so that everyone here will benefit from it and the entire community will be the better for it.

Leading questions

1. The following is the summary of the lessons you highlighted in our last session. Kindly make appropriate corrections where necessary and if you have additional insight you can also share.
2. In your opinion how can this community benefit from these lessons?
3. How can the suggestions you have agreed on be applied successfully in this community? Who will be responsible for what, when, etc.?
4. How will you get feedback? How will you sustain the process for other areas not included in these two or three that we have focused on?

Session 5

The fifth and final scheduled session was for the purpose of evaluating the whole process. The research participants were led to evaluate the entire process, highlighting the benefits and challenges they encountered in the entire process. The researcher used their feedback to analyze, interpret, and to also evaluate the outcome of the research.

Introduction

You have been committed to this project through the last four sessions. This session is the last scheduled session for the purpose of this study. It is my hope that you will continue with the process to consider the other issues we had to leave out in order to limit ourselves to the selected ones. Once again, thank you for your commitment.

Leading questions

1. What has been the outcome, so far, from the decisions and action plans you agreed upon in our last session?
2. What have been the high points for you personally through these past four sessions? What lessons and personal benefits have you gained?
3. In your personal opinion in what way(s) can this exercise be of use for the progressive improvement of the total well-being of individuals, families, and the community as a whole?
4. Through the sessions, which aspects have you found most challenging?
5. In which way(s) can this exercise not benefit individuals, families, and the community as a whole?
6. What suggestions do you have that could be used to improve the entire process?

Concluding remarks

I thank each one of you for actively participating in this study. It is my honest and sincere prayer that each of you has benefitted from the entire program. I also hope you will use the lessons learned to enhance your personal development, your family development, and the progressive development of the community. It is my hope that you will continue as a team, with the support of the religious and community leaders and the entire community, to apply the lessons learned to other issues for the progressive development of the total well-being of your community. You may as well consider how you can help neighboring communities with the insights you have gained from this exercise.

Conceptual Framework for Data Analysis

The qualitative data collected through the focus group discussions is analyzed using a thematic analysis method. A thematic data analysis approach is applied to analyze and interpret the primary data. Thematic analysis seeks to weave together themes drawn from empirical data "to tell a coherent and persuasive story about the data and contextualizing it in relation to existing literature."[28] Thematic analysis consists of six phases in the process: (1) familiarization with the data, (2) coding or labelling important features of the data relevant to the research question, (3) the process of coding reduces and identifies the data into coherent and meaningful patterns relevant to the research question, (4) reviewing the identified themes, (5) defining the themes, and (6) weaving the themes together to present a coherent and persuasive interpretation of the empirical data.[29] This guideline served as a step-by-step guide in the process of doing the thematic analysis. Note that a guideline simply helps to describe the activities involved in a process.[30] The guideline helped the researcher to identify the themes presented in chapter 4. Note here that the process of thematic analysis is not a linear process it is rather a more recursive or iterative process.

Themes drawn from the diachronic data sets are presented and described in chapter 4. Hence chapter 4 focuses on the description of the themes drawn from the diachronic data sets. Chapter 5 focuses on interpreting the themes described in chapter 4. According to Virginia Braun and Victoria Clarke, ideally the thematic analysis process involves progression from description to interpretation. The description phase shows patterns in the diachronic data content and the interpretation phase attempts "to theorize the significance of the patterns and their broader meanings and interpretations."[31]

The conceptual framework that guided the analytic rigor was the theoretical framework proposed by Braun and Clarke.[32] Following Braun's and Clarke's theoretical guidelines the following choices were made for application in the thematic analysis process. First, themes were identified as "something important about the data in relation to the research question, and represents some level of patterned response or meaning within the data set."[33] Second, it was not the prevalence of responses that was considered as the basis of determining something to be a theme, rather it was "on whether the responses

---

28. Clarke and Braun, "Teaching Thematic Analysis," 120–123.

29. Clarke and Braun, 121–122; Braun and Clarke, "Using Thematic Analysis," 84.

30. Braun and Clarke, "Using Thematic Analysis," 86.

31. Braun and Clarke, 77–101.

32. In "Using Thematic Analysis," Braun and Clarke outline the theory, application, and evaluation of thematic analysis to "provide a vocabulary and 'recipe' for people to undertake thematic analysis in a way that is theoretically and methodologically sound." Braun and Clarke, 78.

33. Braun and Clarke, 82.

capture something important in relation to the overall research question."[34] Therefore each theme presented an overall description of the diachronic data set in which it occurs. The researcher decided, as a third consideration, to identify the themes from an inductive perspective rather than a deductive perspective. Identifying themes from a deductive perspective entails coding the data to fit a pre-existing coding frame. Therefore, in the deductive approach, thematic analysis is driven by the analytic interest of the theory, hence the approach is analyst driven. Whereas in the inductive approach, themes are identified directly from the data hence the inductive analysis approach is data-driven rather than theory driven. The themes identified are latent themes. A latent theme is a theme that goes beyond the semantic presentation of data. A latent theme presents "the underlying ideas, assumptions, and conceptualizations, and ideologies"[35] that shape or inform the semantic content of the data. Therefore, though the data in the study was generated through the application of a theoretical framework, the themes identify the features that give the data their particular form and meaning. The themes were drawn from coding, collating, and reducing the data sets that were responses to the questions that guided the focus group discussions.

The data collected by the researcher, which was mostly in the Hausa language and a little in the Ham language, and recorded in a video was translated into English in the process of transcription as a first and essential step. The portion of the data collected in the Ham language was translated and transcribed by the research assistant of the researcher. The process of transcription, translation, reading, and re-reading of the data set constituted the first phase of becoming familiar with the data. Coding features of the data that appear interesting for the study using Atlas.ti8 software as a tool to help in storing, organizing, reviewing, and retrieving codes and themes in the process was part of the process.[36] The codes were collated into potential themes that were constantly reviewed in order to generate clearly defined themes that could be interpreted and discussed to achieve the purpose of the study.

---

34. Braun and Clarke, 82.

35. Braun and Clarke, 83–84.

36. Susanne Friese, "ATLAS.ti8 Windows Literature Review" note for African Doctoral Academy, Stellenbosch University, 2017. This researcher attended a training for the use of the ATLAS.ti8 software at the African Doctoral Academy of the Stellenbosch University, South Africa in January 2017 where the notes were presented.

Worldview themes of the communities were identified using Hiebert's model for worldview analysis.[37] The analysis of the worldview of each community was based on the assumption that worldview transformation is essential to achieve a sustainable process for holistic transformational development and the application of biblical shalom in each of the communities.

Hiebert's model for worldview analysis combines diachronic and synchronic approaches. The diachronic approach is an approach that gathers data through human stories. Human stories describe the complexities of human experiences and provide explanation for and give meaning to life.[38] Hence, human stories provide the diachronic data needed for the analysis of worldviews. The stories of the rural communities in the study provide the diachronic data that are synchronically analyzed. The analysis of the worldview of each community draws up descriptions of the identity, values, goals, and expectations of each community as it relates to their community's development. It is the worldview analysis that makes it possible to provide the framework for engaging each community's worldview on development and the biblical worldview on holistic transformational development. The biblical metanarrative provides the biblical diachronic data for synchronic analysis on the biblical worldview on holistic transformational development. An analysis of the identified themes for this study are presented in chapter 4 and interpreted to address the research question in chapter 5.

Biblical Metanarrative as Normative Framework of Evaluation

Part of the process of data collection includes participants identifying what ought to be going on in their community's situation in the light of the biblical metanarrative. This process is similar to Vincent J. Donovan's principle of first evangelization. Donovan's principle of first evangelization involves mentioning a religious theme or thought and asking to hear the opinion of the audience.[39] In this study the biblical metanarrative served as the normative framework by which the participants can evaluate and identify what ought

---

37. Hiebert, *Transforming Worldviews*, 31–69, 335.

38. Hiebert, 31.

39. Donovan, *Christianity Rediscovered*, 32.

to be going on in their community's situation. The researcher therefore presented the following condensed summary of the biblical metanarrative that highlights the biblical themes of creation, the fall, redemption, people of God, and kingdom of God. The condensed summary of the biblical metanarrative is immediately followed by the guideline the researcher provided for the focus groups to apply in executing the project(s) each group selected.

> The Bible does have many stories, which include the history of the people of Israel. The summary I am presenting here is to give you the big picture of what God reveals in the Bible. The Bible story is about God's plan and actions from creation through the process by which to redeem human beings from sin and the consequences of sin to the final state where there will be total harmony and peaceful coexistence. From this Bible story you will be able to see where your community fits in God's plan in the light of what God has said and done.
>
> The Bible story shows that God created the world and everything that exists. The story also shows that man fell into sin. That after the fall, difficulties in life were introduced. Since then people are struggling and striving to survive and to be comfortable. People are striving and struggling to make progress.
>
> The Bible story continues to show that there is something God did following the fall. In the story God revealed to Adam and Eve that he plans that someday someone will come into the world to deal with the situation sin has generated in creation.
>
> The Bible story reveals how God went about his plan to send that someone who will come to deal with the human and creation situation. God chose a particular group of people, descendants of a man named Abraham. God used these people as a model to show how he wants to deal with the world and how God wants people of the world to relate with him. The people of Israel are the descendants of Abraham. It is through the history of Israel that God completed his plan to deal with the human situation after the fall.
>
> Through the history of the people of Israel God illustrates how people should relate with God, how people should relate with others and how to relate with nature as they engage in

activities for their welfare on earth. God showed the Israelites how they are to develop their economic activities, how they are to conduct themselves, how they are to make money, how they are to transact money and the rest. God showed them how they are to farm and how they are to deal with their farm produce. In the biblical metanarrative God reveals the methods or principles for living before the final establishment of the perfect state for all of creation.[40]

In the Bible story God shows that the children of Israel were not able to perfectly follow all God's plans. For example, when God gave them the Ten Commandments the Israelites were not able to keep them perfectly. There were consequences for the failures of the Israelites. One of the major consequences recorded in the Old Testament section of the Bible story was that the Israelites were taken into exile. They were sent into exile in Babylon. Yet God brought them back seventy years later. The New Testament section of the Bible shows that the Israelites, even after being brought back from exile continued to fail in keeping God's commands. The consequence of their continued failure was that years later the Romans defeated and dominated the Israelites militarily and politically.

The story of the Israelites demonstrates that God chooses to work with people. The people God works with are people he has invited and who have responded to his invitation to become his people. God works with his chosen people by guiding them on how to live and what to do in the different aspects of their daily lives. The Bible story consists of God's commands and teachings on how his chosen people should live. God expects his people to obey him by faith, trusting God as they live according to his guidelines. The story further shows that God gives his people identity in both name and their acts. God gives his people values by the laws and principles God prescribes. God demonstrates his will to save mankind from the bondages that sin has brought about in their lives and existence on earth.

---

40. God's commands concerning the year of Jubilee recorded in Lev 2:1–55 is an example.

The Bible story reveals that God completed his plan by the death and resurrection from the dead of Jesus Christ. Jesus Christ is the third person of the one and only true God. Jesus Christ incarnated and was born as a human being. Through his life, teaching, and many miracles Jesus Christ demonstrates his power to bring about a change in the troubled situation that sin generated in creation. It is through the death and resurrection of Jesus Christ that God provides the remedy for human beings and creation that sin generated. This event concluded God's plan for the salvation of human beings, the plan God had revealed to Adam and Eve, the plan which God used the history of the people of Israel to illustrate.

People who believe in the person and work of Jesus Christ, the Bible story further reveals, God makes them his special people. God provides redemption for his special people from the power of sin which the fall brought for human beings and the whole of creation. The story shows that God is working out his final activity to bring people into a perfect state of living without struggles.

The Bible story about Jesus Christ demonstrates God's will to redeem human beings and the whole of his creation from sin and its consequences. In addition to the story of the incarnation of Jesus Christ, his works and teachings, his death and resurrection as the Son of God the Bible story tells of God's promise for an expected eternity with God. God promises to recreate the world and transform his special people to be with him in a perfect state of peace, harmony, and holistically fulfilling life forever.

Therefore, the Bible story reveals that God sets for his people the goal of obeying him. His people are to be the model that invites people to faith and obedience to God. God's people partner with God by obeying him and inviting other people to respond to God's executed plan of redemption by faith; and to also anticipate the future state of peace, harmony, and holistically fulfilling life for eternity with God.

The research participants in Kurmin Gwaza selected three community goals and those of Kurmin Jatau selected one community goal. They applied the guideline given below to plan, execute, and evaluate a selected project or projects. They will execute the project(s) to achieve that the community goal or goals they have selected for the project(s) to achieve the community goal or goals they selected. The aim of the guideline is to help the communities plan how to partner with God in his plan to bring about development and for them to realize their expectations from the development project(s) they embark on.

The following is the guideline the researcher gave the focus groups, in writing, to use in executing their selected project(s):

1. Does our identity fit with the identity of God's people you identified in the Bible story? What are the similarities and what are the differences? What do we need to amend and how can we do so?

2. Do our values fit with God's values you identified in the Bible story for his people? What are the similarities and what are the differences? What do we need to amend and how can we do so?

3. Do our goals fit with God's goals in the Bible story for his people? What are the similarities and what are the differences? What do we need to amend and how can we do so?

4. Do your expectations fit with God's plan for his people you have identified in the Bible story? What are the similarities and what are the differences? What do we need to amend and how can we do so?

5. After examining your identity, values, goals, and expectations you will then set out your plans on how to go about working in partnership with God to achieve your development goals based on how the biblical metanarrative has described how people can partner with God in executing his plan.

6. You will record the answers to all the questions 1–4 above and the plans you set out for achieving your development goals.

7. Finally, you will record what you have done and what outcomes you have experienced based on the guideline in number 5 above.

The foregoing provided the framework the research participants were required to apply in guiding the community to participate in appreciative dialogues. The dialogues were to lead the communities to plan, execute, and evaluate the project(s) each focus group selected in the focus group discussions with the researcher.

CHAPTER 4

Data Presentation

Introduction

There were five themes drawn from a diachronic analysis of the primary data. It has been stated in chapter 3 that the primary data was sorted out, organized, reviewed, and categorized using Atlas.ti8 software as a tool. The following themes emerged: community self-identity, community goals and aspirations, community decisions, community actions and outcomes, and community feedback.

Communities' Self-Identity

The first theme from the primary data is the communities' self-identity. A community's self-conception of its characteristic qualities can be expressed in the descriptions members of the community give about the community. In this study the focus groups expressed, in response to an interview questions, their self-understanding from their history, vocation, relationships, commitments, religion, values, goals, and expectations. The discussions revealed the community's self-understanding of the what, the why, what ought to be, and what needs to be done in regards to the community's self-identity. In this section the data that reveals the Kurmin Gwaza and Kurmin Jatau communities' self-identity is presented. Note that to protect the identity of the respondents the names mentioned in this section are pseudonyms and not the actual names of the respondents.

An analysis of the diachronic data reveals the communities' self-identity theme suggests that the self-identity of both communities is that: (1) the communities consist of industrious people; (2) the communities, as families and as respective communities, fend for their physical and material needs; (3) the communities are harmonious societies that maintain social cohesion through support for one another; and (4) the people's lifestyle is regulated by their religious beliefs and practices.

The Kurmin Jatau respondents described the community as a people with a sense of self-determination to prove the community's self-worth. This arose as a result of the community's historical background. Historically the Kurmin Jatau were sent on exile from Gyani, a Jaba community north of the present location of Kurmin Jatau. The exiles consisted of a clan with four families. In the words of Amashama,[1] "The four families were accused of being responsible for the mysterious death of a young maiden in their clan and were therefore sent on exile." According to Amashama and Ayuta, a sixty-two-year-old man, the accusation was based on the traditional religious beliefs that such a mysterious death was due to the practice of witchcraft.

The experience of the exile promoted a collective sense of community and communal living because, according to Amashama, the exile took place in the dry season and the exiles were mocked by the others that remained. Those who remained in Gyani taunted the exiles by telling the exiles to go and die. They taunted the exiles by mocking them with the question, "what will you eat?" To this question the exiles responded, according to Amashama, "*Nhyi Khyal*"[2] which is in the Ham language. *Nhyi Khyal* means "we will eat stones." Hence, the traditional name of Kurmin Jatau is *Nhyi Khyal*. The experience of the exile led the Kurmin Jatau to develop a sense of unity which promoted a collective sense of community and communal living. Asjon,[3] a forty-year-old widow who was not born in Kurmin Jatau but was married to an indigene of Kurmin Jatau corroborates Amashama's story. Asjon said her parents did not want her to get married to a man from *Nhyi Khyal* because the name denotes

---

1. Amashama was a fifty-two-year-old man who was born in Kurmin Jatau where he had lived all his life.

2. The spelling of the word *Nhyi Khyal* was given by the research assistant. Philip Hayab John, presents an alternative spelling as *Ghikyaar* in "Narratives of Identity," 88. John, is an indigene of Kurmin Jatau.

3. Asjon, was born in Daddu, a Jaba community north east of Kurmin Jatau.

that Kurmin Jatau was a place of poverty but she discovered that "the people of Kurmin Jatau were indeed a people who demonstrate loving fellowship with one another, especially in times of crisis."

Helping others was cultivated as community value. Riphil, a twenty-year-old youth also states that, "the people desire to support each other to progress." According to Amashama, when he was a child attending school, children were given financial assistance by different families without segregation. Ganyam, a fifty-seven-year-old man, describes Kurmin Jatau people as people who have over time demonstrate love for one another "and welcome visitors warmly." According to Ganyam, the people of Kurmin Jatau are traditionally subsistence farmers, farming for the sustenance of life in the community. In Kurmin Jatau, families assist each other in times of need. For example, Asjon explains that where a family's grain reserves in the barn was finished before the next harvest, other families assisted such families in need in a manner that does not expose the head of that family to shame. In the words of Asjon, "Others bring grains in the night to place in the barn of the family in need." Asjon, states that she learned that there is value in unity and sharing from this historical antecedent of the Kurmin Jatau people.

The historical backdrop of the Kurmin Jatau community has had an impact on the community's worldview concerning the promotion and maintenance of a sense of community and collective community well-being. The understanding of this worldview gives insight and provides explanation for what the Kurmin Jatau community define as development. The traditional worldview of the Kurmin Jatau community on development consists of promoting and maintaining a healthy state of community and the promotion of communal living to ensure the physical, material, and educational well-being of members of the community in their sociocultural relationships. There has been a shift from traditional worldview to a modern worldview that lays more emphasis on the well-being of the individual in the context of community cohesion. A more detailed discussion on this shift of worldview is in the next chapter. We now turn to the data set from the Kurmin Gwaza focus group's discussion.

The Kurmin Gwaza community is historically also a vocationally subsistence farming community, in addition, they were hunters. The history of Kurmin Gwaza is the history of migrants but for a different reason than that of the people of Kurmin Jatau. Greshaho, an eighty-three-year-old man, explains that historically the people of Kurmin Gwaza were a community of hunters and farmers who migrated to their present location in search of arable land. Shuyari, an eighty-two-year-old man, also stated that "our parents were both hunters and farmers." Kukandadi an eighty-two-year-old woman, stated that, "our parents were great farmers. Often there was bountiful harvest of all that is cultivated in Kurmin Gwaza." Marmadu, a fifty-two-year-old woman, tells the story she was told about a chief of the community by name Sok. Sok, according to Marmadu, was reported to be a person who inspired hard work and commitment to farming. Marmadu tells how Sok is reported to "visit homes to make sure everyone goes to farm. He visited on horseback." Sok was reported to compel all, except those who were ill, to go to the farm. Shuyari confirmed that he personally knew Sok and confirmed that, "I personally witnessed his commitment to spur everyone to commit themselves to farm work." In the words of Marmadu, "this laid the foundation for the Kurmin Gwaza philosophy that everyone must commit himself or herself to farm work."

Maintaining and promoting community unity and communal activities is another historical characteristic of the Kurmin Gwaza community. Greshaho said the Kurmin Gwaza people practiced communal farming of a food crop, *acca*,[4] on rotational basis. Greshaho explained further that "the person on whose farm the community will farm normally provided food and brewed alcohol for the farmers on that day." Shuyari, an eighty-two-year-old man, extends the philosophy of communal farming as he further explained that "a farmer who finishes his farm work before the rains stop was required to assist others in the community who had not." Mardaku, thirty-seven years old, attributed the sense of community to have been instilled by the *Dodo* religious cult of the people of Kurmin Gwaza. Mardaku stated that "The *Dodo* cult played a vital role in ensuring discipline. Though Christianity was not established in the community then, yet the taboos established by the *Dodo* cult were respected and observed out of fear." Mardaku also added that communal farming also promoted the sense of unity and support for one another. Ezeyo, a seventeen-year-old male, said that he learned that "the ancestors were attached to each other." The ancestors, Ezeyo further posited, engaged

---

4. *Acca* is a cereal of tiny grains which is a staple food among the Jaba people of North Central Nigeria.

in communal activities. Therefore, he concluded that the older generations have experiences and ways of avoiding conflict in the community.

The Kurmin Gwaza people were a hospitable people. Binjjani, an eighty-year-old woman, reports that people from other communities visit Kurmin Gwaza during periods of scarcity of food in other areas of Jaba land to request assistance. This was so, Binjjani said, because "the people of Kurmin Gwaza love accommodating visitors wholeheartedly." Mardaku states that, "Kurmin Gwaza community welcomes and accommodates visitors. Visitors from Katsina, Kano, Saminaka, and other places come to practice dry season farming using our lands and water resources."[5]

It is concluded here that the historical self-identity of both the Kurmin Jatau and Kurmin Gwaza communities is harmonious and hospitable communal communities with binding religious beliefs and common vocations, commitments, values, goals, and aspirations. A diachronic analysis of the data focused on the historical backdrop of these communities suggests that the worldview of both communities on development is the promotion of harmonious relationships and communal partnership for the religious, social, material, and physical well-being of members of the community. A synchronic analysis of the data suggests that historically both communities cognitively, affectively, and morally consider themselves as communities that live in harmonious relationships and in communal partnership for the well-being of their respective communities.

Communities' Goals and Aspirations

The second theme from the focus groups discussions is the development goals and the aspirations of the Kurmin Gwaza and Kurmin Jatau communities. The production of sufficient food, the promotion and maintenance of harmonious relationships, communal living, the sustenance of common religious beliefs, and the holistic well-being of members of the community characterized the traditional development goals and aspirations of both the Kurmin Gwaza and Kurmin Jatau communities. However, the data reveals a set of modern

---

5. Katsina and Kano are cities in northern Nigeria. Saminaka is a town in north central Nigeria and north of Jaba land. The Kurmin Gwaza community live near a dammed river hence Mardaku's mention of "our water resources."

development goals characterized by economic, infrastructural, and social, aspirations. This, as will be discussed in chapter 5, was an expression of a change or transformation of the communities' worldview on development. The data reveals that the introduction of Western education, Christianity, Western technology, and political democracy in the wider Nigerian context are factors responsible for the change or transformation of the communities' goals for development. These factors are presented in more details in the following four sub-sections.

Communities' Goal and Aspirations Following the Introduction of Western Education

In both Kurmin Gwaza and Kurmin Jatau communities there is a quest for Western education through formal schooling. Although the Kurmin Gwaza community has this quest, there is no evidence of a community-based communal approach or cooperation to realize this aspiration unlike the Kurmin Jatau community, which has an approach that promotes cooperation to encourage and support individual members to pursue Western education.

The quest for Western education in Kurmin Gwaza is expressed in the form of laments. Even though the interview question sought for an appreciative description of what has brought about the present understanding of development in the community, the research participants responded by lamenting on the state of interest concerning the pursuit for Western education through formal schooling. All the ten participants made lamenting comments about the lack of progress in the area of acquiring Western education through schooling. Some of the older respondents lamented about not being allowed by their parents to go to school. For example, both Shuyari, eighty-two years old, and Greshaho, eighty-three years old, lamented that their parents did not allow them to go to school. Mardaku's statement summarizes and describes the lament on Western education through formal schooling in the Kurmin Gwaza community. Mardaku states that, "It is a well-known fact that in the entire Jaba land that Kurmin Gwaza community has the least number of educated people."

The attitude of the early settlers of the Kurmin Jatau community toward Western education was more positive than was the case in Kurmin Gwaza. Tassbak, fifty-five years old, stated that,

> I was told that my father also attended school in Kwoi for adult literacy education . . . Our father told us it was his father's decision for him to go to school. Because of our father's example, we also determined to go to school too! We therefore started school in Kurmin Dangana.[6] When the school in our community was started, we returned to be the pioneers.

Tassbak went on to state that, "In the community, it was the business of everyone to ensure that every child attended school. It is because of the insistence on education that today the community has people who now hold positions of responsibilities in different organizations."

The Kurmin Jatau community has a cooperative but not necessarily a communal approach for the acquisition of Western education through schooling. Josam, twenty-six years old, states that the Kurmin Jatau community has a goal to develop to become professors in different fields of study. Tassbak states that the Kurmin Jatau community has the goal of seeing "that more, if not all, girls complete their secondary education." Ayuta also states that in pursuit of this goal the community has set

> a goal that by the year 2020 there should be no less than ten people graduating from the University annually . . . and in five years from now (2017) there should be holders of Doctor of Philosophy degrees (PhDs) that come from this community.

To this end, according to Josam, the Kurmin Jatau Development Association (KUJADA)[7] makes efforts to cooperate in order to provide scholarship for students of Kurmin Jatau origin to pursue their education. The impact of Western form of education on the communities' worldview on development is discussed in chapter 5.

Communities' Goal and Aspirations Following the Introduction of Christianity

The introduction of Christianity to both Kurmin Gwaza and Kurmin Jatau brought about a transformation of both communities and introduced some

---

6. Kurmin Dangana is a neighboring Jaba community to the west of both Kurmin Gwaza and Kurmin Jatau.

7. KUJADA is an organization of indigenes of Kurmin Jatau residing in towns and cities.

other form of aspiration considered to be developmental, which is the training of pastors and priests for the churches. Ganyam states that "Mallam Dawa, Mallam Kure, and Hayab were people who worked tirelessly for the establishment of Christianity in Kurmin Jatau." There are now different church denominations in Kurmin Jatau including Evangelical Church Winning All (ECWA), Roman Catholic, and Baptist. A long quotation of Amashama's contribution throws more light on the transformation Christianity brought about in Kurmin Jatau. Amashama, states in part that:

> Now let us consider our traditional religion before and after the advent of Christianity in this community. I grew in our traditional religion. Today there is virtually no man or woman that will claim to belong to the *Dodo* traditional religious cult. There is no priest of the old *Dodo* traditional religious cult in this community. There were until two weeks ago only two persons that hold to the *Dodo* traditional religion. One of them, Yakubu Dodo, died two weeks ago. There is none of his children that is associated with the *Dodo* religious cult. The only surviving religious traditionalist is Kanwa. The *Dodo* traditional religion has faded out, Christianity is now the dominant religion of the community. This shows that the gospel that was brought has had positive effect on the community. The people have been brought from darkness to light. That is why we have the high expectations we have in this community. Glory to Jesus!

Both Kurmin Gwaza and Kurmin Jatau express a desire to have their sons and daughters trained as pastors, priests, and sisters of the Catholic Christian faith. Amashama states that,

> In the Catholic Church there has been only one Kurmin Jatau indigene that has been trained as a Catholic Priest. He has been serving elsewhere for the past fifteen (15) years. Besides this man, there have not been a single Catholic Reverend Sister or other Catholic Priests trained from this community. It is our hope that in the near future such will be produced for the advance of the gospel.

Yogaj, fifty-three years old, states that in Kurmin Gwaza so far

> only two indigenes have trained as pastors therefore we consider
> this issue an important issue . . . we consider ways to encourage
> our children to pursue theological training so that our commu-
> nity can grow not only materially but spiritually as well.

The effect of the advent of Christianity on the communities' worldview and practice of development are discussed in chapter 5.

Communities' Goal and Aspirations for Technological Development

The acquisition of technological products from the Western world and the quest for the development of technological equipment to facilitate greater cultivation of ginger[8] are considered aspects of development. These were not considered as issues in the earlier worldview on development in these communities. Greshaho comments that in Kurmin Gwaza "our youth do not want to go to school but they are committed to farming. Farming generates income for them. These youth buy cars and build modern houses." Ganyam states that the community desires the acquisition of equipment for mechanized farming because, "we understand that through the use of machines work done with a machine within one hour will cover the work of a hundred people in one year. Therefore, we have the desire for such machines so that Kurmin Jatau will progress." Amashama also states that the community needs

> machines that can help us especially for ginger cultivation . . .
> This will lead to the continuous expansion of ginger production.
> We want to be relieved of our form of manual farming and to go
> into mechanized form of farming like in the advanced countries.

The quest for improved technology to facilitate increase of and ease in the cultivation of ginger has implication for the form of education that should be introduced in the Kurmin Gwaza and Kurmin Jatau communities. This is considered in chapter 5.

---

8. Ginger is a spicy root-crop. It is a crop that is industrially processed to produce spices therefore it is cultivated as economic crop, hence it has economic value.

Communities' Goal and Aspirations for Involvement in Socio-Political Governance

Aspiration for involvement in socio-political governance in the wider society beyond the respective communities is expressed in two different ways. First, by being employed in government jobs, and second, in being represented in the democratic political system of the country. The Kurmin Gwaza focus group mentioned only government employment without mentioning political representation. The Kurmin Jatau group mentioned both government employment and political representation though with greater emphasis on government employment. Government employment is considered a means of securing pension in old age, according to both Greshaho and Marmadu. In the words of Greshaho, "those who work for government do have pension to fall back on in their old age." Josam, from Kurmin Jatau, mentioned that education makes it possible for people to secure government employment and to be placed in positions of influence. Josam gave examples of indigenes of Kurmin Jatau who were in such positions of influence and had used that influence to facilitate government job employment for about six other indigenes of Kurmin Jatau. Ayuta mentioned the desire of the Kurmin Jatau community for a "selfless political representation of the community for the progress of Kurmin Jatau."

Though the focus of discussion was from an appreciative perspective, yet in the process of discussion participants expressed negative experiences. There were laments about some breakdown in the level of commitment to communal living and expressed a sense of helplessness. One example from each focus group describe the sense of helplessness. Yogaj from Kurmin Gwaza, stated that "Kurmin Gwaza is a community that needs help. The youth are not keen on education. Most of the youth are school dropouts. All efforts to get them to acquire education has proved abortive. We need help in this direction." Ganyam, from the Kurmin Jatau focus group, stated that

> We do not have people who stand to help us as a community. For example, our burden is that we do not have fertilizer and we do not have money to buy fertilizer. This has brought great hardship on us. This is something we need your help with.

Concerning changes that have occurred in traditional communal living in the two communities, two examples from Kurmin Gwaza and one from Kurmin Jatau illustrate the changes. Marduk, from Kurmin Gwaza, stated that a spirit of competition has become part of the community as "people want to show that they are better than others." Kukandadi, also from Kurmin Gwaza, laments that "today's generation are no longer obedient to parents." Amashama, from Kurmin Jatau, observes about changes in the state of communal living in Kurmin Jatau that "today things seem to be changing. Today it is more difficult to share your pain with even your brother." These examples show, as discussed in chapter 5, negative effects of the encounter of the traditional worldviews of the communities though there are positive effects as well.

The data identified development goals and aspirations of both Kurmin Gwaza and Kurmin Jatau communities were influenced by Western forms of education, Christianity, technology, and political systems. These factors influenced the extension and transformation of the communities' traditional worldview on development. This is discussed further in chapter 5.

Communities' Decisions

Each focus group in this study decided on specific projects to engage in to facilitate its community development therefore the third theme is the communities' decisions. The groups were required to apply the principles of appreciative dialogue in the process. They were to use the discussion guideline the researcher provided. The Kurmin Gwaza focus group chose three projects. The projects were economic, infrastructural, and educational in focus. The Kurmin Jatau focus group limited itself to just one project, a project with economic focus.

Both the Kurmin Gwaza and the Kurmin Jatau focus groups chose to facilitate the revival of their respective community markets as a means of facilitating economic development. The Kurmin Gwaza focus group selected an addition of two other projects: the repair of an access road into the village from the main tarred road and facilitating the training of indigenes of Kurmin Gwaza in theological institutions to become pastors and evangelists. The following section presents additional details on the selected projects.

Communities' Actions and Outcomes

Each focus group planned its approach and engaged its community in a process to execute its chosen project(s) for the purpose of this study. The communities' actions and the outcomes thereof are the fourth theme. The researcher and each of the focus group agreed to a three-month time frame for the group to go through the process then to discuss the outcomes with the researcher thereafter. The researcher provided the focus group with a written guideline to help them maintain the framework for the study.[9] The following two sub-sections describe reported actions for and the outcomes of the actions of each of the communities on the projects they embarked on for the purpose of this study. The third sub-section presents a summary of the actions and outcomes from the two communities.

Kurmin Gwaza Community Actions and Outcomes

The Kurmin Gwaza focus group met four times to plan their course of action and three times to evaluate the outcome of their respective actions for the three projects the group facilitated community participation. The group recorded the minutes of its meetings and made the minutes available to the researcher at the last interaction between the focus group and the researcher and his assistant. What follows is a description of the meetings, plans, and actions of the Kurmin Gwaza focus group and Kurmin Gwaza community.

The Kurmin Gwaza focus group engaged the community's participation in two ways. One of the ways was to consult with selected stakeholders in the affairs of running the community market. The Kurmin Gwaza focus group invited some recognized leaders and key stakeholders for the market revival project to consult with them as part of the planning process. The second way was to invite members of the community to a community meeting in front of the district head's palace.

The community held three meetings to plan and decide their course of action. The first was to examine, using the guidelines given to the focus group by the researcher, the community's self-identity, the community's values, the community's goals, and the community's aspirations. The second was to

---

9. The discussion guideline for engaging the focus groups' selected projects in the process of participatory appreciative dialogue has been described above under the biblical metanarrative theme section of this chapter.

consider the road rehabilitation project. The community met two times to execute their plan for the rehabilitation of the road through communal efforts. The third community meeting was to consider the community market resuscitation project. The community discussed and agreed on the guidelines for conducting trading activities in the market in order to develop and sustain trading activities in the market. However, in the case of the mobilization for indigenes to train as pastors the focus group did not involve the community in the discussion and planning but executed its own plan.

The minutes of the Kurmin Gwaza focus group show that members of the community were invited for community meetings. At the first meeting the community discussed the similarities and differences the community has with the community of people called the people of God in the Bible, their values, their goals, and their aspirations. Prior to the community discussions facilitated by the focus group the researcher facilitated three focus group discussions. The following are the conclusions drawn from the focus group discussion the researcher facilitated:

1. Identity: The discussions show that the Kurmin Gwaza community describes its people as creatures of God.[10] A people that God has continued to provide for both spiritually and physically. A community that God is still taking care of just as he took care of his earlier people. Though they are God's creation the community thinks that God was closer to the people of God in the past than now because, according to the community, God spoke to his people in the past directly and the people heard him and saw signs of his visible presence through light or fire. In addition, the people of God of the past loved God more than the people of Kurmin Gwaza. Therefore, the people of Kurmin Gwaza consider it essential for them to devote themselves to obeying God by doing what he commands his people to do and to stop doing what God forbids. On this basis the people assumed that by so doing they can be closer to God.

---

10. Both the Kurmin Gwaza and Kurmin Jatau communities have already embraced Christianity as their common religion. Therefore, God as revealed in the biblical metanarrative is who the community refer to here.

2. Values: The Kurmin Gwaza community value farming in order to feed themselves and to be able to use some of the produce to provide for other needs. The community cites the biblical saying that that the person who does not work should not be given food (2 Thess 3:10). In addition to this the community values love for and obedience to elders as well as love for one another. Though in recent times the community has observed that there is a gross reduction of love for one another. There is a loss of obedience for older people. There is increase in love for selves more than love for God. The community also values agricultural inputs that make farming easier and more productive. For example the availability and the use of tractors, chemical fertilizer, pesticides, and so on.[11] However the community has expressed that there is a need for the people to modify the way they live by cultivating a life of love and obedience, pay more attention to prayer, work together as it used to be, for example, communal work.

3. Goal: The goal of the community is to provide a comfortable life just as the community has observed is the same with God's goal for his people. God's goal for his people in the past is to provide for his people a comfortable life. A comfortable life for the community is to have food, shelter, and other comforts such as the use of cars and television. Though the community acknowledges that today the people have these things more than the people in the past. However, the people are misusing these things by failing to use them for the glory of God. So, the people need to correct these through cultivating the fear of God. Thus, the community envisages that this is achievable by organizing teachings that will bring this about in the lives of the people.

4. Aspirations: Good roads, potable water, constant electricity supply, good education, and good health, are what the Kurmin Gwaza community aspire for. Since the community was engaged in interaction with the biblical metanarrative as they examined

---

11. Note that the adverse aspects of these products were not discussed with the communities. This was so because discussing the effects of these products was beyond the scope of this study.

their aspirations, the community assumes that these aspirations are in line with the will of God for his people. This assumption is based on the biblical story of creation that God made provision for the sustenance of human beings with ease in the garden of Eden (Gen 2:4–16). Therefore, the community assumed that God who created man gave man the ability to do these things to make life comfortable for human beings.

The first community discussion led to the decision to embark on the first project, which was to repair the access road into the village. Members of the community agreed on dates to dig a drainage for the road leading into the village. The objective was to improve the accessibility of the road in the rainy season and prevent erosion of the road. Therefore, following an example in the Bible story in the history of the Israelites recorded in Nehemiah 3:1–31, the work was divided, responsibilities were shared, and people were delegated with different responsibilities. The work was completed in two days.

The Kurmin Gwaza focus group invited a selected group of stakeholders to consider ways the community can work together as God's people to revive and sustain the community market. This meeting was convened after the completion of the road rehabilitation project. It was also held prior to the second community meeting to consider the community market resuscitation project. Five people, representatives for ginger farmers, ginger sellers, and market middle men, were invited to discuss and make suggestions. The outcome of the discussion are as follows (a) diligent processing of the ginger by the farmers, that is the farmers must make sure the ginger that is brought to the market is well dried. (b) The standard bags used for measuring the ginger must be filled appropriately. (c) A market vigilante group is to monitor the quality of products brought for sale. (d) There was to be an agreed on and maintained standard and uniform price for the ginger. The purpose for these regulations is to ensure the presentation of quality products for buyers, to serve as a model market, to attract more customers, and for the farmers to have a fair value for their labor.

Following this discussion with the selected stakeholders, the suggestions agreed upon were used as the framework to discuss with the community. At the third community meeting the people discussed the issue of resuscitating the community market. The suggestions proposed as an outcome of the focus group discussion with the selected representatives of the stakeholders in the market business were considered and accepted by the community, though there were dissenting voices who felt they do not need to go through the process of bringing ginger to the market. Such persons prefer selling their ginger unprocessed and directly in the farm. The buyer is left with the responsibility of deciding how to market the goods.

Encouraging indigenes to go for theological training so as to serve as pastors and evangelist is the third project the Kurmin Gwaza focus group selected. The plan and approach the focus group applied did not engage the community in the decision making. Instead the focus group simply sent out announcements to be made in the churches.

The outcome of the Kurmin Gwaza focus group is that the road project was successfully executed to the level of the initial plan. The market project has not been successful because the focus group reports that there was lack of cooperation among the people on what has been agreed to be the collective approach to maintain standards in order to serve as a model market. The theological training support project has not yielded any result yet because there is no one who has responded to the encouragement. The implication of this outcome is discussed in chapter 5.

Kurmin Jatau Community Actions and Outcomes

The Kurmin Jatau focus group also planned its approach to empower the Kurmin Jatau community to revive its community market. Prior to the action of the focus group the researcher facilitated a focus group discussion. The following is a summary of the discussion:

1. Identity: A hospitable, industrious, and determined people who have been delivered from the worship of *Dodo* spirits through the introduction of Christianity.

2. Values: A community that values self-worth, communal living in unity and solidarity, the Christian faith, and visionary leadership.

3. Goal: The goals of the community include facilitating the education of the indigenes of the community and developing ways for sustainable economic empowerment.

4. Aspirations: The community aspires to have indigenes who are professors in different fields of studies. The community also

aspires for industrialization and urbanization based on ginger production and other economic activities.[12]

The Kurmin Jatau focus group met two times to plan and one time to evaluate the outcome of their respective actions for the single project the group facilitated. The minutes of the focus group discussions and report of action revealed that the group used the agency of the traditional leadership of the community and the church to execute its plans. At the meeting with the traditional leaders the focus group solicited the approval and support of the leaders to call for community meetings. The community leaders were present at the community meetings but the meetings were facilitated by the focus group.

The Kurmin Jatau focus group met with the council of chiefs of the Kurmin Jatau district in the district head's palace. The focus group stated that its objective is to educate and inspire the people of Kurmin Jatau to revive the Kurmin Jatau market with the help of God. The council of chiefs welcomed the move of the group and granted the group its blessings. The council of chiefs mandated one of the chiefs, the Babban Dakaci, to invite the people to a community meeting to discuss and decide on the actions to be taken to revive the Kurmin Jatau community market.

Prior to the day set for the community meeting the focus group undertook advocacy visits to all the churches of the five denominations in Kurmin Jatau: Anglican, Baptist, Catholic, Deeper Life, and Evangelical Church Winning All. The focus group had the following as a framework for informing, educating, and inspiring the people to participate in the project.

1. State the objective of the visit. The visit is to invite the people to come together to revive the Kurmin Jatau market with the help of God. The market provides a means of economic empowerment to guard against poverty and to promote the progress of the community in general.
2. Draw attention to the identity of the Kurmin Jatau community. The people of Kurmin Jatau are a people who have been liberated from *Dodo* traditional beliefs and integrated into a relationship

---

12. The effects of industrialization and urbanization were not discussed because this was beyond the scope and purpose of this study.

with God through Christ. The people of Kurmin Jatau have the tradition of partnering together to assist one another. This characteristic aligns with God's command for his people as recorded in Deuteronomy 15:1–18. Therefore, on the basis of these the people need to take a collective action to achieve the identified objective.

3. Inspire the people to take action. The required action is for the people to come together as a liberated people who love one another and are hospitable to visitors to work in partnership for the revival of the Kurmin Jatau market.

4. Invite the people to participate in deciding and taking decisive action to achieve the stated objective. The action needed is to work in partnership to repair the dilapidated and abandoned makeshift market stalls and to re-establish trading activities in the market.

After these advocacy visits to the churches by the focus group the community meeting was held to consider the proposal by the focus group which the council of chiefs had endorsed.

At the end of the meeting the community agreed on the day to assemble and repair the makeshift stalls. On the appointed day the community was organized in groups to make the repairs. The community had a traditional pattern for organizing community work, the pattern is similar to the pattern described in the Bible story of the Israelites dividing responsibilities to rebuild the walls of Jerusalem as recorded in Nehemiah 3:1–31. After the completion of the repairs the community accepted the date the district head proposed for the commencement of trading activities in the market. The focus group reports in the minutes that "the market has become operational and is gradually developing."[13]

Summary of Communities' Actions and Outcomes

The following is a summary of the actions both the focus groups and the respective communities took with the consequent outcomes.

---

13. The researcher visited the community market before and after its resuscitation.

1. The focus groups of each of the communities held meetings to plan how to mobilize their respective communities to engage in their selected projects using the appreciative dialogue guideline they were given by the researcher. Also, the focus groups met to evaluate the outcome of their respective projects and to decide their next line of action.

2. The focus groups held consultative meetings with others before taking further action.

    a) The Kurmin Gwaza focus group held a consultative meeting with some selected stakeholders on the Kurmin Gwaza market. The objective was to have a clear understanding of the market operation.

    b) The Kurmin Jatau focus group held a consultative meeting with the Kurmin Jatau council of chiefs to achieve two objectives. First, to intimate the chiefs on the market revival project the focus group plans to initiate based on the guidelines they were given by the researcher. Second, to solicit the approval and support of the chiefs.

    c) The Kurmin Jatau focus group undertook advocacy visits to all the local churches of the different denominations in the Kurmin Jatau community. The objective was to inform, motivate, and inspire the people to participate in the Kurmin Jatau market resuscitation project in conjunction with the guidelines the researcher gave the focus group.

3. The focus groups held meetings with members of the community in community assemblies. The objectives included informing the communities of the selected projects, stating the reasons for the projects, considering the guidelines for the projects, and for the community members to decide on the lines of action to be taken. Note here that the Kurmin Gwaza applied this for the road rehabilitation project but did not apply the same for both the market and the theological education projects the focus group selected.

4. The respective communities discussed, accepted, and implemented their respective action plans. The Kurmin Gwaza community participated in communal work on the road

rehabilitation project. The Kurmin Jatau community participated in communal work on the repair of the market stalls and began trading activities in the market.

Communities' Feedback

The final theme drawn from the primary data is the communities' feedback. Each of the focus groups reports that the greatest impact of the dialogical appreciative approach was the ease and effectiveness it has in mobilizing the people in the two communities. At the final scheduled focus group discussion facilitated by the researcher there were both verbal comments in addition to the written report of the focus group on the projects the community embarked on. The comments quoted in this section were oral comments made during the final scheduled focus group discussion with each of the two focus groups. Some of the oral comments from Kurmin Gwaza include Yogaj's comment that

> one of the joys of this approach is that we truly enjoy coming together to discuss the issues before us . . . (and) responses to invitations for discussions have improved greatly after the *Shugaban Matasa* (Youth Leader) explained the value of the approach you have introduced.

Marmadu, states that, "this program has brought about a unity of purpose in the community. There is indication that decisions are now being taken collectively." Yogama, also comments that,

> What I find joy in is the fact that though in the past there has been cooperation but the level of cooperation has not been as much as now. We seem to be more united now just as our mother mentioned earlier, whenever people are called they assemble in good time. Since the approach you introduced was explained to the people they respond well by attending to calls for meetings and they do so in good time.

Other oral comments from Kurmin Gwaza on the impact of the dialogical appreciative approach on mobilizing people are as follows: Ganyam stated that "the program has re-ignited a beautiful cooperation between us." Asjon, in her comment stated that "your coming has brought out issues of interest that inspired people to come and attend to it." Admus added that, "God has used you to enlighten us and God is using this group to enlighten the community."

Marmadu, from Kurmin Gwaza stated that,

> I wish to thank God for the time you took to guide us in this program since last year . . . We have seen the handwork of God in guiding us . . . You said it is with our own hands that we can work to help ourselves. It was these words and explanation that the people were mobilized and the people showed their acceptance of the idea by coming out. We witnessed the power of God and the guidance of the Spirit of God . . . we thank God and pray that this will motivate us to take steps to help ourselves rather than looking up to others.

Gaibu, also from Kurmin Gwaza, added that,

> The approach has changed our orientation of waiting for someone else or government to come and do development work for us but that we can put our heads together to do something beneficial for our community. In my view if we continue in this manner we will progress and in some areas we will only require support . . . We did not realize this before but with the introduction of this approach it has helped us to understand this. Therefore, the approach will accelerate our development . . . We are able to understand that within us we can do something that we imagine could be done. We have been empowered to use our own initiative.

Admus, from Kurmin Jatau, stated that,

> This program led me to understand that making progress alone does not necessarily mean bringing about progress in the community. The program has made me realize that if many people with the intention of bringing about the progress of a community come together, they can achieve more within a relatively shorter time . . . We have indeed benefitted from this program in just the little time that the program has been instituted.

> We may not gain the full benefit of this program but certainly our children will gain positive benefits of the program.

Admus, from Kurmin Jatau. Admus further stated that, "We are already thinking of strategies to expand the market to make it popular." Ayuta, also from Kurmin Jatau, stated that "This program has started enlightening us and our children are making good effort . . . We are hoping that God will give us additional insight so that our youth will make more progress in life." Yogaj, from Kurmin Gwaza stated that, "This approach is going to be a model for our children to follow." Yogam, also from Kurmin Gwaza, also stated that "this approach is providing an avenue for our children to receive some discipline they therefore will become models for others." The implication of this feedback is discussed in chapter 5.

Summary

This chapter is descriptive. It presents five themes. The themes are drawn from the data sets transcribed from the focus groups discussions. The five themes are: community self-identity, community goals and aspirations, community decisions, community actions and outcomes, and community feedback. The next chapter interprets the data presented and described in this chapter.

Data Analysis

Introduction

This chapter consists of an iterative interpretation of the themes drawn from the primary data and presented in chapter 4. The analysis is presented in five sections: The Kurmin Gwaza and Kurmin Jatau communities' worldview on development; biblical transformation of Kurmin Gwaza and Kurmin Jatau communities' worldview on development; the application of the biblical shalom through participatory appreciative dialogue in rural communities; summary; and contribution of this study. It has been mentioned in chapter 1 that it is assume in this study that a biblically transformed worldview on holistic transformational development will advance a progressive application of biblical shalom in the life of the people. Therefore, before analyzing the data a description of a biblical worldview on development is presented.

Biblical Worldview on
Transformational Development

The biblical worldview is understood as the conceptual framework for understanding the design, purposes, and actions of God for his creation. It is the worldview that is based on the biblical events that are part of one great story that is a central diachronic worldview theme – the Bible.[1] Synchronically the Bible reveals the origin, nature, purpose, and end to all that exists. The Bible

---

1. Hiebert, *Transforming Worldviews*, 266.

reveals the metanarrative of what God has done in the past, what he is doing in the present, and what he will do in the future as the sovereign owner of all that exists. Therefore, as Bartholomew and Goheen posit, the biblical metanarrative provides the large background story essential for people to understand themselves, understand others, and understand the world they live in.[2] This is so because the Bible presents the most fundamental and encompassing view of reality. Sample explained that the Christian worldview, also referred to as the biblical worldview, "comes from a dramatic account set forth in the Bible that includes the great narrative of historic actions and events involving God and His relation to humanity."[3] Hiebert also posits that Christians "must re-examine any worldview, our own or someone else's, in the light of Scripture."[4] Hence the biblical worldview is the overarching divine lens through which to evaluate other worldviews.

In view of the foregoing the definition of a biblical worldview on holistic transformational development can be described as the conceptual framework for understanding the design, purposes, and actions of God for the progressive application of God's shalom in God's fallen, though redeemable and transformable, creation in the present historical context. God's shalom as God originally intended for creation. It has a future eschatological perfect state of God's shalom.

The biblical worldview is the non-negotiable worldview that the people of God can use to reach out to different worldviews as part of their acts of participating with God in his holistic mission of redemption and progressive transformation of God's creation in anticipation of the final, complete, and perfect establishment of God's shalom. It is on the premise that the biblical worldview is non-negotiable that the biblical worldview on holistic transformational development is to be engaged in dialogue with the communities' worldview on development.

---

2. Bartholomew and Goheen, *Drama of Scripture*, 11, 13, 18.

3. Samples, *World of Difference*, 88.

4. Hiebert, *Anthropological Reflections*, 11.

Communities' Worldview on Development

This section analyzes the worldview of the communities on development. The assumption of this study is that the engagement of the worldview of the Kurmin Gwaza and Kurmin Jatau on development in a participatory appreciative dialogue with the biblical metanarrative on holistic transformational development can result in the progressive application of biblical shalom.

One of the purposes of this study was to facilitate the engagement of the Kurmin Gwaza and Kurmin Jatau communities' worldview on development in a participatory appreciative dialogue with the biblical worldview on holistic transformational development. Hence it is essential to analyze the communities' worldview on development. Hiebert's framework for studying both the synchronic and the diachronic themes and stories of those who hold a worldview is applied.[5]

Community Self-Identity and the Traditional Communities' Worldview on Development

The diachronic data, presented in chapter 4, shows that the self-identity of Kurmin Gwaza and Kurmin Jatau communities is characterized by industrious people who collectively fend for their physical and material needs, while maintaining harmony and social cohesion through support for one another, and whose lifestyle is regulated by their religious beliefs and practices. An analysis of the traditional worldview of both communities on development shows that the communities have a traditional worldview on development that has been overshadowed, though not lost, by a modern worldview on development. The traditional worldview of both communities on development presupposes development to entail the promotion of harmonious relationships and communal partnership for the holistic well-being of members of the community. This sub-section discusses and analyzes the communities' self-identity to identify their traditional worldview on development.

The data from both the Kurmin Gwaza and Kurmin Jatau communities' stories provide a description of the communities' historical backdrop. An analysis of the data reveals the communities' self-identity. Yan Chen and Sherry Xin Li state that identity provides an explanation for the psychological

---

5. Hiebert, *Transforming Worldviews*, 28.

basis for group discrimination.[6] Hiebert states that "narratives combine rationality and imagination to integrate the cognitive, affective, and evaluative dimensions of life in a single whole."[7] Hence the self-identity of the Kurmin Gwaza and Kurmin Jatau communities is not only a set of observable characteristics of the communities but is also the communities' reflective understanding of their biography.[8] The self-identity of communities, as will be discussed in more detail in the light of social psychological theory below, is developed through social interaction, over time, between members of the communities to provide the communities with the collective cognitive self-understanding, affective cohesion, and self-value. It has also been shown that the framework of a community's identity as well as the community's worldview consist of the set of cognitive interpretation and affective evaluation the community members ascribe as a description of who they are as a community.[9] Therefore the self-identity of the Kurmin Gwaza and Kurmin Jatau communities has an impact on the communities' worldview on development.

The Kurmin Gwaza and Kurmin Jatau communities' self-identity and self-interest are pointers to the communities' worldview on development. The communities' self-interest is expressed in the communities' goals and aspirations. Richard Jenkins argues that self-interest has a direct bearing with self-identification.[10] Therefore, it can be argued that from the diachronic data the Kurmin Gwaza and Kurmin Jatau communities' traditional worldview on development can be synchronically interpreted to cognitively, affectively, and morally presuppose development to consist of growth, refinement, and maturation of harmonious relationships and communal partnership to cultivate the holistic well-being of the community and individuals in the community.[11]

The communities' traditional worldview however has not been static. There has been an identifiable shift. The shift is to what is described in the next sub-section as the communities' modern worldview on development.

---

6. Chen and Xin Li, "Group Identity."

7. Hiebert, *Transforming Worldviews*, 66.

8. Gauntlett, "Anthony Giddens." Kehily, "What is Identity?," cites Gidden's definition of identity.

9. Stets and Burke, "Sociological Approach to Self."

10. Jenkins, *Social Identity*, 7.

11. Hiebert, *Transforming Worldviews*, 335.

The Modern Kurmin Gwaza and Kurmin Jatau Communities' Worldview on Development

The traditional worldview of the Kurmin Gwaza and Kurmin Jatau communities on development has not remained static. The analysis of the data from both the Kurmin Gwaza and Kurmin Jatau communities' stories also reveal a shift from the communities' traditional worldview on development. While the communities' traditional worldview on development presupposes development to entail the promotion of harmonious relationships and communal partnership for the holistic well-being of members of the community, the modern worldview of the communities on development presupposes development to be the pursuit and acquisition of economic, educational, and political statuses for individuals in the context of harmonious community.

The shift, or modification, in the worldview of the Kurmin Gwaza and Kurmin Jatau communities' worldview on development occurred due to the engagement of the communities' traditional worldview on development in interaction with modern concepts on development. Hiebert argues that the worldviews of cultures, though organic wholes, are ever-changing systems rather than static, harmonious systems.[12] Kehily, citing social scientist Bauman, also states that identities are constantly being developed because "who we are, what we do, and what we become changes over the life course."[13] Sociologists Luloff and Krannich, as noted earlier, have argued that the rise of modernization, industrialization, and urbanization to address different facets of human lives since the mid-twentieth century had effects on the concept, nature, and social order of human communities.[14] So from the perspective of the social psychological theory it is through social interaction, over time, that the cognitive perceptions, affective cohesion, and value systems of a community are formed and transformed. Therefore, it is through the process of social interaction with other ideas, discussed below, over time, which has transformed and can be applied to transform the worldview of the Kurmin Gwaza and Kurmin Jatau communities on development. It is in the light of this that the deliberate effort to facilitate an appreciative dialogue between the

---

12. Hiebert, *Transforming Worldviews*, 46.
13. Kehily, "What is Identity?," 2.
14. Luloff and Krannich, "Introduction," 1.

biblical worldview on transformational development and the worldview of the Kurmin Gwaza and Kurmin Jatau communities was applied in this study.

The worldview of the two communities on development at the time of this study can be described as the communities' modern worldview on development. The community goals and aspiration theme presented in chapter 4 shows that the development aspirations of the communities had changed. It had changed from the traditional emphasis on sociological harmony and communal activities to sustain the communities' well-being and the well-being of individuals in the community. It has changed to emphasize economic, infrastructural, and social progress for individual members of the communities in the context of cohesive sociocultural relationships. The modern worldview views the individual as an autonomous entity rather than an individual-in-community. While the elements of social cohesion and harmony in the traditional worldview on development are retained, the element of communal partnership for the holistic well-being of members of the community is de-emphasized. Therefore, the emphasis in the modern worldview on development is on personal or individualistic pursuit and acquisition of economic, educational, and political status. This change or transformation occurred with the introduction of Western education and Western form of Christianity in the wider Nigerian context. The following sections discuss the impact of these factors in the transformation of the Kurmin Gwaza and Kurmin Jatau communities' worldview on development.

The role of education in worldview shift in Kurmin Gwaza and Kurmin Jatau communities

This sub-section is concerned with the role of Western form of formal education in worldview shift in the Kurmin Gwaza and Kurmin Jatau communities. The data presented under the goals and aspiration theme in chapter 4 show that in both Kurmin Gwaza and Kurmin Jatau communities there is a quest for Western education through formal schooling for individual members of the community without evidence of its pursuit through communal efforts. The data from Kurmin Gwaza community does not show evidence of a community-based cooperation to encourage individual members to pursue Western education. However, the data from the Kurmin Jatau community shows that the community has an approach that promotes cooperation to encourage and support individual members to pursue Western education. It has been argued earlier that the shift of the historical or traditional worldview of the communities on development is due to the engagement of the communities' worldview in dialogue with Western worldview on development. Western forms of formal education is one of the factors that has engaged the Western worldview on development in dialogue with the traditional worldview of the Kurmin Gwaza and Kurmin Jatau communities on development.

Education is a process of learning that provides the means by which to cultivate inherent potentials in human beings for meaningful living on earth. Godpower A. Ikechi Nwogu describes education as knowledge and skills acquired for meaningful life evidenced in changes in conception, attitude, and/or behavior to meet human needs and sustain progress.[15] Ronald R. Yager writes that learning is a fundamental human capability.[16] Davies, Gregory and McGunn posit that human beings are born with inherent and diverse talents, dispositions, propensities, and inclinations that are developed through the process of education.[17] Paulo Freire states that every human society has the potentials and skills for education.[18] Therefore education is an essential tool for creative and innovative approaches to cultivate inherent potentials in human beings to meet human needs and sustain progress in human communities.

The Kurmin Gwaza and Kurmin Jatau communities, like every human community, have practical ways by which they foster and extend knowledge, understanding, and skills among their members for the purpose of meeting human needs and sustaining the improvement of the quality of life in the communities. The primary data shows that modelling, hands-on learning through practice, and story-telling are among the most essential ways the Kurmin Gwaza and Kurmin Jatau communities extend knowledge, understanding, and skills from older, more experienced adults to children and

---

15. Nwogu, "Education and National Development," 266–276.

16. Yager, "Participatory Learning."

17. Davies, Gregory, and McGunn, *Key Debates in Education*, 12.

18. Paulo Freire was a Brazilian educationist and activist. Freire believed that education is an exclusively human phenomenon that can be applied to liberate humans from dehumanizing experiences. Freire's philosophy was developed in the context of reaction against poverty, which Freire blames on the economic activities of Europe and America. See Freire, "Education and Community," 83. Freire, makes a similar assertion as Davies, Gregory, and McGunn. He writes that "educational practice is a necessary dimension of social practice (as are productive, cultural practices)." Freire, "Education and Community,"83.

young adults. Understanding the traditional philosophy of education of these communities gave an insight to determine the kind of philosophy of education that may be considered appropriate to facilitate a process for sustainable holistic transformational development.

The traditional philosophy of education of the Kurmin Gwaza and Kurmin Jatau communities is a non-formal philosophy with discernible goals, curriculum content, and pedagogical methodology. An analysis of the primary data reveals a non-formal philosophy of education in these communities. The analysis reveals the aims, concepts, and methodology of education applied as a vehicle for the transmission of the communities' worldview. The histories, the economic practices, and the cultural expectations of both communities have been passed from older generations to the present generation through apprenticeship, which include story-telling and modelling as is common in oral societies. According to Erin Hanson, oral transmission of stories, histories, lessons, and other knowledge serves to maintain historical records and sustain cultures and identities.[19] Hence story-telling in and among the Kurmin Gwaza and Kurmin Jatau communities transmitted the substantive knowledge needed. The modelling by older persons demonstrated required skills for achieving both personal and community goals. The intercourse of the Kurmin Gwaza and Kurmin Jatau communities' traditional philosophy of education and the Nigerian National Policy of Education (NPE) brought about the shift of their worldview on development. The NPE provides the conceptual framework for understanding and planning educational enterprises to meet human needs in the Nigerian context.

J. D. Okoh argues that the NPE is "a hybrid of Euro-American thinking about reality, knowledge, and values."[20] That the NPE is an educational philosophy that is alien to the Nigerian socio-political context and that the national goals are set based on that philosophy are equally based on worldviews that are alien to the Nigerian context.[21] This argument suggests that the goals, the curriculum content, and the pedagogical methodologies of the NPE is not contextually appropriate or relevant for the Nigerian socio-political context. At the national level, the Nigerian nation has five main

---

19. Hanson, "Oral Traditions."

20. Okoh, *Risk of An Educational System*, 20.

21. Okoh, 20.

national goals, which include: (1) a free and democratic society; (2) a just and egalitarian society; (3) a united, strong, and self-reliant nation; (4) a great and dynamic economy; and (5) a land of bright and full opportunities for all citizens.[22] These national goals express the kind of society envisioned for the Nigerian people and communities. These goals suggest the development of autonomous individuals who think for themselves without due regard to the communal norms and beliefs of the communities they are a part of. This is evident in the educational goals of the NPE.

The NPE goals lay emphasis on the principles to be inculcated through education to achieve the five national goals. The NPE goals are: (1) "The inculcation of national consciousness and national unity."[23] (2) "The inculcation of the type of values and attitudes for the survival of the individual and the Nigerian society."[24] This is an ethical goal concerned with the conduct of mankind.[25] This goal also requires religious education which also prescribes ethical behavior. (3) "The training of the mind in the understanding of the world around."[26] The goal of training the mind for understanding the world around is based on a metaphysical philosophy that is concerned with the intellectual comprehension of non-concrete concepts.[27] And (4) "The acquisition of appropriate skills and the development of mental, physical and social abilities and competencies as equipment for the individual to live in and contribute to the development of the society."[28] These NPE goals lay emphasis on the individual in society rather than the individual as a seamless part of the community. Hence the emphasis on the individual promotes the sense of individualism that has priority over a sense of individual-in-community and communalism.

Rowland Onyenali's[29] appraisal of problems in Nigeria through education and religious education provides an insight on the consequences of

---

22. Federal Republic of Nigeria, National Policy on Education, 1; Ozurumba and Ebuara, "Appraisal of Education," 31.

23. Federal Republic of Nigeria, National Policy on Education, 2.

24. Federal Republic of Nigeria, 2.

25. Sharma and Hyland, *Philosophy of Education*, 22.

26. Federal Republic of Nigeria, National Policy on Education, 2.

27. Sharma and Hyland, 14.

28. Federal Republic of Nigeria, National Policy on Education, 2.

29. Onyenali, *Appraising the Nigerian Problem*.

the self-autonomy that the NPE goals emphasize in a multi-cultural and multi-religious nation like Nigeria. Onyenali argues that Nigeria consists of different, previously unrelated, nationalities that were amalgamated into one political entity without a common ideological framework to hold them together. He further argues that Nigeria is a commonwealth of different nations with natural and ideological demarcations that were not put into consideration in the creation of the nation. Therefore, there was no religious, sociocultural, or ideological framework for the development of the nation as a united entity. The result is that the educational structure and content in the Nigerian context does not provide the Nigerian populace the cognitive skills with which to critically review and digest information and knowledge needed for the establishment of unity in diversity. Therefore, just as Okoh argues, the NPE lacks a clear-cut guide for action leading to the establishment of unity in diversity and it is beclouded with ambiguities and serious logical contradictions in attempts to address the peculiar development needs of particular communities in the nation.[30]

If Onyenali's and Okoh's arguments are true then formal education, as guided by the NPE, has influenced the development of the sense of individualism in the Kurmin Gwaza and Kurmin Jatau communities. More so that it is clearly stated that the NPE seeks to inculcate "types of values and attitudes for the survival of the individual."[31] Autonomous individuals developed on the basis of this philosophy think more of their own interest and can challenge communal norms and beliefs. This weakens sociocultural bonds within the communities the individuals belong to. Note here that it is the sociocultural bonds that are weakened but the sense of community is not lost in these communities. It has been argued earlier that though the elements of social cohesion and harmony in the traditional worldview on development are retained, the element of communal partnership for the holistic well-being of members of the community is de-emphasized. Instead the emphasis in the modern worldview on development is on personal or individualistic pursuit and acquisition of economic, educational, and political status.

It is thus argued that the intercourse between the communities' traditional philosophy of education, which sustains the communities' traditional

---

30. Okoh, *Risk of an Educational System*, 20.

31. Federal Republic of Nigeria, National Policy on Education, 2.

cultures and identities, and the NPE, which guides the implementation of formal education that promotes the autonomy of individuals in Nigeria, has been responsible for influencing the shift in the worldview of the communities. The shift tilts the communities' worldview toward "Euro-American thinking about reality, knowledge and values."[32] It seems obvious that the engagement of the traditional philosophy of education and formal education guided by the NPE in Nigeria has led to cognitive, affective, and value change concerning development in Kurmin Gwaza and Kurmin Jatau communities. Both formal and non-formal education as tools for transforming people's and societies' worldviews have been responsible for transmitting and transforming Kurmin Gwaza and Kurmin Jatau communities. Therefore, through the instrumentality of Western philosophy of education there is a shift of the cognitive perception and passionate pursuit of what is considered and valued as development in these communities.

The role of Christianity in worldview shift in Kurmin Gwaza and Kurmin Jatau communities

This sub-section discusses the role of Christianity in the shift of the traditional worldview of both communities toward a modern worldview on development. The data reveals that in both communities Christianity, as was introduced, is viewed as a liberator from their cultural beliefs and practices so the communities had other aspirations. The people describe those other aspiration as "high expectations" because, according to them, "the people have been brought from darkness to light."[33] Religion is an integral component of the social tapestry of societies and worldviews. Paul G. Hiebert, R. Daniel Shaw, and Tite Tienou, posit that religion is an essential component of culture.[34] Clarke posits that religious belief is a common human characteristic with 80 percent of the world's population professing religious faith.[35] Jeffery Haynes adds that "throughout the developing world, it is implausible to believe that the religious factor can be isolated from life's general context" because religion provides

---

32. Okoh, *Risk of an Educational System*, 20.

33. Comment of one of the respondents, Amashama, from Kurmin Jatau, quoted above.

34. Hiebert, Shaw, and Tienou, *Understanding Folk Religion*, 36.

35. Clarke, *Development and Religion*, 6, 1. Clarke, in his work argues "for a realistic appreciation of the centrality that religion holds in certain communities and for some individuals" as it relates to advance of human dignity, freedom, social equity and self-determination.

the necessary concepts and ideas that answer people's existential questions.[36] It is presupposed in this study that Christianity played and can still play a role if deliberately applied to achieve the transformation of the worldview of the Kurmin Gwaza and Kurmin Jatau communities on development.

Christianity with its values and beliefs, like any other religion, influences and motivates the actions of individuals and those of a community that subscribe to it. According to Haynes, citing M. Marty, focus on human "ultimate concern," the building of community, and demands for certain behavior from its adherents is some of the characteristics of religion.[37] Hiebert, Shaw, and Tienou, also state that anthropologists associate religion with "beliefs about the ultimate nature of things, as deep feelings and motivations, and as fundamental values and allegiances."[38] Clarke also argues that religion consists of beliefs and practices that reflect the values that facilitate human well-being.[39] In addition, according to Clarke religious beliefs serve as a reference point for its adherents to interpret their own circumstances or make decisions in the light of those beliefs.[40] Therefore any change in religious beliefs and practices in any individual or community brings about changes in conceptions about ultimate human concerns, about their circumstances, about community, about behavioral expectations, and changes in feelings, motivations, fundamental values, and allegiances.

The Kurmin Gwaza and Kurmin Jatau communities historically, like any other community in Nigeria in particular, have religion as an integral component of their worldview. The history of both communities, as described in the focus groups' discussions, indicate that before the advent of Christianity the *Dodo* religious cult was the dominant religion. Mardaku, of Kurmin Gwaza, mentions that before the advent of Christianity in Kurmin Gwaza the *Dodo* traditional religion was in existence and played a role in the lifestyle of the community. In his own words Marduk, stated that historically "the *Dodo* cult played a vital role in ensuring discipline in the community. Though Christianity was not established in the community then, yet the

---

36. Haynes, *Religion and Development*, 14.

37. Haynes, 14.

38. Hiebert, Shaw, and Tienou, *Understanding Folk Religion*, 35.

39. Clarke, *Development and Religion*, 2–3.

40. Clarke, 1.

taboos established by the *Dodo* cult were respected and observed out of fear." Amashama, of Kurmin Jatau, stated that he grew in "our traditional religion" and narrates that,

> Today there is virtually no man or woman that will claim to belong to the *Dodo* traditional religious cult. There is no priest of the old *Dodo* traditional religious cult in this community. There were until two weeks ago only two persons that hold to the *Dodo* traditional religion. One of them, Yakubu Dodo, died two weeks ago. There is none of his children that is associated with the *Dodo* religious cult. The only surviving religious traditionalist is Kanwa. The *Dodo* traditional religion has faded out, Christianity is now the dominant religion of the community.

The foregoing shows that in the history of both Kurmin Gwaza and Kurmin Jatau communities the *Dodo* religion influenced the lifestyle of the communities and the advent of Christianity brought changes in the lifestyles of the communities. Amashama, of Kurmin Jatau, admits that, "The *Dodo* traditional religion has faded out, Christianity is now the dominant religion of the community . . . That is why we have the high expectations we have in this community."

The form of Christianity brought to the Kurmin Gwaza and Kurmin Jatau communities was clothed in Western perspective or culture. Bosch writes that Christianity in the West was influenced by the enlightenment concept "that everyone was an emancipated, autonomous individual" which resulted in "the rampant individualism which soon pervaded Protestantism in particular."[41] The assumption was that an individual had the right and the ability to know God's revealed will and to make independent decision without reference to the community they belong to. Thus, the Western form of Christianity focuses on the individual above the community as a seamless constituency of individuals. It emphasizes the redemption of individuals at the expense of the redemption of whole families and whole communities. The salvation of individuals, rather the salvation of families or whole communities or societies, was historically the primary evangelistic focus of Western form of Christianity. This focus ignores the fact that the biblical metanarrative demonstrates the redemption

---

41. Bosch, *Transforming Mission*, 273.

of whole families. Noah and his family, Rahab and her family, Cornelius and his household, and the Philippian Jailer and his family[42] are some biblical examples of redemption of whole families. The biblical metanarrative also demonstrates the redemption of whole nations, especially the Jewish nation. For example, the Israelites redemption from the Egyptian slavery and their redemption from the Babylonian captivity.[43] Hence Christianity as introduced in both communities lacks the capacity to transform the worldview of the communities towards holistic transformational development for the communities and individuals-in-community. The individualism promoted by the Western form of Christianity promoted the dismantling family bonds and societal norms that held individuals-in-community in the context of community bound together in harmony.

Instead of critically examining the societal norms in the light of biblical principles to facilitate the contextualization of biblical Christianity in the non-Western context the Western missionaries condemned, rejected, and promoted the rejection of the entire cultures of these non-Western societies. Thus, they promoted the disintegration of cultural bonds of relationships and the principles that promote community and communal living in the non-Western societies. Therefore, the Western form of Christianity, which focuses on the individual above the community as a seamless constituency of individuals, seems to be inadequate in transforming people-in-communities. Individualism is antithetical to the sociocultural practices of communalism. The traditional worldview on development of the Kurmin Gwaza and Kurmin Jatau communities upholds the practices of communalism where the interest of the individual is subsumed in the interest of the community without denying the individual his or her individuality.

While the Western form of Christianity does not deny the place of participation and exercise of faith in community as part of the expectations of the Christian faith yet it did not, like the *Dodo* traditional religion, provide for the means to hold the individual accountable for disrupting community cultural bonds without unpleasant consequences on the individual. The *Dodo* religious beliefs and practices sustained and promoted harmony in the communities as noted by Marduk, of Kurmin Gwaza. The Kurmin Gwaza and

---

42. Gen 7:1; 8:18; Josh 2:8–14; 6:25; Acts 10:44–48; 16:29–34.
43. Exod 12:31–33, 40; 2 Chron 36:22–23.

Kurmin Jatau communities consider Christianity, which has replaced the traditional *Dodo* religious cult, as having a positive impact on the state of development of their respective communities. It introduced the people to the worship of God through faith in Jesus Christ. Amashama, from Kurmin Jatau, states that the introduction of Christianity and its dominance in the Kurmin Jatau community "shows that the gospel that was brought has had positive effect on the community. People have been brought from darkness to light . . . (and have changed) the expectations we have in this community."

However, Christianity as understood by the people seems to have some negative effect on the traditional social relationship. It watered down the enforcement of the traditional social control mechanism that instilled discipline and respect for elders. Kukandadi, of Kurmin Gwaza, laments that "Today's generation are no longer obedient to parents. We now witness the present generation being engaged in drunkenness and disobedience to parents." The foregoing lament does not imply that Christianity and its beliefs are directly responsible for the loss of discipline but it suggests that the way Christianity is practiced does not enforce discipline in a manner that makes sense to the people. The lament indicates that the form of Christianity introduced in the communities did not enforce community discipline for communal living. Hence because of the influence of the form of Christianity introduced in the communities there is a shift from the sense of communality, which is part of the traditional worldview on development of the communities.

Another characteristic of Western forms of Christianity is emphasis on rationalism. Christianity practiced in a Western context is grounded in rational propositions.[44] It insisted on correct formulation of doctrine so that it became important to uphold "creeds in an absolutely unaltered and unalterable form, ascribing to them comprehensive validity for all times and settings."[45] These creeds became the basis for excluding or including groups as orthodox or non-orthodox. This approach dismissed the possibility of any future doctrinal development therefore it foreclosed the possibility of contextualizing theology. It has been stated in the review of literature that theology is formulated in specific sociocultural contexts in order to arrive at

---

44. Hiebert, *Gospel in Human Contexts*, 39–44.
45. Bosch, *Transforming Mission*, 240.

a meaningful understanding of the faith prescribed in the biblical metanarrative.[46] Christianity, wherever it is practiced, must be informed by the biblical metanarrative not creeds and doctrines formed in other contexts. The biblical metanarrative is the supreme and normative standard for Christianity. The practice of Christianity can and should take shape in different cultures in contextually relevant forms without compromising the biblical normative. Hiebert argues for the development of contextual forms of Christianity that applies the principles of missional theology. Missional theology seeks for "a way of thinking biblically about God's universal mission in the context of the world here and now, with all its particularities, paradoxes, and confusions."[47] The practice of Christianity can and should be contextualized in the different context to make it authentic, practical, and meaningful in the different contexts. Therefore, the theology of development for the Kurmin Gwaza and Kurmin Jatau communities should be biblical and be contextually developed, therefore authentic, practical, and meaningful.

The Western form of Christianity introduced in the Kurmin Gwaza and Kurmin Jatau communities emphasized the autonomy of the individual. This weakened the principle of communalism that subsumes the autonomy of the individual into the seamless community of individuals with a common concern for the welfare of the whole without neglecting the welfare of the individual.

It is therefore argued that the fusion of the sense of personal autonomy to make individual decisions and choices without reference to the community as introduced and promoted by the Western form of Christian practice has impact on the shift of the communities' traditional worldview on development to their modern worldview on development. It is a shift from emphasis on sociological harmony and communal activities to sustain the communities' well-being. It is a shift to emphasis on economic, infrastructural, and social progress for individual members of the communities in the context of cohesive sociocultural relationships.

---

46. Allen, *Theological Method*, 97; Netland, "Introduction," 16–18; Bevans, *Models of Contextual Theology*, 3.

47. Hiebert, *Gospel in Human Contexts*, 44.

Biblical Transformation of Kurmin Gwaza and Kurmin Jatau Communities' Worldview on Development

It has been established through the literature review in chapter 2 that world-views can be transformed. It has been argued above that Western form of formal education and Western form of Christianity transformed the Kurmin Gwaza and Kurmin Jatau communities' worldview on development. The assumption of this study is that the worldview of Kurmin Gwaza and Kurmin Jatau communities on development can be transformed through a process that engages the communities' worldview on development in dialogue with the biblical worldview on holistic transformational development. Hiebert argues that it was through their history that God shaped and refined the "Jewish understanding of sin, sacrifice, salvation, Messiah, and other concepts essential for an understanding of the gospel."[48] Similarly it is through the process of engaging in dialogue with the biblical metanarrative that the worldview of the Kurmin Gwaza and Kurmin Jatau communities on the concept of development can be biblically reshaped, refined, and transformed. The aim of developing a biblically transformed worldview of the communities on development is to facilitate a sustainable process for holistic development process that progressively applies biblical shalom in both communities.

It has been stated in chapter 2 that the biblical worldview on holistic transformational development presupposes the beginning and a process of transforming every aspect of the human life towards the state God originally intended it to be at creation. In chapter 2 it was also established that the biblical metanarrative reveals that human life consists of a spiritual relationship with God, a psychological perception of one's self-identity, social relationship with other human beings, and one's vocation in the ecological or physical context in which human beings exist all in a state of perfect harmony. It was also established that the biblical metanarrative reveals God's plan to re-establish human beings and all of his creation in a state of shalom. In addition, that God in his plan invites people to a special spiritual relationship with God so that they can participate with him in unfolding his plan. Therefore, from the biblical metanarrative the process of holistic transformational development begins with the re-instatement of the spiritual relationship between God and

---

48. Hiebert, *Transforming Worldviews*, 266.

human beings in a state of perfect harmony and continues as God unfolds his plans to reinstate the whole of God's creation in a state of harmony through his people.

The Kurmin Gwaza and Kurmin Jatau communities' self-identity was presented in chapter 4. It has been argued above that a community's self-identity and self-interests theoretically provides the conceptual understanding of the community's worldview on development. It is therefore necessary to identify the self-identity of both communities. The communities' self-identity, presented in chapter 4, was focused on both the communities' sociocultural relationships and their vocation to sustain life. Although the communities were not ignorant of the existence of God nor of the existence of some relationship with God yet their relationship with God was not factored in the communities' self-identity. Through the application of the participatory appreciative dialogue the communities' self-identity was engaged in a dialogical interaction with the biblical metanarrative. The process was aimed at facilitating the communities' examination of their relationship with God. The intent was to get the communities to define their self-identity in the light of the identity of the people of God described in the biblical narrative. The dialogue was facilitated by the community responding to the questions: does our identity fit with the identity of God's people you identified in the Bible story? What are the similarities and what are the differences? What do we need to amend and how can we do so?

The responses of the people in the light of the biblical metanarrative presented in chapter 4 showed the people in the communities view themselves as creatures of God. The people view themselves as God's creatures who are continually being taken care of by God both spiritually and physically. They also viewed themselves as a people who have been liberated from the worship of *Dodo* spirits and therefore have been integrated into a relationship with God as Christians through Christ.

The biblical metanarrative reveals further, that God stated the purpose of inviting people into a special spiritual relationship with himself. The invitation was for God to execute his plan to bless other people through his own people. The revelation in the biblical metanarrative is that God executed his plan through the people of Israel by guiding them with his will, through a covenant relationship that consists of the guidelines for living in relationship with him to experience shalom. The biblical metanarrative also reveals that through the people of Israel the Son of God, Jesus Christ, became incarnate. Jesus Christ taught and modelled the quality of life God wills for his people. Then he established a new covenant relationship that extends God's invitation to other people. Jesus Christ, the biblical metanarrative further reveals, completed the task necessary for re-establishing the spiritual relationship with God. The biblical metanarrative reveals further that people who respond to the invitation to enter into the special spiritual relation with God also become God's special people. In addition, the people of God in the biblical metanarrative were under obligation to assist and support one another. Therefore, members of the communities were encouraged by the fact that, like the people of God in the biblical metanarrative, it was in their culture to partner and to assist one another. Hence the members of the community saw the need to continue to take collective action to achieve their community goals.

In the area of differences, the responses showed that the communities think that God was closer to the people of God in the biblical metanarrative because they heard God and saw signs of his visible presence through light or fire. It also showed that the people of God in the biblical metanarrative loved God more than the people in their communities do today. Therefore, to improve their relationship with God and to make progress the communities considered it essential for the people to devote themselves to obeying God so that they can be closer to God.

The responses to the participatory appreciative dialogue questions reveal that the process of appreciative dialogue facilitated, first, the people's self-appreciation, then, a willingness to improve their self-identity to align with the qualities of the people of God in the biblical metanarrative. The appreciative approach, as argued by Booy and Sena, celebrates past successes and builds upon the best of the past and the successes of the present.[49] Marmadu, of Kurmin Gwaza, in her comment stated that the participatory appreciative dialogue approach introduced through the study has been helpful. She said:

> We have seen the handwork of God in guiding us. We witnessed the power of God and the guidance of the Spirit of God. We thank God and pray that this will motivate us to take steps to help ourselves rather than looking up to others.

---

49. Booy and Sena, "Capacity Building," 38–41.

Gaibu, also from Kurmin Gwaza, commented that through the application of the participatory appreciative dialogue approach, "We are able to understand that within us we can do something that we imagine could be done. We have been empowered to use our own initiative." Thus, the people, through the participatory appreciative dialogue came to the realization that they can celebrate their special spiritual relationship with God through their confession of faith in Jesus Christ.

Therefore, through the use of the participatory appreciative dialogue the communities' self-perception demonstrates a process of transformation taking place. The communities no longer view their identity as weak communities infested with many problems in need of someone else to help them. Rather they are communities with resources within their reach and with capacities to develop themselves in line with prescriptions in the biblical metanarrative rather than being dependent. Thus, this is an indication that a fusion of the biblical worldview on the identity of the people of God and the communities' worldview on their self-identity has occurred. The communities' worldview on development consequently is being transformed from being focused on sociocultural relationships and vocation to sustain life. It is transformed to perceive development to include being in a special spiritual relationship with God while they strive to live their sociocultural relationships and vocation in accord with the guidance of the principles revealed in the biblical metanarrative. This is indicative that holistic transformational development must begin with a people's covenant relationship with God. This is the cornerstone for holistic transformational development in any community.

Good values contribute to the stability and harmony that exists in a community. The Kurmin Gwaza and Kurmin Jatau communities have values that facilitate the communities' perception of development. These communities value the sustenance of their social relationships through respect and obedience by younger persons to older persons. The data presented in chapter 4 shows that in the Kurmin Gwaza community the community values love for and obedience to elders, as well as love for one another. In the Kurmin Jatau community they value communal living in unity and solidarity. Hence the maintenance and sustenance of harmonious relationships are of great value to both communities. Another outstanding value in both communities is farming. It should be noted that both communities are engaged in subsistence farming to meet their survival needs. Both communities are also engaged in the cultivation of ginger for commercial purposes. The farming methods of these communities are not characterized by the use of machines, like tractors, but by manual use of hand tools like hoes. Therefore, farming to meet the survival needs of the community has great value and promotes a sense of self-worth as indicated in the narrative of the Kurmin Jatau focus group discussion.

For the purpose of applying the participatory appreciative dialogue approach to facilitate the evaluation and the possible biblical transformation of the values of both communities, the research participants were required to answer the following questions: do our values fit with God's values you identified in the Bible story for his people? What are the similarities and what are the differences? What do we need to amend and how can we do so? The responses presented in chapter 4 show that the Kurmin Gwaza focus group conceded that biblical teaching is necessary for their transformational development. They also indicated that love for one another and respect for elders are in consonance with the teaching of the Bible.

The Kurmin Gwaza focus group described their commitment to communal living in unity and solidarity to be in consonance with the Christian faith. The self-identity of these communities analyzed above does give expression to these values of harmony in social relationships and commitment to their vocation to sustain life and uphold self-respect. The research participants in both communities agreed that there is a decline in the quality of relationships compared to their previous histories. Therefore, there is a need for the people to modify the way they live by cultivating a life of love and obedience, paying more attention to prayer, working together as it used to be, for example with communal work.

This study has attempted to establish some of the goals both the Kurmin Gwaza and Kurmin Jatau communities had set for themselves to aim at for the development of their respective communities. The goals the Kurmin Gwaza community set for themselves prior to their interaction with the biblical metanarrative were to establish and sustain a comfortable life which consists of having food, shelter, and the use of cars and televisions. The Kurmin Jatau community set for themselves the goals of having community members acquiring academic degrees and developing ways for sustainable economic empowerment. The following questions guided the dialogical discussion with the biblical metanarrative on the issue of the goals of the communities: do our goals fit with God's goals in the Bible story for his people? What are the similarities and what are the differences? What do we need to amend and how can we do so? The response to these questions is that their goals are similar to God's goal for his people. The research participants conceded that from the biblical metanarrative God sought to provide his people food, shelter, and a harmonious atmosphere. The data shows that the communities acknowledged that though people in their communities have more of these material resources like food, shelter, cars, and television than was the case in the past, these materials are not used to glorify God. Therefore, they opined that, they need to correct the ways they use these things by cultivating the fear of God through teaching the word of God. These communities being communities that consider religion as an essential component of development were able to have a reorientation concerning their community goals. Following their interaction with the biblical metanarrative the communities seem to have reconsidered their perception of the priority they were giving to material wealth in comparison to their religious life. It seems to have brought out an understanding that the pursuit of material wealth must not be given priority over their relationship with God. This is in itself is cognitive, affective, and evaluative transformation of the communities' perception of material wealth.

The Kurmin Gwaza and Kurmin Jatau communities have visions and aspirations beyond the communities' immediate goals of development. The research participants in both communities expressed visions and aspirations for their communities that included good roads, potable water, stable electricity, good education with professors in different fields of study, and industrialization and urbanization. It has been argued earlier that modern development thinking has been introduced in these communities through Western form of education. Therefore, these visions and aspirations can be said to be influenced by modernization thinking.

Both focus groups evaluated their visions and aspirations in the light of the biblical metanarrative. The following questions served as a tool to guide the evaluation: do your expectations fit with God's plan for his people you have identified in the Bible story? What are the similarities and what are the differences? What do we need to amend and how can we do so? The response was that the aspirations were in line with the will of God for his people. The research participants considered the biblical narrative of creation recorded in Genesis 2:4–16 and came to the conclusion that God had made provision for the sustenance of human beings with ease in the garden of Eden. They also concluded that God gave human beings the ability to create things for their comfort therefore to aspire for the things that will make life comfortable was in line with God's plan for them. The research participants did not evaluate their aspirations on moral grounds. However, considering their prioritization of the need to fear God while pursuing the communities' goals it is assumed that the same standard is applied for evaluating their community aspirations. The positive and negative implication of industrialization and urbanization was not discussed because it was beyond the scope of this study.

The process of applying biblical shalom among human beings in their historical and spatial context has a starting point, a progressive process, and a final destination. The process begins with a positive response to God's invitation to believe in the person and work of Jesus Christ as revealed in the biblical metanarrative. A positive response to believing in the person and work of Jesus Christ generates positive results, especially in the area of holistic transformational development. The outcome of faith response is entering into a special spiritual relationship with God, becoming part of God's people. The special spiritual relationship with God manifests in a process of progressive transformation of the psychological, intellectual, social, emotional, moral, and vocational aspects of the lives of people in that relationship with God. These aspects of human life are progressively transformed to align with God's designed purposes until they are finally brought into God's goal of a state of biblical shalom. The progressive transformation occurs as the people in the special spiritual relationship with God commit to and obey the will of God as revealed in the biblical metanarrative. Thus, there is a progressive application of biblical shalom in the community where the process of facilitating holistic transformational development is applied.

Application of Biblical Shalom through the Participatory Appreciative Dialogue in Rural Communities

This study integrates an AI approach to move from the mode of constant focusing on problems and into a mode of continuous innovation.[50] This section

---

50. Booy and Sena, 43.

applies Myers's framework for holistic development. The study assumed God's mission characterized by God's invitation of his people to participate with him in the process of holistic transformational development.[51] God invites people regardless of their sociocultural, historical, and geographical location to become his people. They become his people on the basis of faith in and redemption by the action of God in Christ. The study also applies and extends Matarrita-Cascante and Brennan's self-help model of community development for the study. Lastly, the study integrates Scriptures, which is the catalyst and the norm, for the process of holistic transformational development.

There are approaches that seek to facilitate the transformational development through the integration of Scriptures in the process. Two of such approaches are the Scripture Search approach developed in the Philippines and The Seven Steps approach developed in Brazil. Alvarez, Avarientos, and McAlpine, drawing from Bradshaw and McAlpine, describe the characteristics of the Scripture Search approach to include the people themselves discovering the relevance of Scripture to the issues of life they are wrestling with. The facilitator "comes prepared to introduce a Scripture reading during the reflection period, when experience sharing is at a high point." The reflection is guided by three fundamental questions: (1) what are the similarities between experience in biblical times and our experience now? (2) What light does that experience cast upon our current experience? And (3) as individuals and as a group, what should we do about these insights?[52] The Scripture Search approach brings life issues to the Bible. However, it is the facilitator who predetermines which passage of Scripture or aspect of the metanarrative to be reflected upon.

The Seven Step approach is a Bible reading, not Bible study, approach. The method requires a small group of people meeting to read, reflect upon, share insight from the Bible, and decide course of action. The method consists of seven steps. In this approach the Bible is taken to address the issues of life. The method follows a predetermined Bible reading plan, the *lectio divina* (divine reading) developed by the Lumko Institute in the Republic of South Africa.[53]

---

51. Wright, *Mission of God*, 23.

52. Alvarez, Avarientos, and McAlpine, "Our Experience," 63–64.

53. Alvarez, Avarientos, and McAlpine, 72–74.

According to Alvarez, Avarientos, and McAlpine, the application of these approaches has made it possible for Scripture to play a vital and irreplaceable role in community development project as it addresses individual and group values and behaviors. "In the Philippines, where participative methods have had a chance to mature, Scripture has become a major motor for institutional learning and transformation."[54] Alvarez, Avarientos, and McAlpine, opine that there is need to "to expand our 'tool kit' of participative ways of reading the Bible among ourselves and with communities."[55] This study examined the possibility of integrating the biblical metanarrative in the process of facilitating holistic transformational development in two homogeneous rural communities.

The participatory appreciative dialogue approach facilitated a direct dialogical interaction of the biblical worldview on transformational development and the communities' worldview on development. It is participatory because it is the people that are engaged in the dialogue. Freire's philosophy of education advocates for rigorous dialogue on practical issues that arise from everyday experiences.[56] Therefore the research tool applied to facilitate focus group discussions integrated Freire's philosophy of education to create dialogical interaction between the biblical worldview on transformational development and the communities' worldview on development. The dialogue in this study is described as appreciative because it focuses on continuous innovation using the principles that have given success in the past. The interaction with the biblical worldview is similar to the Scripture Search approach.

It has, however, some differences with the Scripture Search approach. In the Scripture Search approach the interaction is focused on isolated biblical passages, whereas in this study the biblical metanarrative is approached based on the creation-fall-redemption-eschatological framework rather than isolated biblical passages. The participatory appreciative dialogue approach provides a mechanism that will enhance the capacity of the people to interact with the biblical metanarrative. This fits in with the Matarrita-Cascante and Brennan self-help model of CD that focuses on the establishment of mechanisms that will enhance the human resources of the community through

---

54. Alvarez, Avarientos, and McAlpine, 76.
55. Alvarez, Avarientos, and McAlpine, 76.
56. Roberts, *Education, Literacy, and Humanization*, 1.

capacity building. The approach empowers the people with the capacity to define their worldview on development, identify the biblical worldview on holistic transformational development drawn from the biblical metanarrative, evaluate their worldview in the light of the biblical worldview, then to chart a course of action aimed at facilitating the progressive well-being of their communities, and finally to evaluate the outcome their action. The mechanisms developed in the process in the self-help model promote the development of skills and know-how for members of the community. Therefore, just like the self-help model, the approach in this study aims for innovation, sustainability, sense of ownership, and encouraging the practice of communality in the sense of community existing in the two rural communities.

It was considered essential to equip the Kurmin Gwaza and Kurmin Jatau communities with the skill to facilitate participatory appreciative dialogue. This is so because the process is to be driven by members of the community. It is also assumed that participatory appreciative dialogue when applied can facilitate the transformation of the communities' worldview on development. Applied to facilitate dialogue between the biblical worldview on holistic transformational development the communities' perceptions, attitudes, and practices can be biblically transformed. It has the capacity in helping them to set goals, make plans, implement processes for, and evaluate holistic transformational development. Finally, it is assumed that a biblically transformed perception, attitudes, and practices can facilitate the application of biblical shalom. Therefore, it was essential to equip both communities with the skill for engaging their perceptions, attitudes, and practices to facilitate community well-being in participatory appreciative dialogue with the biblical metanarrative.

Rather than focusing on and facilitating CD processes to diagnose, plan for, and take actions to solve community problems, the approach in this study focused on appreciating and facilitating a CD process to build on and further develop the good in communities in the light of the biblical metanarrative. Principles drawn from Osmer's method of doing theology, Freire's philosophy of education and Cooperrider's Appreciative Inquiry informed the development of the interview protocol that was used as a research tool in this study. The following is the analyzes on how the participatory appreciative dialogue approach was applied in the study. The applied approach consisted of four phases. Each of the phases has specific objectives and two or three different actions. The phases are analyzed in the following four sub-sections.

Participatory Appreciative Dialogue Approach for the Identification of the Worldview of Rural Communities' Worldview on Development

The objective of the first phase was for the communities to diachronically describe their present strengths and identify their sources from their history. The research participants embarked on three actions for the first phase. The research participants in this study were asked two questions. (1) How will you describe your community? (2) Each one of you may have witnessed or learned of an event or events that occurred in this community which you or the community as a whole considers to have brought about and/or is bringing progressive development for the well-being of this community. I requested that each of them take as much as five minutes or less to describe such an event or events. These questions gave the research participants the opportunity to present their communities' stories of successes. The questions help to bring to the surface and to consciously examine the deep, unexamined assumptions the people have, "therefore making explicit what is implicit."[57] Synchronically this approach provides for cognitive explanation and inspires affective appreciation of the values of the communities. The analysis of the research participants' story revealed both the traditional and the modern worldview of the communities on development. It is the communities' worldview on development that was engaged in an appreciative dialogue with the biblical worldview on transformational development.

Chapter 4 presents the actions the research participants took to mobilize their respective communities to participate in activities aimed at planning for and implementing actions to facilitate the execution of the development project they selected for this study in their respective communities. The actions were initiated by the research participants in the focus groups without the direct involvement of the researcher. The researcher simply provided a written framework to help the participants. The written framework is presented in chapter 4 under the theme biblical metanarrative.

---

57. Hiebert, *Transforming Worldviews*, 319.

The first action the research participants took was to hold a strategy meeting within themselves to plan how to mobilize their respective communities to participate in executing the projects they selected. Both groups of research participants demonstrated a clear understanding of the value of consultative dialogue to plan. This is not a new development since the chiefs and elders of the communities do hold consultative meetings therefore the focus group participants were applying the approach to achieve their objectives.

The second action was that each of the research participants held consultative meeting with selected leaders in their respective communities. For the market project, for instance, the Kurmin Gwaza focus group held consultative meeting with selected market leaders to gain an understanding of how the market system was conducted. The Kurmin Gwaza focus group chose two other projects: road rehabilitation project and the theological students support project. However, the group did not hold consultative meetings before summoning the members of the community for dialogue on both projects. The Kurmin Jatau focus group held consultative meeting with the Kurmin Gwaza community council of chiefs under the leadership of the Kurmin Jatau district head. The group met with the council of chiefs to inform them of the proposed plan, the method of implementing the plan, the goal of the plan, and to solicit the backing of the chiefs.

Both communities value and respect their community leaders. The data describing the factors responsible for the successes of the communities indicated that there were key charismatic leaders who inspired individual and community action that instilled values and inspired actions that led to such successes. For example, the commitment to farming in Kurmin Gwaza is attributed to the inspiration of Sok, a chief of the community. In the Kurmin Jatau community the commitment to acquire Western education and to embrace Christianity were inspired by community leaders like Mallam Dawa, Mallam Kure, and John Hayab. The community chief that inspired the establishment of the community market was identified by the focus group as Simon Kura. Therefore, the research participants saw the need to first dialogue with the respective community leaders to gain their support and insights. Engaging community leaders first to mobilize their support is an essential factor in the process of facilitating meetings with members of the community for any interaction.

The third action the research participants took was to mobilize members of their respective communities for action. The Kurmin Jatau focus group, after receiving the assurance of support from the community's council of chiefs, undertook advocacy visits to all the local churches of the different denominations in the Kurmin Jatau community. The objective was to inform, motivate, and inspire the people to participate in a community meeting to consider how and to take actions to resuscitate the Kurmin Jatau community market successfully. The Kurmin Gwaza focus group, unlike the Kurmin Jatau focus group, did not consider undertaking any advocacy visits to the churches in their community. However, both focus groups scheduled and conducted community meetings to dialogue on the projects they selected for the purpose of this study.

Each of the two groups of research participants reported the application of the discussion guide provided by the researcher. The communities were led to identify their place in God's plan as outlined in the biblical metanarrative. As reported earlier in chapter 4, the community now considered their identity in relationship with the God that revealed himself in the biblical metanarrative.

In summary, the communities consider themselves as creatures of God for whom God provides for both their spiritual and physical needs just as he took care of his people in biblical times as narrated in the biblical metanarrative. The communities recognized the need to listen more closely to God, to love God more, and to be focused on obeying God. Therefore, the participatory appreciative dialogue facilitated the communities to have an explicit understanding of their self-identity in the light of the biblical metanarrative. This self-identity is that the communities are related to God through faith in Jesus Christ. They have the responsibility of partnering with God through obedience to him for every goal, every aspiration, and every action related to the facilitation of development or improvement of the holistic well-being of the communities.

Participatory Appreciative Dialogue Approach for the Analysis, Interpretation, and Transformation of Communities' Worldview on Development

The objective of the second phase in the participatory appreciative dialogue is for the communities to analyze and interpret their story. The analysis and interpretation were aimed at helping the people to cognitively understand and affectively appreciate the successes and reasons for the successes that facilitated their communities' development at that point in time. The first action in this second phase was the analysis of the stories the research participants narrated. The analysis was guided by four open-ended questions: (1) what were the benefits derived in your community from the events you described at the last session? (2) How did the events bring about progress and development for the well-being of the community? (3) Who in your opinion were responsible for the occurrence of the events? (4) What other factors do you think contributed to the realization of these benefits? The research participants interpreted their communities' stories by analyzing the successes in their stories, the factors that served as catalysts for the successes, and the communities' aspirations or vision for a better future. Inspiring leaders, community cohesion brought about by respect for the rules established by the *Dodo* religious practices before the advent of Christianity, communal activities, hard work, apprenticeship, Christianity, and Western education were the factors identified from the analysis of the stories the research participants narrated. Hence the research participants were able to provide a cognitive description of their communities' traditional and modern worldview on development described above. It is the communities' modern worldview on development, however, that could be engaged in dialogue with the biblical worldview on holistic transformational development because it is now the dominant communities' worldview.

The second action in this second phase of the participatory appreciative dialogue was the participants interpreting their communities' worldview on development in the light of the biblical worldview on transformational development. The research participants compared and contrasted their communities' self-identity, values, goals, and aspirations with corresponding elements drawn from the biblical metanarrative to arrive at a biblical and contextual holistic transformational development. The following questions guided the discussion to help the research participants to interpret their stories in the light of the biblical metanarrative. (1) What are the similarities between the experiences of the biblical story and the experience of your community that we have focused our discussion on in the past sessions? (2) What are the differences? (3) What lessons have you learned from these comparisons? The participants identified from the biblical metanarrative their communities' place in God's mission plan. It has been stated earlier that the participants identified their communities as related to God through faith in Christ. They identified their communities as a people who now have the responsibility to partner with God through obedience to his will in every aspect of their effort aimed at facilitating the development or improvement of the holistic well-being of their communities. Hence this interpretation highlighted to the participants the idea that their communities needed to align with God's will as a people with a special relationship with God through Christ. This conceptual understanding of the communities' self-identity and responsibility in the light of the biblical metanarrative led to three identifiable benefits for the research participants.

First, the research participants developed an intellectual and spiritual understanding of the process leading to the holistic well-being of their respective communities. The following comments from the research participants, as presented in chapter 4 are pointers. Comments like: "We were able to understand that within us we can do something that we imagine"; "If many people have the intention of bringing about progress in their community, they can achieve more within a relatively shorter time"; "We have seen the handiwork of God in guiding us . . . We witness the power of God and the guidance of the Holy Spirit"; and "God has used you to enlighten us and God is using this group to enlighten the community."

Second, the research participants realized that the values of the communities' modern worldview on development had distorted the community's traditional values. This realization made it easier for the people to appreciate their traditional worldview on development. It has been stated earlier that religion is recognized to have valuable influence in the lifestyle of a people. It has also been stated that the research participants claim that Christianity is the dominant religion of the communities. Through the participatory appreciative dialogue, the research participants could see, from the biblical metanarrative, that it is not archaic to be engaged in communal labor for the well-being of the community. Thus, the communities' value for religion as part of its traditional worldview provided a platform for the research participants to consider the model of the biblical metanarrative to revive the community's comatose sense of communality.

Third, the participatory appreciative dialogue between the biblical worldview on transformational development and the communities' worldview on development led to better understanding of the power of the biblical world-view on transformational development in the communities. Models in the biblical metanarrative inspired the communities to appreciate their traditional worldview and practices for the well-being of their respective communities. For example, the principle of supporting and restoring members of the Israelite community laid down in the Jubilee narrative in Leviticus 25. The Jubilee narrative provides a biblical model for economic, social, theological, and christological understanding of the meaning of communal living that does not violate the individuality of persons yet provides for a collective well-being for all members of the community.[58]

Finally, the research participants expressed a joyful appreciation of the participatory appreciative dialogue in the restoration of a sense of communal cooperation. For example, Yogaj, from Kurmin Gwaza states that "one of the joys of this approach is that we truly enjoy coming together to discuss the issues before us." Marmadu, also from Kurmin Gwaza states that, "this program has brought about unity of purpose in the community. Decisions are now being taken collectively." Yogama, also from Kurmin Gwaza comments that,

> What I find joy in is the fact that though in the past there has been cooperation but the level of cooperation has not been as much as now. We seem to be more united now just as our mother mentioned earlier, whenever people are called, they assemble in good time. Since the approach you introduced was explained to the people, they respond well by attending to calls for meetings and they do so in good time.

Ganyam from Kurmin Jatau states that "the program has re-ignited a beautiful cooperation between us." Asjo, also from Kurmin Jatau, in her comment stated that "your coming has brought out issues of interest that inspired people to come and attend to it." The foregoing joyful appreciation of the participatory appreciative dialogue in the restoration of a sense of communal cooperation may be explained to mean a lack of satisfaction with the communities' modern worldview on development. Not only does the communities' modern worldview disrupt the quality of relationships in the communities it does not promote the nurture of the peoples' religiosity nor

---

58. Wright, "Biblical Paradigms of Redemption," 83–90.

the people's spiritual relationship with God as revealed in the biblical meta-narrative. Therefore, the research participants realized that patterning their community's worldview on communality after the revealed biblical pattern amounts to partnering with God in their redemption from an approach that was taking them away from each other and from God.

The objectives of changing people and transforming their relationships in the process of holistic transformational development as proposed in Myers's framework for holistic transformational development were being achieved in this process.[59] This is highlighted in comments such as,

> The approach has changed our orientation of waiting for some-one else or government to come and does development work for us but that we can put our heads together to do something beneficial for our community. In my view if we continue in this manner we will progress and in some areas we will only require support . . . We did not realize this before but with the introduction of this approach it has helped us to understand this. Therefore, the approach will accelerate our development . . . We are able to understand that within us we can do something that we imagine could be done. We have been empowered to use our own initiative.

The above comment was made by Gaibu, from Kurmin Gwaza. The following comment was made by Marmadu, also from Kurmin Gwaza.

> I wish to thank God for the time you took to guide us in this program since last year . . . We have seen the handwork of God in guiding us . . . You said it is with our own hands that we can work to help ourselves. It was these words and explanation that the people were mobilized and the people showed their accep-tance of the idea by coming out. We witnessed the power of God and the guidance of the Spirit of God . . . We thank God and pray that this will motivate us to take steps to help ourselves rather than looking up to others.

Also to be noted here is the comment of Admus, from Kurmin Jatau,

---

59. Myers, *Walking with the Poor*, 202.

> The program has made me realize that if many people with the intention of bringing about the progress of a community come together, they can achieve more within a relatively shorter time . . . We have indeed benefitted from this program in just the little time that the program has been instituted.

The above comments illustrate the fact that the primary participants in community transformational development are members of the community and God. Therefore, the communities' contextual theology of development is a collective effort through divine guidance.

The communities' contextual theology on development views holistic transformational development as a process of their communities, being in a special spiritual relationship with God through faith in Christ, participating with God to facilitated the application of God's plan for the progressive application of biblical shalom in the communities. The ultimate goal of God's plan is the re-instatement of God's people in an eschatological state of shalom. The participation takes place through the people in the community communally setting community development goals, drawing up community development plans, and implementing the community development plans in accord with God's model revealed in the biblical metanarrative. Hence the communities' biblically transformed worldview on holistic development portrays transformational development to consist of: (1) reinstating and deepening harmonious spiritual relationship with God as God's people; (2) reinstating and deepening social relationship within human societies; and (3) responsible stewardship, under biblical or divine guidance, of the material resources available to people for the well-being of their respective communities. This aligns with the *missio Dei* which was described in chapter 2, the idea of the triune God's goal, plan, and process of establishing an eschatological kingdom through the person and work of Christ. The *missio Dei* is achieved through the redemption and reconciliation of people to God. The *missio Dei* is being extended by the person of the Holy Spirit to all humanity regardless of their physical, economic, and sociocultural context. Therefore the re-instatement and the deepening of harmonious spiritual relationship with God as God's people, the re-instatement and deepening of social relationships within the Kurmin Gwaza and Kurmin Jatau communities, and the collective responsible stewardship of the material resources available to the communities for their well-being demonstrates the application of biblical shalom in both communities through the process of participatory appreciative dialogue to promote a sustainable holistic transformational development.

Second, the participatory appreciative dialogue facilitated a new understanding of the communities' modern worldview on development vis-à-vis the biblical worldview on transformational development. In the transformed mode of their worldview on development, the communities view God as an essential, indispensable stakeholder and active participant they must engage with in their communal efforts to facilitate holistic community development and/or well-being.

Therefore, the transformed worldview of the Kurmin Gwaza and Kurmin Jatau communities on development now consists of restored spiritual relationship with God, which guides and transforms harmonious social relationships and strengthens communal partnership to sustain life in their respective vocations for the well-being of the community according to God's revealed pattern in the biblical metanarrative. The application of the participatory appreciative dialogue that led to the transformed worldview of the Kurmin Gwaza and Kurmin Jatau communities on development is a means by which biblical shalom can be progressively applied in both communities.

Applying Participatory Appreciative Dialogue Approach for Holistic Transformational Development and Application of Biblical Shalom in Rural Communities

The third phase of the participatory appreciative dialogue, the action phase, was guided by Osmer's framework for doing practical theology described in chapter 3. The contextual theology of development in Kurmin Gwaza and Kurmin Jatau communities described above inspired the research participants to take initiatives. The initiatives were to facilitate the application of the participatory appreciative dialogue approach in their respective communities to facilitate projects aimed at a holistic transformational development. The research participants applied the participatory appreciative dialogue to mobilize members of their communities to engage in a process that promises holistic transformational development for the well-being of their communities.

The projects the research participants selected were influenced by the communities' modern worldview on development but the process for facilitating the achievement of the developmental goals was guided by the application of the participatory appreciative dialogue. The immediate concern of the research participants was to facilitate projects that were of economic and material interest. It has been argued earlier that economic and material concerns are the primary focus of modern development thinking. The process for facilitating the achievement of the development goals proposed in the participatory appreciative dialogue approach has been described as the setting of community goals through communal discourse, communal planning, and communal action in partnership with God for the holistic well-being of the community and individuals-in-community. In the data presented in chapter 4, Marmadu, of Kurmin Gwaza, is reported to have stated that the participatory appreciative dialogue approach "has brought about a unity of purpose in the community. There is indication that decisions are now being taken collectively." The two groups of research participants reported the application of the discussion guide provided by the researcher to facilitate community meetings. The next section evaluates the actions of the communities through the first three phases of applying the participatory appreciative dialogue approach in Kurmin Gwaza and Kurmin Jatau.

Evaluating the Application of Participatory Appreciative Dialogue Approach for Holistic Transformational Development and Its Implication for the Application of Biblical Shalom in Rural Communities

The final phase of the participatory appreciative dialogue approach is the evaluative phase. The feedback presented in chapter 4 shows that the participatory appreciative dialogue approach facilitated greater participation of members of the community in dialoguing, planning, and taking collective action in the communal projects identified in this study. This section provides an evaluative summary of the outcome of the application of the participatory appreciative dialogue in the Kurmin Gwaza and Kurmin Jatau communities.

First, the communities learned to appreciate their spiritual relationship with God. It has been stated earlier that through the process of the participatory appreciative dialogue the communities' self-identity became more explicit to the research participants. The communities could see that by virtue of their religious confession as Christians they are supposedly spiritually related to God through faith in Jesus Christ. And as a people they have the responsibility of partnering with God through obedience to him for every goal, every aspiration, and every action related to the facilitation of development or improvement of the holistic well-being of the communities.

Second, the communities learned to appreciate the importance of making deliberate effort to partner with God in his mission, which is his plan and action to facilitate the communities' holistic well-being. In the analysis above on the description of the communities' worldview it has been shown that the communities acknowledged the handwork of God in guiding to identify how they can work with God to help themselves.

Third, partnership with God involves the application of principles deduced from the biblical metanarratives for the well-being of God's people. The feedback from the communities indicate, for example the comment by Ayuta of Kurmin Jatau that, "We are hoping that God will give us additional insight so that our youth will make more progress in life," the communities' understanding and value of partnership with God in community development projects.

Fourth, re-orienting community development goals go beyond immediate economic and material gain and elevation of social status for either the individual-in-community or the community as a body. Hence, they place the divine goal above self-centered goals of meeting personal or community economic or material gains. It has been indicated that the Kurmin Gwaza community consider the setting of standard for the community market will serve, not only as a model to attract traders but will so serve as a moral model.

Fifth, the communities appreciated the value of their cultural practices that promote communal cooperation for the well-being of the community. A number of comments presented in the feedback theme in chapter 4 confirm this. For example, Yogama of Kurmin Gwaza stated that, "since the approach you introduced was explained to the people they responded well by attending to calls for meetings and they do so in good time." Asjo, of Kurmin Jatau, in her comment stated that "your coming has brought out issues of interest that inspired people to come and attend to it." This goes to show that the approach re-emphasized the community's cultural practice of communal cooperation for the common good of the community and for individuals-in-community.[60]

---

60. The communities' communal cooperation was presented in chapter 4 under the theme Communities' Self-Identity.

Sixth, the appreciation of the value of the wisdom and authority of elders and community leaders who inspire, harness, and give direction toward communal action for the common good of all in the communities. The research participants mentioned the names of leaders who inspired development in their communities in the past. The approaches of the research participants to seek support and insights from community leaders, as was the case in Kurmin Jatau, as well as seek the input of leaders in the community market, as was the case in Kurmin Gwaza, mentioned earlier are indications of the communities' appreciation of their community leaders.

Seventh, the people appreciated and learned how to apply the biblical principle of sharing labor for different sets of people to achieve the community development goal for any specific project. In both Kurmin Gwaza (the road rehabilitation project) and Kurmin Jatau communities (the market resuscitation project) this principle was applied. The process is sustainable because the quest for development or improvement of the well-being of communities and individuals is insatiable. The quest is insatiable because the eschatological state of shalom revealed in the biblical metanarrative is yet to be established.

Eighth, dissenting voices reveal their commitment to the modern goal of development to be centered on the interest of the individual. This was the case in Kurmin Gwaza where there were dissenting voices against monitoring the quality of the ginger brought to the Kurmin Gwaza community market. It is an indication that they are unable to see that there can be a well-being of the community which also provides for the well-being of the individual-in-community.

Ninth, the community needs more time for the approach to take root and increase the community's dexterity for applying the approach. It has been presented in chapter 4 the failure of the research participants to engage the community in a discussion on the theological training project selected by the group in Kurmin Gwaza. The research participants failed to apply the guideline for conducting a community participatory appreciative dialogue on this project. And the research participants did not provide an explanation, yet two likely reasons for this failure are assumed. First, the agreed time frame with the researcher was inadequate for all three projects the research participants selected. Therefore, they may have approached it by way of announcement to keep to time. Second, the participants may have not understood how to handle the discussion on a matter related to religion and therefore felt inadequate. Therefore, since the community was not engaged in dialogue there was no community decision and thus there was no agreed communal line of action so this approach proves ineffective.

Tenth, to demonstrate a strategy that can be applied by CRDOs in rural communities to facilitate a participatory appreciative dialogue approach through community leaders and church leaders. The Kurmin Jatau focus group began their advocacy aimed at mobilizing the participation of their community in the participatory appreciative dialogue to facilitate the community market resuscitation project by first approaching the community traditional leaders then through visit to the local churches in the community. This approach demonstrates a strategy of inviting the community to participate in the participatory appreciative dialogue through both the traditional leaders in the community and the religious institutions in that community.

Eleventh, a cultivation of appreciative resources rather than cultivating problem-solving resources as a supplementary approach has been demonstrated. Unlike the problem-solving approach that seeks to identify resources for solving community is physical, economic, social, and religious or spiritual problems, the participatory appreciative dialogue approach seeks to identify the good in the community – and to engage the community in dialogue with the plan of God for holistic transformational development at play within the community. This leads to the transformation of the community in all development to align with the biblical concept that avoids syncretism and avoids areas of its existence. Hence, through the process of applying participatory appreciative dialogue to facilitate holistic transformational development, the people in both communities have begun to experience change in their conception of development. It is hoped that the communities' modern worldview on development would be discarded with time and a biblically transformed worldview will take predominance.

Summary

The participatory appreciative dialogue approach applied in this study demonstrates the potential for the progressive application of biblical shalom in a sustainable holistic transformational development process. In the participatory appreciative dialogue approach the Kurmin Gwaza and Kurmin Jatau communities' worldview on development is being transformed. The approach has great potentials to create a sustainable holistic transformational development worldview in these two communities. The spiritual relationship with God guides and transforms harmonious social relationships and strengthens communal partnership to sustain life in their respective vocations for the well-being of the community.

The revival of the traditional communal practices for development in both Kurmin Gwaza and Kurmin Jatau communities in partnership with God in the process of participatory appreciative dialogue guarantees the progressive application of biblical shalom in the community. The approach is thus transformational. The approach promotes a holistic view of development to include interpersonal relationships, spiritual relationships, and moderates emphasis on physical and material interests, which otherwise overshadows the other aspects in the modern worldview of development.

The Kurmin Gwaza and Kurmin Jatau communities' worldview on development that is being biblically transformed through the application of the participatory appreciative dialogue approach is achieving the following:

1. Re-affirming the positive aspects of the communities' traditional worldview on development, which is the application of communal activities that facilitate a seamless well-being of individuals and the community. The communal activities facilitate the holistic well-being of the community and that of individuals-in-community.

2. De-emphasizing the element of individualism that is evident in the communities' modern worldview on development described earlier as focusing on the individual's well-being rather than the community's well-being. In the modern worldview on development social cohesion of the communities for the benefit of the communities is not a matter of priority rather the social cohesion is to be considered only for the benefit of the individual. In the communities' worldview the individual exists and has personal interests that are not violated so long as those personal interests do not infringe on the communities' well-being. The individual exists as an individual-in-community. Therefore, the communities' worldview on transformational development being biblically transformed de-emphasizes social

status, economic, and material development that is centered
on the well-being of individuals. Instead it promotes holistic
transformational development that is community-centered
and allows for the holistic transformational development of the
individual-in-community.

3. Integrating the biblical worldview on holistic transformational
development. The biblical worldview on holistic transformational
development emphasizes restoration and continuous nurture of
harmonious spiritual and social relationships in the context of
responsible stewardship of the ecological context for the holistic
well-being of human communities. Thus, the communities'
worldview on development being biblically transformed is
indicating that development consists of promoting harmonious
relationships and communal partnership based on a harmonious
spiritual relationship with God and the application of principles
and models drawn from the biblical metanarrative for the holistic
well-being of the communities and individuals-in-community.

Research participants in the two focus group discussions were equipped
with the skills to mobilize and engage members of their respective communities in a participatory appreciative dialogue. They facilitated the participation
of members of their communities through the worldview transforming process earlier described. The process of equipping members of the community
with the skill is a means by which to sustain the progressive application of
biblical shalom as they applied it in the projects they undertook. The sustainability of the process of biblical transformation of communities' worldview
on development in other aspects of life is based on the continual engagement of the community's worldview on development drawn from analyti-
cal understanding of the community's conceptual, affective, and volitional
comprehension of the issue at hand.

The outcome of the application of a participatory appreciative dialogue
for the purpose of engaging the Kurmin Gwaza and Kurmin Jatau worldview
on development with the biblical worldview on holistic transformational
development has demonstrated great potential for being a means of applying
biblical shalom in rural communities. The approach has demonstrated how
the biblical metanarrative on holistic transformational development can bring

about the biblical fusion and transformation of rural communities' worldview on development. The approach promises the potential for the progressive application of biblical shalom in rural communities through the process of sustainable holistic transformational development that is contextually relevant and meaningful to the people and their communities.

Contribution of This Study

The study provides valuable insight on facilitating the progressive application of biblical shalom for holistic transformational development in rural communities in Nigeria in particular and Africa in general. The focus of the study was to facilitate the progressive application of biblical shalom in two rural communities in North Central Nigeria: Kurmin Gwaza and Kurmin Jatau. These communities are representative to similar rural communities in Nigeria in particular and Africa in general.

The result of the study suggests that the progressive application of biblical shalom can be achieved by means of a participatory appreciative dialogue approach in a seamless process that facilitates the engagement of the worldview of socio-culturally and spatially homogeneous rural communities on development in a dialogical interaction with the biblical worldview on development. Hence a participatory appreciative dialogue approach is a relevant supplementary means of facilitating the application of biblical shalom for holistic transformational development.

Therefore, the study adds to the body of knowledge available to Christian relief and development practitioners, organizations, policy makers, and denominational and local church leaders. The knowledge is also available to mission students, educators, and researchers.

CHAPTER 6

Summary, Conclusion, Implications, and Recommendations of the Study

Introduction

This study argues for the application of biblical shalom through an appreciative and dialogical approach for a sustainable process of holistic transformational development in rural communities. The study has attempted to provide valuable insight on the processes of transforming people who are active participants in the development of rural communities.

The study proposed and applied the use of a participatory appreciative dialogue approach to facilitate a biblical transformation of rural communities' worldview on development as a sustainable process of holistic transformational development. The approach is a means for developing a biblical, contextually relevant, and meaningful theology of holistic transformational development that provides cognitive and spiritual explanations for the acts of God as he executes his plan for the holistic transformation of communities, as described in the principles of the *missio Dei*. The acts of God facilitate the application of biblical shalom. Therefore, the goal of applying the participatory appreciative dialogue approach in a holistic transformational development process is to achieve a progressive application of biblical shalom until its eschatological fulfilment.

A review of relevant literature was undertaken to understand and situate the research problem and to provide conceptual tools for analyzing primary data. Christian relief and development organizations (CRDOs) apply participatory, problem-solving approaches in rural communities in Nigeria to facilitate holistic development in those communities. The participatory, problem-solving approaches do not seem to adequately engage the people's worldview and perception of development in a direct dialogue with the biblical worldview and concept of holistic transformational development. Hence relevant theories, concepts, and ideas from different fields of study like practical theology, philosophy of education, organizational development, sociology, anthropology, biblical theology, and hermeneutics were reviewed to gain requisite insight and conceptual tools that helped in the analysis of the primary data. The data was collected through the qualitative empirical focus group discussion research methodology. The data was collated in five themes. A thematic data analysis framework was applied to interpret the data and to draw up conclusions.

Summary of the Study

The literature review in chapter 2 demonstrates that global theories that guide approaches to development are focused on economic growth. The approaches use science and technology, world economic system, and human ingenuity to promote human physical and social well-being. The application of science and technology enhance economic growth of Western nations. The production of goods is based on the exploitation, rather than the cultivation, of natural resources using science and technology. Therefore, the approach, rather than cultivate, exploits and rather than conserve, squanders the natural infrastructure for supporting the physical aspect of life and ignores the spiritual aspect of human life from a biblical perspective.

The scope of the global theories revolved around nations and institutions without giving attention to micro settings of rural communities. The application of global theories in non-Western contexts promotes mass consumption of manufactured goods and produces social transformation in the non-Western communities. However, there is no resultant eradication of economic and material poverty in the non-Western communities, especially in Nigeria in particular and Africa in general. Rather there is a disruption of the traditional and sociocultural structures of the non-Western communities. There is also no evident promotion of spiritual and moral transformation in the communities. The spiritual dimension of human well-being, though beginning to draw interest, has traditionally not been part of the focus of global theories that guide the approaches to development.

The global theories impose scientific, technological, and economic policies at the national level of non-Western polities but they do not engage rural communities. Hence rural communities are not directly engaged as participants in planning, execution of plans, and evaluating the outcome of development efforts. The outcome of the application of global theories of development is limited to the promotion of mass consumption of manufactured goods without necessarily eradicating economic and material poverty. Increase in mass consumption of manufactured goods imported from the West deepens the poverty level of rural communities.

The literature review led to the identification of three major flaws associated with the application of global theories of development in non-Western nations. These are, first, the failure to engage rural communities as stakeholders in the process of development. Second, the failure to eradicate economic and material poverty. And third, the neglect of the spiritual dimension of the well-being of communities. These flaws have social and cultural implication for rural communities as the analysis of the study shows. The approaches of CRDOs addressed some of these failures.

The review of the CRDOs approaches to holistic development, also in chapter 2, indicates that they apply principles of community development (CD). CD principles are concerned with the promotion of communal coherence, which enables communities to relate to one another peacefully in order to make collective decisions and take collective actions to promote the community's well-being on issues of social, economic, political, vocational, religious, and other interests. CD approaches were reviewed in the light of Matarrita-Cascante and Brennan's three broad models of CD – imposed, directed, and self-help models.

The review of the CRDOs approaches show that the CRDOs apply a directed method of CD for facilitating holistic development in rural communities. The directed model of CD, like both the imposed and self-help models, applies problem-solving approaches that often engage the community in the CD activities but based on predetermined options from which a group of stakeholders within the community may choose. The CRDOs seek to introduce the gospel through evangelism and through partnership with local churches in the communities to model the kingdom of God. The CRDOs avoid coercing the target communities to accept the gospel. The approaches of the CRDOs have both similarities and differences with the global theories for development.

The approaches of the CRDOs, unlike the approaches of the global theories, engage rural communities in the CD processes. Another difference is that the CRDOs include efforts to facilitate the transformation of the spiritual and moral dimension of community well-being. The CRDOs aim for the spiritual and moral well-being that accord with Christian beliefs and practices. The approaches of the CRDOs do have similarities with the approaches of the global theories. The key similarity between the approaches of global theories and that of the CRDOs is that both approaches have predetermined goals, not by the communities but by the global development organizations or governments and CRDOs. The rural communities' choices, where they are involved, was based on predetermined projects, thus it is based on limited options proposed by the CRDOs.

A document analysis of the three selected CRDOs in this study reveals that the CRDOs have a biblically based theology of development. It is a theology that has the kingdom of God as its goal. It also led to the identification of two inadequacies in the CRDOs approaches. First, the CRDOs propose holistic development projects that are predetermined from the perspective of the CRDOs on development rather than from the contextual perspective of the communities. Second, which arises from the first, is that the approaches of the CRDOs do not engage the communities' worldview on development in a direct dialogical interaction with the biblical worldview on holistic transformational development.

An analysis of the primary data made explicit the communities' implicit traditional worldview on development. The primary data collected through focus groups discussions was collated into five themes presented in chapter 4 and analyzed in chapter 5. The traditional worldview of the communities on development entails the promotion of harmonious relationships and communal partnership for the holistic well-being of members of the community. The primary data collection method described in chapter 3 was guided by the application of an interview protocol. The interview protocol was drawn based on insights from Osmer's method of doing practical theology, Freire's philosophy of education, and the principles of Cooperrider's Appreciative Inquiry.

Braun's and Clarke's framework for thematic analysis provided the conceptual framework that guided the analytic rigor applied for the data analysis. The framework describes the process of analysis as a progression from description to interpretation. Insight from the following were used to interpret the data: (1) Hiebert's anthropological framework for analyzing worldviews and Mead's social psychology theory were synthesized and applied to identify the communities' traditional and modern worldview on development; (2) Freire's philosophy of education provided the epistemological framework for the development and application of the interview protocol applied in this study; (3) Wright's biblical theology that describes the biblical metanarrative informed the use of the biblical metanarrative as the normative source of the contextual theology of development identified in the study; (4) the eschatological-christocentric-trinitarian understanding of the *missio Dei* provided the understanding on the process and eschatological goal of the mission of God; and (5) Gadamer's hermeneutical concept of the fusion of horizons was applied to demonstrate how the communities' worldview on development can be successfully transformed through a participatory appreciative dialogue. Wright's biblical theology, the Eschatological-Christocentric-Trinitarian understanding of the *missio Dei*, and Gadamer's hermeneutical concept of the fusion of horizons provided the basis for drawing up a contextual theology of development in the study sites.

An interview protocol was applied to facilitate a direct dialogue of the communities' modern worldview and perception on development with the biblical worldview and concept of holistic transformational development. Hence the dialogue exposes the communities' worldview on development to the biblical worldview on holistic transformational development. Based on the assumption of Gadamer's fusion of horizons through dialogue the aim of the direct dialogue was to facilitate the transformation of the communities' worldview on development by the normative biblical worldview on holistic transformational development.

The study identified that (1) the biblical worldview of holistic development posits God as actively involved in transforming the holistic state of his creation for the purpose of reinstating a state of shalom in God's creation. (2) God is acting on the basis of the redemptive death and resurrection of Jesus Christ. (3) God is also acting through the agencies of the biblical metanarrative, the convicting and guiding ministry of the Holy Spirit, and the active participation of God's people who live and ac according to God's revealed will in the biblical metanarrative.

The facilitated dialogue between the communities' modern worldview on development and the biblical worldview on holistic transformational development initiated the transformation of the communities' worldview and perception of development. The communities' transformed worldview informed the application of acceptable and meaningful social and cultural practices in the light of biblical principles. The acceptable and meaningful social and cultural practices were inherent in the communities' traditional worldview of development. Though inherent in the communities' traditional worldview of development the practices were now infused with a biblically transformed motivation, to experience God's shalom. It has been stated earlier that holistic transformational development is about the progressive transformation of the total well-being of individuals and communities for the application of biblical shalom.

It has been argued earlier that holistic transformational development is about the progressive transformation of the total well-being of individuals and communities for the application of biblical shalom. The result of this study shows that the communities' traditional worldview on development in the study sites consists of harmonious interpersonal relationships and cooperative communal labor. The harmonious interpersonal relationships and cooperative manual labor are essentials for facilitating the well-being of individuals and the community. This is in contrast to the communities' modern worldview on development, which presupposes development to be the pursuit and acquisition of economic, educational, and political status for individuals in the context of harmonious community. Through the application of the interview protocol the communities' modern worldview on development was engaged in dialogical interaction with the biblical metanarrative to arrive at the communities' biblically transformed and contextually relevant theology of development.

The dialogical interaction integrated the biblical principle of a harmonious spiritual relationship with God as foundational for the communities' sociocultural focus on harmony and communal action. This provided the impetus by which the research participants, not the researcher, mobilized their respective communities to engage in selected development projects.

Within the period of twelve weeks the communities' reported success in most of the selected projects. The Kurmin Gwaza community succeeded in the repair of the access road to the community and in resuscitating the community's ginger market with a biblically informed moral principle to guide marketing activities. The Kurmin Jatau community succeeded in resuscitating their community market for the purpose of economic empowerment of the community and also as an avenue for demonstrating godly values. The report of the focus groups indicates the excitement of the communities for the success they achieved within the relatively short period of time. The excitement includes a desire to continue with the participatory appreciative dialogue approach to facilitate development in other aspects of the communities' life in the light of the biblical metanarrative.

The human resources for mobilizing the communities are not technical experts with predetermined answers to problems identified by experts outside the communities. The experts are members of the community who identify their community's strengths that can be applied in partnership with God in his *missio Dei* to facilitate holistic transformational development and to progressively apply biblical shalom within their communities.

Financially, the cost of facilitating the participatory appreciative dialogue approach is low. In this study, the researcher and his assistant travelled to the study sites and purchased recording equipment for the purpose of recording conversation and data collection. Except for the cultural expectation of demonstrating appreciation to the community leaders for allowing the research participants to access the community for the study, there was no financial obligation on the researcher for the focus group participants. There was no need to rent any facilities to conduct the focus group discussions. The discussions in Kurmin Gwaza were held in the palace of the district head. The discussion in Kurmin Jatau was held in the home of one of the focus group participants. Therefore, the cost for conducting the field study was low. This indicates that the cost for applying participatory appreciative dialogue to facilitate holistic transformational development in rural communities is low.

The positive results achieved within the short period of twelve weeks indicate that the participatory appreciative dialogue approach is effective and fruitful for holistic transformational development in rural communities for the progressive application of biblical shalom. The result holds promise for a more qualitative impact within a relatively shorter time frame for biblical shalom to be progressively experienced in a process of holistic transformational development that is sustainable. Hence the application of a participatory appreciative dialogue approach facilitates the progressive application of biblical shalom in the communities.

Conclusion of the Study

The data analysis in chapter 5 demonstrates that the application of a participatory appreciative dialogue in this study reveals four outcomes. First, the approach brought to the fore the study communities' worldview on development to the fore. Second, the engagement of the communities' worldview on development in dialogue with the biblical worldview on transformational development led to the fusion of the communities' worldview on development. The fusion led to the development of the communities' biblical, contextual, and meaningful theology of development. Third, the communities' contextual theology of development guided the communities' traditional sociocultural approaches in partnership with God as modelled and patterned in the biblical metanarrative. Fourth, a promise of the progressive application of biblical shalom as the approach is applied consistently to achieve desired development goals in the communities.

Hence it can be concluded that:

1. The study attempted to demonstrate that the application of the participatory appreciative dialogue approach is effective for the application of biblical shalom. This is achieved through engaging the worldview of the Kurmin Gwaza and Kurmin Jatau communities on development in a dialogical interaction. The process leads to the development of a biblical, contextual, and meaningful theology of development, which guides the communities' activities to facilitate people's well-being. A theology of development that enhances partnership with God in his *missio Dei*, which aims for the progressive application of God's shalom in the history of creation until it is fully realized in the eschatological future revealed in the biblical metanarrative.

2. It is evident that the participatory appreciative dialogue approach is helpful for engaging the communities to initiate and sustain the

process that facilitates holistic transformational development in partnership with God. This promises the possibility of progressive application of biblical shalom in the communities as the approach is applied consistently.

3. The response of the communities for the success they achieved within the twelve-week period of their engagement in the process suggests that the people owned the project and found the approach fulfilling.

Therefore, a participatory appreciative dialogue approach to facilitate the application of biblical shalom for sustainable transformational development is a supplementary approach. It is a supplementary approach to the participatory problem-solving approach as to apply biblical shalom for sustainable transformational development in rural communities in Nigeria. The approach has at least five advantages.

First, the approach is cheap and produces positive results within a short time frame compared to the cost, the quality of results, and the time frame for the other approaches. Second, the approach applies a contextually developed, biblically based, and relevant theology of development that guides the community to facilitate its holistic transformational development in socioculturally acceptable ways. Third, the approach empowers rural communities with the skills to highlight and engage their worldview on development in an appreciative dialogue with the normative biblical worldview on holistic transformational development drawn from the biblical metanarrative. Fourth, the dialogue makes it possible for the communities to be able to identify the acts of God in his *missio Dei* to re-establish biblical shalom in their immediate contexts. And fifth, the dialogue leads to a fusion of the communities' worldview on development with the biblical worldview on holistic transformational development. The consequences of the fusion of the communities' worldview include: the development of a biblically based contextual and relevant theology of development; the developed theology guides the communities to willingly and joyfully apply their sociocultural approaches for holistic transformational development from a new and biblical perspective. The goal of the new biblical perspective is the progressive application of biblical shalom in the communities.

Implications of the Study

The application of the participatory appreciative dialogue approach is a supplementary to a participatory problem-solving approach in rural communities, particularly in Nigeria and in Africa in general. This supplementary approach can be applied to achieve the missional goal of facilitating the progressive experience of biblical shalom "while we wait for the blessed hope – the glorious appearing of . . . our great God and Savior, Jesus Christ"[1] when the anticipated eschatological goal of the mission of God to reinstate the state of shalom for God's creation shall be realized.

Policy makers for CRDOs and church denominations may consider developing policies that aim at equipping rural communities with skills for a participatory appreciative dialogue approach for holistic transformational development. The policy can provide for resident participatory appreciative dialogue approach facilitators for a given period of time. The facilitators are to ensure that the approach is well rooted in a community or a number of communities before being moved to another community or sets of communities. Hence more rural communities can be directly equipped rather than indirectly through training seminars and workshops for church leaders and community leaders which seems to be the preferred strategy for CRDOs.

Donors who support the ministries of CRDOs serving in rural communities may need to redirect their support for the approach in more rural communities in a manner that is cost-effective. The support may be in the form of cash or kind. Materials like vehicles, generators, audio-visual gadgets will be needed.

This researcher has acquired both conceptual and practical skills for facilitating participatory appreciative dialogue in rural communities for the purpose of the progressive application of biblical shalom. These place the researcher in a good position to be able to train people who can serve as facilitators for the application of the participatory appreciative dialogue in rural communities. Therefore, the researcher can serve as a consultant and/ or trainer for CRDOs practitioners of holistic development in rural communities, policy makers for CRDOs, donors who support CRDOs, and church denominations considering the application of the participatory appreciative dialogue approach in rural communities in Nigeria. In addition,

---

1. Titus 2:13 NIV.

the researcher can be fruitfully engaged in further studies and research to facilitate participatory appreciative dialogue for the application of biblical shalom in other contexts such as communities resident in urban areas or other community sub-sets.

Recommendations for Further Study

This study does not claim to have exhaustively examined the application of the participatory appreciative dialogue approach. The contexts within which this study was conducted had existing local churches and no known CRDO activities. The contexts were already exposed to the biblical metanarrative through the local churches in the communities. This may have been responsible for the ease with which the study's communities readily accepted the interaction with the biblical metanarrative. This raises the question on whether or not rural communities not familiar with the biblical metanarrative will readily accept to dialogue with the biblical metanarrative as was the case in the communities where this study was conducted. It is therefore recommended that a further investigation on the applicability of the participatory appreciative dialogue approach that engages the biblical metanarrative can be adapted for different community sub-sets such as rural communities not familiar with the biblical metanarrative and/or communities living in suburbs/shanty towns of cities.

Bibliography

Abidan, David. "People Oriented Development of ECWA: Mid-Term Evaluation: September, 1991."

———. "Report of Church and Community Mobilization Process (CCMP) Empowerment Activities January-July, 2011."

Allen, Paul L. *Theological Method: A Guide for the Perplexed*. London: T&T Clark, 2012.

Alvarez, Joy, Elnora Avarientos, and Thomas H. McAlpine. "Our Experience with the Bible and Transformational Development." In *Working with the Poor: New Insights and Learnings from Development Practitioners*, edited by Bryant L. Myers, 56–77. Colorado Springs: Authentic, 2008.

Andrew Kidd (with input from Zakka Chomock and Istifanus Gimba). "Participatory Rural Appraisal." Presentation at a Workshop organized by POD and CRUDAN on Participatory Rural Appraisal, Community Organizing, and Participatory Evaluation, 30 May – 6 June 1994.

Applerouth, Scott, and Laura Desfor Edles. *Sociological Theory in the Contemporary Era: Text and Readings*. 2nd ed. Thousand Oaks, CA: Sage and Pine Forge Press, 2011.

Arthur, Eddie. "Missio Dei and the Mission of the Church." *Wycliffe Global Alliance*. Accessed 16 January 2018. https://www.wycliffe.net/more-about-what-we-do/papers-and-articles/missio-dei-and-the-mission-of-the-church/.

Ashford, Bruce Riley. "Introduction." In *Theology and Practice of Mission: God, the Church, and the Nations*, edited by Bruce Riley Ashford, 1–4. Nashville, TN: B&H Academic, 2011.

Ashford, Bruce Riley, and David P. Nelson. "The Story of Mission: The Grand Biblical Narrative." In *Theology and Practice of Mission: God, the Church, and the Nations*, edited by Bruce Riley Ashford, 6–16. Nashville, TN: B&H Academic, 2011.

Baran, Paul. *The Political Economy of Growth*. Harmondsworth: Penguin Books, 1973.

Bartholomew, Craig G., and Michael W. Goheen. *The Drama of Scripture: Finding Our Place in the Biblical Story*. Grand Rapids, MI: Baker Academic, 2004.

Baxter, Brian. *A Darwinian Worldview: Sociobiology, Environmental Ethics and the Work of Edward O. Wilson*. Aldershot: Ashgate, 2007.

Bevans, Stephen B. *Models of Contextual Theology: Faith and Cultures*. Revised and expanded edition. Maryknoll, NY: Orbis Books, 2002.

Bloor, Michel, Jane Frankland, Michelle Thomas, and Kate Robson. *Focus Group in Social Research*. London; Thousand Oaks, CA: Sage, 2001.

Booy, Dirk, and Sarone Ole Sena. "Capacity Building Using the Appreciative Inquiry Approach." In *Working with the poor: New Insights and Learnings from Development Practitioners*, edited by Bryant L. Myers, 38–55. Colorado Springs: Authentic, 2008.

Bosch, David J. *Transforming Mission: Paradigm Shifts in Theology of Mission*. Maryknoll, NY: Orbis Books, 1991.

Braun, Virginia, and Victoria Clarke. "Using Thematic Analysis in Psychology." *Qualitative Research in Psychology* 3, no. 2 (2006): 77–101.

Bridger, Jeffrey C., A. E. Luloff, and Richard S. Krannich. "Community Change and Community Theory." In *Persistence and Change in Rural Communities: A 50 year Follow Up To Six Classic Studies*, edited by A. E. Luloff and R. S. Krannich, 9–22. New York: CABI, 2002.

Burke, Peter J., and Jan E. Stets. *Identity Theory*. New York: Oxford University Press, 2009.

Bushe, Gervase R. "Advances in Appreciative Inquiry as an Organization Development Intervention." *Organization Development Journal* 13, no. 3 (1995):14–22.

Chase-Dunn, Christopher. "Contemporary Semiperipheral Development: The Regimes and the Movements." IROWS Working Paper 78, presented at the Santa Barbara Global Studies Conference session on Rising Powers: Reproduction or Transformation? 22–23 February 2013. https://irows.ucr.edu/papers/irows78/irows78.htm.

Chen, Yan, and Sherry Xin Li. "Group Identity and Social Preferences." *American Economic Review* 99, no. 1 (2009): 431–457.

Chinitz, Jacob. "The Three Tenses in the Kingdom of God: God of Israel or of the World." *Jewish Bible Quarterly* 38, no. 4 (2010): 255–260.

Choji, Ezekiel. "Development Aids and Relief." Report of RURCON International Wholistic Development Course 2015, held 7–18 September 2015.

Christian Rural & Urban Development Association of Nigeria (CRUDAN). "Constitution and Bye-Laws." Revised: April 2010.

———. "CRUDAN Services: Reduced poverty, Improved equity for Sustainable Development in Nigeria." See also www.crudan.org.

———. "2015 Annual Report for the Year Ended 31st Dec. 2015." n.d.

Chrome IAS Academy. "Sociology – G. H. Mead – Self and Identity." ChromeIAS. Accessed 27 October 2017. https://chromeias.com/sociology-g-h-mead-self-and-identity/.

Clarke, Matthew. *Development and Religion: Theology and Practice*. Cheltenham: Edward Elgar, 2011.

Clarke, V., and V. Braun. "Teaching Thematic Analysis: Overcoming Challenges and Developing Strategies for Effective Learning." *The Psychologist* 26, no. 2 (2013): 120–123.

Coleman, Doug. "The Agents of Mission: Humanity." In *Theology and Practice of Mission: God, the Church, and the Nations*, edited by Bruce Riley Ashford, 36–47. Nashville, TN: B&H Academic, 2011

Cooperrider, David L., Diana Whitney, and Jacqueline M. Stavros. *Appreciative Inquiry Handbook for Leaders of Change*. 2nd ed. Brunswick, OH: Crown Custom Publishing, 2008.

Cooperrider, David L., and Diana Whitney. "A Positive Revolution in Change: Appreciative Inquiry." www.appreciativeinquiry.case.edu/uploads/whatisai. pdf. Accessed June 12, 2012.

Cooperrider, David L., and Diana Whitney. *Appreciative Inquiry: A Positive Revolution in Change*. San Francisco: Brett-Koehler, 2005.

Coppenger, Jedidiah. "The Community of Mission: The Church." In *Theology and Practice of Mission: God, the Church, and the Nations*, edited by Bruce Riley Ashford, 60–75. Nashville, TN: B&H Academic, 2011.

Crewe, Emma, and Richard Axelby. *Anthropology and Development: Culture, Morality and Politics in a Globalised World*. Cambridge: Cambridge University Press, 2013.

Dale, John, and Emery J. Hyslop-Margison. *Paulo Freire: Teaching for Freedom and Transformation*. Explorations of Educational Purpose. New York: Springer, 2010.

Darragh, Neil. "The Practice of Practical Theology: Key Decisions and Abiding Hazards in Doing Practical Theology." *Australian eJournal of Theology* 9 (March 2007): 1–13. aejt.com.au/__data/assets/pdf_file/0006/395736/AEJT_9.9_Darragh_Practice.pdf.

Davies, Ian, Ian Gregory, and Nick McGuinn. *Key Debates in Education*. London: Continuum, 2002.

De Rivero, Oswaldo. *The Myth of Development: Non-Viable Economies and the Crisis of Civilization*. 2nd ed. London: ZEDD, 2010.

Dhlamini, Philani Hlophe. "Modernization Theory Versus Dependency Theory." Accessed 4 March 2017. http://www.academia.edu/4605873/Modernization_Theory_Versus_Dependency_Theory.

Donovan, Vincent J. *Christianity Rediscovered*. 25th anniversary ed. Maryknoll, NY: Orbis Books, 2003.

Dos Santos, Theotonio. "The Structure of Dependence." *The American Economic Review* 60, no. 2 (May 1970): 231–236, www.jstor.org/stable/181581.

Eckhardt, Ivan. "Immanuel Wallerstein: World Systems Analysis: An Introduction." *Perspectives* 25 (Winter 2005/2006): 95–98. www.jstor.org/stable/23616037?seq=1#page_Scan_tab_contents.

ECWA People Oriented Development. "Church and Community Mobilization Process (CCMP)." POD of ECWA Newsletter 2, no. 1, 1 June 2014.

Edelman, Marc, and Angelique Haugerud. "Introduction: The Anthropology of Development and Globalization." In *The Anthropology of Development and Globalization: From Classical Political Economy to Contemporary Neoliberalism*, edited by Marc Edelman and Angelique Haugerud, 1–73. Malden, MA: Blackwell, 2005.

Ehret, Willi. "Brief Sketch of People Oriented Development of ECWA." 31 August 1991.

———. "Training and Capacity Building within People Oriented Development of ECWA." 28 August 1991.

Elliot, Jennifer A. *An Introduction to Sustainable Development*. 4th ed. London: Routledge, 2013.

Elwell, Frank W. "Wallerstein's World Systems Theory." Accessed 26 July 2017. http://www.faculty.rsu.edu/~felwell/Theorists/Essays/Wallerstein1.htm.

Engelsviken, Tormod. "*Missio Dei*: The Understanding and Mis-Understanding of a Theological Concept in European Churches and Missiology." *International Review of Mission* 92, no. 367 (2003): 481–497.

Falola, Toyin. *The Power of African Cultures*. Rochester, NY: University of Rochester Press, 2003.

Federal Republic of Nigeria. National Policy on Education. 4th ed. Jos, Nigeria: Federal Republic of Nigeria, 2004.

Flint, R. Warren. *Practice of Sustainable Community Development: A Participatory Framework for Change*. New York: Springer, 2013.

Fowler, Floyd J., Jr. *Survey Research Methods*. 4th ed. London: Sage, 2009.

Franko, Patrice M. *Puzzle of Latin American Economic Development*. Lanham, MD: Rowman & Littlefield, 2007.

Freire, Paulo. "Education and Community Involvement." *In Critical Education in the New Information Age*, by Manuel Castells, Rámon Flecha, Paulo Freire, Henry A. Giroux, Donaldo Macedo, and Paul Wallis, 83–92. Lanham, MD: Rowman & Littlefield, 1999.

Friese, Susanne. "ATLAS.ti8 Windows Literature Review." Unpublished notes for African Doctoral Academy, Stellenbosch University, 2017.

Gadamer, Hans-Georg. *Truth and Method*. 2nd rev. ed. Translated and revised by Joel Weinsheimer and Donald G. Marshall. London: Continuum, 2004.

Gauntlett, David. *Media, Gender and Identity: An Introduction*. London: Routledge, 2002.

Gilchrist, Alison. *The Well-Connected Community: A Networking Approach to Community Development*. 2nd ed. Bristol: Policy Press, 2009.

Gill, David W. "Christian Social Ethics." In *The Portable Seminary: A Master's Level Overview in One Volume*, edited by David Horton, 636–677. Minneapolis, MN: Bethany House, 2006.

Glasser, Arthur F. *Announcing the Kingdom: The Story of God's Mission in the Bible*. Grand Rapids, MI: Baker Academic, 2003.

Goebert, Bonnie. *Beyond Listening: Learning the Secret Language of Focus Groups*. New York: Wiley & Sons, 2002.

Gow, David D. *Countering Development: Indigenous Modernity and the Moral Imagination*. Durham, NC: Duke University Press, 2008.

Grenz, Stanley J. *Theology for the Community of God*. Nashville, TN: Broadman & Holman, 1994.

Grudem, Wayne. *Systematic Theology: An Introduction to Biblical Doctrine*. Leicester: Inter-Varsity Press, 1994.

Haines, Anna. "Asset-Based Community Development." In *An Introduction to Community Development*, edited by Rhonda Phillips and Robert H. Pittman, 38–48. London: Routledge, 2009.

Hancock, Beverly. *An Introduction to Qualitative Research*. Nottingham: Trent Focus Group, 2002.

Hanson, Erin. "Oral Traditions." *IndigenousFoundations*. Accessed 12 December 2017. https://indigenousfoundations.arts.ubc.ca/oral_traditions/.

Harrison, David. *The Sociology of Modernization and Development*. London: Routledge, 1988.

Hart, Roger A. "Stepping Back from 'The Ladder': Reflections on a Model of Participatory Work with Children." In *Participation in Learning: Perspectives on Education and the Environment, Health and Sustainability*, edited by Alan Reid, Bjarne Bruun Jensen, Jutta Nikel, and Venka Simovska, 19–28. New York: Springer, 2008.

Haviland, William A. *Cultural Anthropology*. 10th ed. Fort Worth: Harcourt College Publishers, 2002.

Haynes, Jeffrey. *Religion and Development: Conflict or Cooperation?* New York: Palgrave Macmillan, 2007.

Hendriks, H. Jurgen. *Studying Congregations in Africa*. Wellington: Lux Verbi, 2004.

Hennink, Monique M. *International Focus Group Research: A Handbook for the Health and Social Sciences*. New York: Cambridge University Press, 2007.

Herath, Dhammika. "Development Discourse of the Globalist and Dependency Theorists: Do the Globalisation Theorists Rephrase and Reword the Central

Concepts of the Dependency School?" *Third World Quarterly* 29, no. 4 (2008): 819–834.

Herrera, Rémy. "Theories of Capitalist World-System." In *Critical Companion of Contemporary Marxism*, edited by Jacques Bidet and Stathis Kouvelakis, 209–224. Leiden: Brill, 2008.

Hettne, Bjorn. *Development Theory and the Three Worlds*. New York: Wiley & Sons, 1990.

Hiebert, Paul G. *Anthropological Reflections on Missiological Issues*. Grand Rapids, MI: Baker Academic, 1994.

———. *The Gospel in Human Contexts: Anthropological Explorations for Contemporary Missions*. Grand Rapids, MI: Baker Academic, 2009.

———. *Transforming Worldviews: An Anthropological Understanding of How People Change*. Grand Rapids, MI: Baker Academic, 2008.

Hiebert, Paul G., R. Daniel Shaw, and Tite Tienou. *Understanding Folk Religion: A Christian Response to Popular Beliefs and Practices*. Grand Rapids, MI: Baker Books, 1999.

Hoggett, Paul, Marjorie Mayo, and Chris Miller. *The Dilemma of Development Work: Ethical Challenges and Regeneration*. Bristol: Policy Press, 2009.

Hustedde, Ronald J. "Seven Theories for Seven Community Developers." In *An Introduction to Community Development*, edited by Rhonda Phillips and Robert H. Pittman, 20–37. London: Routledge, 2009.

Hyman, Drew. "Six Models of Community Intervention: A Dialectical Synthesis of Social Theory and Social Action." *Sociological Practice* 8, no. 1 (1990): 32–47.

"Jaba." *Joshua Project*. Accessed 16 July 2015. https://www.joshuaproject.net/people_groups/12165/NI.

Jacobsen, Johannes. "Revisiting the Modernization Hypothesis: Longevity and Democracy." *World Development* 67 (2015): 174–185.

Jaison, Jessy. "Practical Theology: A Transformative Praxis in Theological Education Towards Holistic Formation." *Journal of Theological Education and Mission (JOTEAM)* 1, no. 1 (February 2010): 76–86. Accessed 3 October 2016. www.orcuttchristian.org/Practical%20Theology_12+_JOTEAM_Jessy_Jaison.pdf.

Jakonda, Sulaiman Z. *Your Kingdom Come: A Book on Wholistic Christian Development*. Jos: RURCON, 2001.

Jenkins, Richard. *Social Identity*. 3rd ed. London: Routledge, 2008.

Jensen, Robert W. *Systematic Theology: The Works of God*. Volume 2. Oxford: Oxford University Press, 1999.

Johansson, Ulla, and Jill Woodilla. "Bridging Design and Management for Sustainability: Epistemological Problems and Possibilities." In *Positive Design and Appreciative Construction: From Sustainable Development to Sustainable*

Value, edited by Tojo Thatchenkery, David L. Cooperrider, and Michal Avital, 57–75. Bingley: Emerald Group Publishing, 2010.

John, Philip Hayab. "Narratives of Identity and Sociocultural Worldview in Song Texts of the Ham of Nigeria: A Discourse Analysis Investigation." PhD dissertation, Stellenbosch University, South Africa, March 2017.

Johnson, Ian. "Introduction." In *Bridging Diversity: Participatory Learning for Responsive Development*, by Lawrence F. Salem and Eileen Kane. Washington, DC: World Bank, 2006.

Kasai, Joshua D. "Evangelical Church of West Africa Information on the Ministry of People Oriented Development." May 2008.

Kehily, Mary Jane. "What is Identity? A Sociological Perspective." ESRC Seminar Series: The Educational and Social Impact of New Technologies on Young People in Britain, 2 March 2009. Accessed 1 March 2017. http://oro.open. ac.uk/16372/2/What_is_Identity.pdf.

Kesuwo, Adamu Kevin. *Insight into Development Administration*. Jos: Quality Function Publishers, 2009.

Kunhiyop, Samuel Waje. *African Christian Theology*. Nairobi: HippoBooks, 2012.

Lamingo, Joel. "Community Organizing." A presentation at a Workshop organized by POD and CRUDAN on Participatory Rural Appraisal, Community Organizing, and Participatory Evaluation, 30 May – 6 June 1994.

Larrain, Jorgen. *Theories of Development: Capitalism, Colonialism, and Dependency*. Cambridge: Polity Press, 1989.

Laszlo, Chris, and David Cooperrider. "Creating Sustainable Value: A Strength-Based Whole System Approach." In *Positive Design and Appreciative Construction: From Sustainable Development to Sustainable Value*, edited by Tojo Thatchenkery, David L. Cooperrider, and Michal Avital, 17–33. Bingley: Emerald Group Publishing, 2010.

Lingenfelter, Sherwood. *Transforming Culture: A Challenge for Christian Mission*. 2nd ed. Grand Rapids, MI: Baker Books, 1998.

Luloff, A. E., and Richard S. Krannich. "Introduction." In *Persistence and Change in Rural Communities: A 50 year Follow Up to Six Classic Studies*, edited by A. E. Luloff and R. S. Krannich, 1–8. New York: CABI, 2002.

Marczyk, Geoffrey R., David DeMatteo, and David Festinger. *Essentials of Research Design and Methodology*. Hoboken, NJ: Wiley & Sons, 2005.

Martínez-Vela, Carlos A. "World Systems Theory." Accessed 21 July 2017. https:// web.mit.edu/esd.83/www/notebook/WorldSystem.pdf.

Matarrita-Cascante, David, and Mark A. Brennan. "Conceptualizing Community Development in the Twenty-First Century." *Community Development* 43, no. 3 (2012): 293–305.

Mattessich, Paul W. "Social Capital and Community Building." In *An Introduction to Community Development*, edited by Rhonda Phillips and Robert H. Pittman, 49–57. London: Routledge, 2009.

McGonigal, Terry. "If You Only Knew What Would Bring Peace: Shalom Theology as the Biblical Foundation for Diversity." Accessed 8 March 2017, www. citeseerx.ist.psu.edu.

McKinzie, Greg. "An Abbreviated Introduction to the Concept of *Missio Dei.*" *Journal of Missional Theology and Praxis* 1 (August 2010): 10–11. Accessed 16 January 2018. http://missiodeijournal.com/issues/md-1/authors/md-1-mckinzie.

Meyer, Raymond K. "An Evangelical Analysis of the Critical Realism and Corollary Hermeneutics of Bernard Lonergan with Application for Evangelical Hermeneutics." Dissertation, Southeastern Baptist Theological Seminary, September 2007.

Miller, Darrow L. *Discipling Nations: The Power of Truth to Transform Cultures.* Seattle, WA: YWAM Publishing, 1998.

Musa, Danladi. "Participatory Evaluation." A presentation at a Workshop organized by POD and CRUDAN on Participatory Rural Appraisal, Community Organizing, and Participatory Evaluation, 30 May – 6 June 1994.

———. *Promoting Christian (W)holistic Development in Nigeria: The Story of CRUDAN 1990-2000* Bukuru, Jos: Africa Christian TextbookS (ACTS), 2011.

Myers, Bryant L. "Setting the Table." In *Working with the Poor: New Insights and Learnings from Development Practitioners*, edited by Bryant. L. Myers, xi–xxii. Colorado Springs: Authentic, 1999

———. *Walking with the Poor: Principles of Transformational Development.* Revised and expanded ed. Maryknoll, NY: Orbis Books, 2011.

Netland, Harold A. "Introduction: Globalization and Theology Today." In *Globalizing Theology: Belief and Practice in an Era of World Christianity*, edited by Craig Ott and Harold A. Netland, 14–35. Grand Rapids, MI: Baker Academic, 2006.

Newbigin, Lesslie. *The Gospel in a Pluralist Society.* Grand Rapids, MI: Eerdmans, 1989.

Note, Nicole, Raul Fornet-Betancout, Josef Eastermann, and Diederik Aerts. "Worldview and Cultures: Philosophical Reflections from an Intercultural Perspective. An Introduction." In *Worldview and Cultures: Philosophical Reflections from an Intercultural Perspective*, edited by Nicole Note, Raul Fornet-Betancout, Josef Eastermann, and Diederik Aerts, 1–10. New York: Springer, 2009.

Nwogu, Godpower A. Ikechi. "Education and National Development in Nigeria: A Philosophical Perspective." *African Research Review* 7, no. 2 (2013): 266–276.

Okoh, J. D. *The Risk of an Educational System Without a Philosophical Base.* Inaugural Lecture Series 38. Port Harcourt: University of Port Harcourt Press, 2005.

Onwuegbuzie, Anthony J., Wendy B. Dikinson, Nancy L. Leeck, and Annmarie G. Zoran. "A Qualitative Framework for Collecting and Analyzing Data in Focus Group Research." *International Journal of Qualitative Method* 8, no. 3 (2009): 1–21.

Onyenali, Rowland. *Appraising the Nigerian Problem Through Education and Religious Dialogue: A Cognitive Approach.* European University Studies Series on Education. Bern: Lang, 2013.

Orji, Joseph Iloabanafor. *New Approaches to Effective Poverty Alleviation in Nigeria.* Kaduna: Joyce Publishers, 2008.

Osmer, Richard R. *Practical Theology: An Introduction.* Grand Rapids, MI: Eerdmans, 2008.

Oyserman, Daphna, Krishen Elmore, and George Smith. "Self, Self-Concept and Identity." In *Handbook of Self and Identity,* edited by Mark R. Leary and June Price Tangney, 69–104. 2nd ed. New York: Guilford Press, 2012.

Ozurumba, C. N., and V. O. Ebuara. "An Appraisal of Education Policy Implementation and Challenge of Leadership in Nigerian Universities." *IOSR Journal of Research & Method in Education* 3, no. 6 (2013): 31–35. Accessed 16 November 2014. https://www.iosrjournals.org/iosr-jrme/papers/Vol-3%20 Issue-6/E0363135.pdf?id=7370.

Patton, Michael Quinn. *Qualitative Research and Evaluation Methods.* 3rd ed. Thousand Oaks, CA: Sage, 2002.

Peet, Richard. *Global Capitalism: Theories of Societal Development.* London: Routledge, 1991.

Peet, Richard, and Elaine Hartwick. *Theories of Development: Contentions, Arguments, Alternatives.* 2nd ed. New York: Guilford Press, 2009.

Phillips, Rhonda, and Robert H. Pittman. "A Framework for Community and Economic Development." In *An Introduction to Community Development,* edited by Rhonda Phillips and Robert H. Pitman, 3–19. London: Routledge, 2009.

Pitchford, Michael. *Making Spaces for Community Development.* Bristol: Policy Press, 2008.

POD of ECWA. "Evaluation Report of Sixth Project Phase: May 2009." ECWA Library, Jos, Nigeria.

———. "Fourth Project Phase 2001–2003 End-Term Evaluation Report." 12–23 May 2003.

———. "Know More About POD of ECWA." POD of ECWA Newsletter 4, no. 1 (Jan–Jun 2014): 2. ECWA Library, Jos, Nigeria.

————. "Notes and Handouts for Participatory Evaluation Process (PEP) Also referred to Church and Community Mobilization Process (CCMP)." July 2004. ECWA Library, Jos, Nigeria.

————. "People Oriented Development of ECWA Fourth Project Phase 2001–2003 End-Term Evaluation Report." 12–23 May 2003. ECWA Library, Jos, Nigeria.

————. "People Oriented Development of ECWA Internal Evaluation." 30 September – 11 October 1996. ECWA Library, Jos, Nigeria.

————. "The Workshop Report on CCMP." POD Head Office, 8–11 December 2014. ECWA Library, Jos, Nigeria.

Rapley, John. *Understanding Development: Theory and Practice in the Third World*. 2nd ed. London: Lynne Rienner, 2002.

Ridderbos, H. N. "Kingdom of God, Kingdom of Heaven." In *New Bible Dictionary*, 2nd ed., edited by J. D. Douglas, N. Hilyer, F. F. Bruce, D. Guthrie, A. R. Millard, J. I. Packer, and D. J. Wiseman, 656–659. Leicester: Inter-Varsity Press, 1982.

Rist, Gilbert. *The History of Development: From Western Origins to Global Faith*. Translated by Patrick Camiller. 3rd ed. London; New York: ZED Books, 2008.

Roberts, J. Timmons, and Amy Hite. "Editor's Introduction." In *From Modernization to Globalization: Perspectives on Development and Social Change*, edited by J. Timmons Roberts and Amy Hite, 1–24. Malden, MA: Blackwell, 2000.

Roberts, Peter. *Education, Literacy, and Humanization: Exploring the Work of Paulo Freire*. Westport, CT: Bergin & Garvey, 2000.

Ross, Alistair. *Curriculum Construction and Critiques*. London: Falmer Press, 2000.

"Rural" in www.dictionary.reference.com/browse/communitiy. Accessed 26 May 2015.

RURCON. "RURCON: A Brief History." in *RURCON*. Accessed 5 June 2017. www.rurcon.org accessed June 5, 2017.

RURCON. "RURCON Long-Range Strategic Plan: 2011–2017." January 2011.

————. "International Development Management Course." Conducted at the RURCON Headquarters, 6–17 March 2017. Notes given to participants.

————. "International Wholistic Development Course." 7–18 September 2015. Notes given to participants.

Saegert, Susan. "Building Civic Capacity in Urban Neighborhood: An Empirically Grounded Anatomy." In *The Community Development Reader*, 2nd ed., edited by James Defilippis and Susan Saegert, 220–227. New York: Routledge, 2012.

Samples, Kenneth Richard. *A World of Difference: Putting Christian Truth-Claims to the Worldview Test*. Grand Rapids, Mi: Baker Books, 2007.

Sharma, A. P., and J. T. Hyland. *Philosophy of Education for Nigeria*. Ibadan: Gbabeks Publishers, 1991.

Siegel, Harvey, D. C. Phillips, And Eamonn Callan. "Philosophy of Education." *The Stanford Encyclopedia of Philosophy*. Accessed 12 December 2017. https://plato.stanford.edu/entries/education-philosophy/.

Sillitoe, Paul, Peter Dixon, and Julian Barr. *Indigenous Knowledge Inquiries: A Methodology Manual for Development*. Warwickshire: Practical Action Publishing, 2005.

Skocpol, Theda. "Wallerstein's World Capitalist System: A Theoretical and Historical Critique." *American Journal of Sociology* 82, no. 5 (1977): 1075–1090.

Smith, Kevin Gary. *Academic Writing and Theological Research: A Guide for Students*. Johannesburg: South African Theological Seminary Press, 2008.

———. "Review of Richard Osmer, Practical Theology: An Introduction." Conspectus: *The Journal of the South African Theological Seminary* 10, no. 1 (2010): 99–115. Accessed 4 October 2016. www.semanticscholar.org.

Smithson, Janet. "Using and Analysing Focus Group: Limitation and Possibilities." *International Journal of Social Research Methodology* 3, no. 2 (2000):103–119.

So, Alvin Y. "Dependency and World Systems Perspectives on Development." UNESCO Encyclopedia Life Support Systems, online. Accessed 3 March 2017. www.eolss.net.

Sorinal, Cosma. "Immanuel Wallerstein's World System Theory." *Annals of Faculty Economics* 1, no. 2 (2010): 220–224. Accessed 24 July 2017. www.steconomiceuoradea.ro/anale/volume/2010/n2/031.pdf.

Stets, Jan E., and Peter J. Burke. "A Sociological Approach to Self and Identity." In *Handbook for Self and Identity*, edited by Mark Leary and June Tangney, 128–152. New York: Guilford Press, 2003. Accessed online 27 October 2017. www.researchgate.net/publication/252385317_A_Sociological_Approach_to_Self_and_Identity.

Stewart, David W., Prem N. Shamdasani, and Dennis W. Rook. *Focus Groups: Theory and Practice*. 2nd ed. Thousand Oaks, CA: Sage Publications, 2007.

Stringer, Ernest T. *Action Research*. 4th ed. London: Sage Publications, 2014.

Stryker, Sheldon. "The Past, Present, and Future of an Identity Theory." *Social Psychology Quarterly* 63, no. 4 (2000): 284–297.

Swinton, John, and Harriet Mowat. *Practical Theology and Qualitative Research*. London: SMC Press, 2006.

Tennent, Timothy C. *Invitation to World Missions: A Trinitarian Missiology for the Twenty-first Century*. Grand Rapids, Mi: Kregel, 2010.

Thompson, Karl. "World Systems Theory." *ReviseSociology*. Accessed 26 July 2017. www.revisesociology.com/2015/12/05/world-systems-theory/.

Tsele, Molefe. "The Role of the Christian Faith in Development." In *Faith in Development: Partnership Between the World Bank and the Churches of Africa*, edited by Deryke Belshaw, Robert Calderisi, Chris Sugden, 219–236. Oxford: Regnum, 2001.

Tucker, Ruth A. *From Jerusalem to Irian Jaya: A Biographical History of Christian Missions*. Grand Rapids, MI: Zondervan, 2004.

Turaki, Yusuf. *Foundations of African Traditional Religions and Worldview*. Nairobi, Kenya: International Bible Society Africa, 2001.

———. *The Trinity of Sin*. Grand Rapids, MI: HippoBooks, 2011.

Ujo, Abdulhameed A. *Theory and Practice of Development Administration*. Rev. ed. Kaduna: Joyce Publishers, 2008.

United Nations Development Programme. "Sustainable Development Goals." *United Nations Development Programme*. Accessed 23 October 2017. http://www.undp.org/content/undp/en/home/sustainable-development-goals.html.

Valenzuela, J. Samuel, and Arturo Valenzuela. "Modernization and Dependency: Alternative Perspectives in the Study of Latin American Underdevelopment." *Comparative Politics* 10, no. 4 (July 1978): 535–557.

Vanhoozer, Kevin J. "One Rule to Rule Them All?: Theological Method in an Era of World Christianity." In *Globalizing Theology: Belief and Practice in an Era of World Christianity*, edited by Craig Ott and Harold A. Netland, 85–126. Grand Rapids, MI: Baker Academic, 2007.

———. "A Reader's Guide." In *Everyday Theology: How to Read Cultural Texts and Interpret Trends*, edited by Kevin J. Vanhoozer, Charles A. Anderson, and Michael J. Sleasman, 7–12. Grand Rapids, MI: Baker Academic, 2007.

———. "What Is Everyday Theology?: How and Why Christians Should Read Culture." In *Everyday Theology: How to Read Cultural Texts and Interpret Trends*, edited by Kevin J. Vanhoozer and Charles A. Anderson, 15–61. Grand Rapids, MI: Baker Academic, 2007.

Vincent II, John W. "Community Development Practice." In *An Introduction to Community Development*, edited by Rhonda Phillips and Robert H. Pittman, 58–74. London: Routledge, 2009.

Wallerstein, Immanuel. *The Modern World System: Capitalist Agriculture and the Origins of the European World-Economy in the Sixteenth Century*. New York: Academic Press, 1976.

———. *World-Systems Analysis: An Introduction*. Durham , NC: Duke University Press, 2004.

Webb, Eugene. *Worldview and Mind: Religious thought and Psychological Development*. Columbia, MO: University of Missouri Press, 2009.

Whitfield, Keith. "The Triune God: The God of Mission." In *Theology and Practice of Mission: God, the Church, and the Nations*, edited by Bruce Riley Ashford, 17–33. Nashville, TN: B&H Academic, 2011.

Whitney, Diana, and Amanda Trosten-Bloom. *The Power of Appreciative Inquiry: A Practical Guide to Positive Change*. 2nd ed., revised and expanded. San Francisco: Berrett-Koehler, 2010.

Wright, Christopher J. H. "Biblical Paradigms of Redemption: Exodus, Jubilee and the Cross." In *Transforming the World? The Gospel and Social Responsibility*, edited by Jamie A. Grant and Dewi A. Hughes, 334–335. Nottingham: Appollos, 2009.

———. *The Mission of God's People: A Biblical Theology of the Church's Mission*. Grand Rapids, MiI: Zondervan, 2010.

———. *The Mission of God: Unlocking the Bible's Grand Narrative*. Grand Rapids, Mi: IVP Academic, 2006.

Wuyep, Nehemiah. "Introducing RURCON." Slides presented at the International Wholistic Development Course organized by RURCON, 7–18 September 2015.

Yager, Ronald R. "Participatory Learning of Propositional Knowledge." *IEEE Transactions on Fuzzy Systems* 20, no. 4 (2012): 715–727.

Yamsat, Pandang. "The Role of the Church in Society and Development." RURCON Advocacy Bulletin, no. 32, July – September, 2012.

Yoms, Ephraim. "Transformational Development as Theological Challenge: An Evaluation of the ECWA People Oriented Development Programme." PhD dissertation, Stellenbosch University, South Africa, December 2015.

Zasha, James. "2016 Evaluative Report 2011–2016." A Report presented at the Christian Rural and Urban Association of Nigeria General Meeting 11 May 2016.

Zhexembayeva, Nadya. "A Whole New Value: Driving Innovation, Sustainability, and Prosperity Through Appreciative Inquiry." In *Positive Design and Appreciative Construction: From Sustainable Development to Sustainable Value*, edited by Tojo Thatchenkery, David L. Cooperrider, and Michal Avital, 77–96. Bingley: Emerald Group Publishing, 2010.

Zuchell, Lisa. "The Theory of International Development." Paper presented at the 79th Annual Meeting of the Speech and Communication Association, Miami Beach, Florida, 18–21 November 1993, www.files.erik.gov.

Langham
PARTNERSHIP

Langham Literature, with its publishing work, is a ministry of Langham Partnership.

Langham Partnership is a global fellowship working in pursuit of the vision God entrusted to its founder John Stott –

to facilitate the growth of the church in maturity and Christ-likeness through raising the standards of biblical preaching and teaching.

Our vision is to see churches in the Majority World equipped for mission and growing to maturity in Christ through the ministry of pastors and leaders who believe, teach and live by the word of God.

Our mission is to strengthen the ministry of the word of God through:
• nurturing national movements for biblical preaching
• fostering the creation and distribution of evangelical literature
• enhancing evangelical theological education
especially in countries where churches are under-resourced.

Our ministry

Langham Preaching partners with national leaders to nurture indigenous biblical preaching movements for pastors and lay preachers all around the world. With the support of a team of trainers from many countries, a multi-level programme of seminars provides practical training, and is followed by a programme for training local facilitators. Local preachers' groups and national and regional networks ensure continuity and ongoing development, seeking to build vigorous movements committed to Bible exposition.

Langham Literature provides Majority World preachers, scholars and seminary libraries with evangelical books and electronic resources through publishing and distribution, grants and discounts. The programme also fosters the creation of indigenous evangelical books in many languages, through writer's grants, strengthening local evangelical publishing houses, and investment in major regional literature projects, such as one volume Bible commentaries like the *Africa Bible Commentary* and the *South Asia Bible Commentary*.

Langham Scholars provides financial support for evangelical doctoral students from the Majority World so that, when they return home, they may train pastors and other Christian leaders with sound, biblical and theological teaching. This programme equips those who equip others. Langham Scholars also works in partnership with Majority World seminaries in strengthening evangelical theological education. A growing number of Langham Scholars study in high quality doctoral programmes in the Majority World itself. As well as teaching the next generation of pastors, graduated Langham Scholars exercise significant influence through their writing and leadership.

To learn more about Langham Partnership and the work we do visit **langham.org**

www.ingramcontent.com/pod-product-compliance
Lightning Source LLC
Chambersburg PA
CBHW050349270326
41926CB00016B/3665